WIND

IN THE

FIRE

A Personal Journey

BOBBI GIBB

The First Woman to Run and Win at Boston

The Institute for the Study of Natural Systems Press
Cambridge Massachusetts

Anniversary Edition
Copyright 2016 by Roberta (Bobbi) Gibb
All Rights Reserved

ISBN: 978-0-9829675-1-5

Book Design: Y42K Publishing Services

http://www.y42k.com/publishing-services/

Books by Bobbi Gibb

Wind in the Fire
The Art of Inflation
To Boston with Love
DiMa
The Art of Meditative Running
The Art of Economics
Visions and Social Consciousness
Seven Years of Seasons

Table of Contents

Foreword

Wind in the Fire is about my experiences from 1964 to 1966, from the time I first saw the Boston Marathon and fell in love with it, to Patriots' Day, April 19, 1966, when I became the first woman ever to run the Boston Marathon.

This book is not just about running, but is about overcoming obstacles, challenging prejudice, making a difference, tenacity, perseverance and love. In this volume I describe my spiritual and philosophical quest as I seek the answers of some of life's biggest questions.

This quest follows its own story line of development in a sequential, logical line of thinking about the nature of existence and about the mind-body problem. This inner story is written in italics, where as the outer story is written in regular type. The inner and outer stories intertwine as they proceed.

Names have been changed to protect the privacy of the people involved. The dialogue has been constructed, not verbatim, but in a way to capture the essence of the people and the ideas.

Your comments and feedback are welcome.

Thank you to all you wonderful people. May your lives be filled with happiness, health, joy and love.

To all my
Beloved friends and family who helped me
On my journey
To my parents who gave me
The gift of life
And to
Future generations

Preface

It's Patriots Day, 1964, only four and a half months after President John Fitzgerald Kennedy's assassination. Under the Dallas sun, for one horrible moment we saw a hideous subterranean river of evil flowing through the world, causing a death that pulled the vision of Camelot away from our eyes and left us disillusioned by the terror of its destructive power. The Vietnam War rages and Kennedy, who fought against communism and supported our involvement in that South Asian country, is dead. So is Diem, South Vietnam's U.S.-supported president, assassinated just three weeks before Kennedy.

We have lived through the disastrous Bay of Pigs fiasco in 1961, as our government attempted a covert operation to help exiled Cubans unseat Fidel Castro. We have survived the 1962 standoff with Premier Nikita Khrushchev and the Soviet Union over their missile installations in Cuba. President Kennedy had put the nation on red alert, and for a few precarious hours we teetered on the brink of nuclear war. Finally, the prayers of millions of people around the world were answered, and the Soviet battleships turned back, our planet was saved, for the time being, but the threat of nuclear holocaust remains. Every large American city is the target of a Soviet missile and every large Soviet city is the target of an American missile. The destruction of countless lives is terrifyingly surreal, and yet it could happen with a simple push of a button. How did we come to this insanity?

I was born in the middle of World War II, and it seems as though we have been at war ever since: the Cold War with the Soviets, the Korean War and now Vietnam. It's not the Soviet people or the Koreans, or the Vietnamese we distrust and fear, but their totalitarian governments. I wonder if we'll ever escape from this madness and learn to live peacefully on the same earth with people who should be our friends. After all, the Soviet people have been in the grip of a ruthless government that they themselves distrust and fear. Stalin wasn't elected, nor was Khrushchev, although he indicates a willingness to correct some of the "excesses" of his predecessor's era. But now their government and the other most powerful totalitarian government in the world, China, have joined in the Communist block, which is perceived as threat to the free world. Yet to them, the free world is a threat. A threat to what? Had we not, only nineteen years ago, freed the Chinese from a cruel Japanese occupation?

Anti-Vietnam War protests have been growing in size and frequency as President Lyndon Johnson escalates our involvement in the conflict. But despite the tragedy of the rising body count in Vietnam, the Peace Corps has become a potent force for spreading American goodwill around the world, and stateside the War on Poverty attempts to help the disenfranchised regain a foothold in society.

In August of 1963, only six and a half months ago, one hundred thousand people had marched on Washington in support of Civil Rights. The Reverend Martin Luther King Jr. spoke eloquently, moving us with the dream he has for America. Black and White are beginning to work together to make civil rights a reality for everyone, no matter their ethnic or racial heritage. Hope is rising up among all races that America can do the impossible: that we can have a truly color and race blind society, where a person's skin color or ethnic background will be only one aspect of who they are, no more important than the accidental place where they were born. Can we have a country where what is important is who you are as a person, not to what group you happen to belong?

There is a new consciousness springing up from a new generation. We are experiencing growing pains as a nation born in colonialism and rising to an entirely new consciousness of human dignity and freedom that will, we hope, inspire the world.

The culture of the times reflects the dizziness of this struggle, the elation, as it looks possible, the despair as once again it is ripped out of our grasp.

In February of this year, the Beatles, with their bowl haircuts and sweet young faces burst upon the stage on the Ed Sullivan Show singing *She l Loves You... Yeah, Yeah, Yeah.* The angelic, stirring voice of Joan Baez, trembles as she sings Dylan's song, Blowin' in the Wind." Peter Paul and Mary croon "We Shall Overcome." The audience joins in, tears rolling down cheeks, feeling a love that expands to all the world. Woody Guthrie leads us in singing, "This land is your land. This land is my land, from the Mississippi to the New York Highland." We are inspired by a vision larger than ourselves.

We are working for a better world, a place where all people can live in harmony, and create vibrant peaceful societies that respect one another and prosper together in freedom and democracy. We know that for each individual to be healed, whole, happy and fully engaged, the whole of society must be healed. We know too that it must be the people themselves who create their own government by means of which they govern themselves, and that unless a government governs for the good of the whole, it cannot long survive.

Bob Dylan sings that "The Times They Are a Changin'," telling us in his nasal whine what we all know; these are deeply trying, transformative times.

Yet, there is no women's movement.

Growing up I had fumed over the injustices and unfairness of what I saw my future role would be as a woman in our society. There were few, if any, opportunities for a woman unless she wanted to be a teacher, nurse or secretary-- jobs she would be expected to give up once she married. And once she did marry a woman often found herself trapped. She couldn't have a credit card in her name, let alone a mortgage. Husband and wife were joined through marriage as one, and the *one* was the husband. Women gave up their names, their identities, and far too often, their dreams. Witnessing my own mother's struggle to retain her identity and her dignity was painful to see.

I read the _Feminine Mystique_ and observed the nameless malady Betty Friedan described swallow up my mother and her friends. I watched as the lunchtime glass of wine expanded into the afternoon glasses of wine. I heard the clink of ice in the evening drink and discovered the bottle of tranquilizers in the closet. I saw her standing with her back hunched away from me facing the sink, a numb zombie-like shell of my real mother, but with an inner rage seething, that sometimes broke through the trance and struck at me with malicious force.

Over the years I watched as my mother's frustration at her situation turned in on herself, and I vowed that if being a woman meant living as my mother lived, I would never do it. I would never drink to dull the pain of an unfulfilled life; I would never take drugs to mute the misery of not being true to my own soul. I would never live as a captive in my own home.

The choice to me was clear—either I would have to find a way to change society, or I would have to escape from society altogether. I fantasized about living close to the earth, perhaps in some remote place like Canada where I would be free. I was determined that if I ever married, the person I chose would be my best friend and lover, someone who would be as wild as I was, someone who would be my equal. I had thought that person was Will, a man I'd met a Tufts School of Special Studies, where I was studying in the Fall of 1962. Will introduced me to cross-country running and sculpture and gave me my first hunk of clay. Will and I were friends, but not lovers. I was, he said, like his younger sister. And Will, as I called him, was, to me, the older brother I never had. But, when he graduated, he joined the Navy and we lost touch. Much as I loved Will, when I met John in the summer of '63, romance burgeoned.

Chapter 1: Love at First Sight

The morning tastes like cold skim milk left out on the back porch all night in the rain. I glance over at the powerfully built man standing next to me. Despite the chilly air his coat is unbuttoned, and when it falls open he briefly lowers his head — hatless so only his short dark hair protects against the cold. New England springs are characterized by too much light and not enough heat. Today is typical — the white sun feels cold, not warm, and the barren trees cast bruise-colored shadows over the pasty brown rubble of last season's leaves. Together we stand, my father and I, on this nearly colorless and stark April day, watching the most extraordinary ritual I've ever seen – the sixty-eighth running of the Boston Marathon.

The scent of damp wool jackets and leather shoes mingles with the smell of burning cigarettes. At least my Father hasn't lit up yet. Like a living creature — heavy, warm, murmuring, shifting and stamping — the crowd closes around us; the vapor of its collective breathing condenses on the moist spring air. Children shout and squeal. The air sounds sharp, high pitched like a note ready to break. I look at the bare trees, buds swelling on every tip, ready to burst into urgent, fragilely-folded green leaves and I think how generations are born, live and die like leaves, while the social order stands like the bare rack of a frozen tree. We are this year's leaves and many generations have gone before us. We here now celebrate this ritual of spring, the return of new life after the long, dark, cold New England winter.

My father's keen blue eyes are focused on a line of Wellesley coeds dressed in pleated skirts, wool coats, white ankle socks and penny loafers. Behind them, are the stately stone buildings and elegantly landscaped conifers of this elite woman's college, which marks the mid point of the twenty-six and two tenths-mile Marathon.

A sudden hush of anticipation falls over the crowd. Heads turn west, craning to see. The Wellesley girls scream. The runners are in sight! A singing, bubbly, fizzy sensation wells up inside me. I lean forward. In the distance I see small wavering patches of white moving along the road. I watch as they near. Sinewy men dressed in white cotton shorts and undershirts race towards me along route 16.

Loud, sharp clapping, shouts of encouragement and screams of excitement explode around me. My breath catches. I've never seen people run like this before. How strong they are! They run with such grace, balancing the motions of their arms and legs— their heads scarcely bobbing. I'm surprised at how quiet their foot falls are. They make hardly any sound at all. They are like wild animals running. I know how they feel; it is the way I feel when I run, turned inward, listening to the inside of their bodies. Here at last are people who feel the same way I do, who have integrated their minds, bodies and spirits into one perfect whole. They too have rediscovered the original unity, which has been all but lost in modern society. Here are people who share a vision of the courage, strength, and dignity it takes to live a life of integrity and to run a race like this. The tremendous energy and power, juxtaposed with the vulnerability and fleetingness of human existence, strikes me with peculiar poignancy.

Something shifts deep inside me. At this moment I know that I am meant to run this race. It makes no sense, there's no logic to my decision; it's a mystical transformation, like falling in love. I see my own self in these runners; I see my future opening up before me. As if called by some divine edict, impelled by some primal unconscious sense, I realize that the decision has already been made deep inside me, by a part of me much more fundamental, than my small ego. I know that I am meant to run the Boston Marathon, the ultimate challenge. Even for men to run is outside the norm, and for a woman to run a marathon is thought impossible.

Fewer runners are passing by now, the Wellesley coeds aren't cheering as often, a few of them have drifted back to the dorm rooms. My father and I turn away and walk back to the car. We don't speak. I don't tell him about my decision to run in the race. He doesn't reveal his thoughts to me. If he knew what I was thinking, he would try to put a halt to it immediately. He and my mother... they would never approve of their daughter daring to step outside the *"normal"* parameters society has laid down for women.

I have a profound love for my father. He's the most brilliant man I've ever known, a research scientist and a professor of Chemistry at Tufts University. He introduced me to the ethereal magic of music and awesome mysteries of nature when I was just a toddler. As a young child I would dance around the house listening to the thunderous music of Bach. I would run through the park where my father first took me to experience the wonders of life rising up from the earth. We would marvel at the animals that crept and flew about, aware that they shared their kingdom with lumbering two-footed creatures. This is where I learned what it felt like to run free, blonde curls bouncing around my head, my legs whirling as fast as a child's possibly could, my young mind filled with a joy and excitement that I was yet too young to verbalize. And my father was there, always there, watching over me.

When I was growing up my father was very motherly, and as I matured, his attitude and behavior led to a dichotomy that caused a rift between us. Although as a scientist and deep-thinker he had encouraged his only daughter to question the *"whys"* of the universe. He was fiercely protective of me, to such an extent that eventually he would distance himself so as not to be over-protective, leaving me confused and feeling vulnerable. He tended to drive off the men in my life believing that none of them were good enough for me, yet he expected me to marry, often telling me that he *"had little use for spinsters."* And despite the fact that he had inspired me to open my mind to the wonders of science and the mathematical lyricism of music, he preferred that my mind be closed to any consideration of my living outside societal norms. My father took a very dim view of any woman, particularly his daughter, having a career. He had let me run loose in the park as a child but as I became a woman, he tried to break my rebellious spirit.

No, as much as I love him, I can't tell my father, … nor can I tell my mother that I'm going to run in the Boston Marathon. I will never confide in them, this will be my secret. But I can't wait to tell John.

Chapter 2: The Minister's Son

My dad and I walk in silence to a pale yellow Volkswagen microbus, his pride and joy. He has overhauled it into something resembling a ship's cabin, replete with a folding bed and table, sink, water tanks and cupboards filled with food, dishes, pots and pans. Despite his successful career, a chemist who had worked during World War II on projects vital to our nation security, he secretly yearns to escape from everything and let himself be the poet and musician his soul yearns to be, living in his converted camper on a tropical island paradise.

He drives us along a tortuous course of back streets, side alleys and seldom-used roads. Dad prides himself on his knowledge of shortcuts; he can get anywhere in Greater Boston without ever using a main road. We wind our way through the landscape of ordinary, two-story homes built in the thirties and forties with their small, dirt-colored lawns, along nondescript roads, flanked by frequently cracked sidewalks and neatly planted shade maples, and finally emerge from the suburban maze in Winchester. We pull up in front of a house with patches of peeling gray paint, and a front porch surmounted by a slanted peaked roof, so that one could, in theory, sit out in the spring rain and contemplate the view.

I jump down out of the microbus and call out, "Gail! We're home!" The children, Lorrie, Jimmy and Lisa skip down the stairs to meet us. "Horsy-back ride! Horsy-back ride!" They shout out, vying to see who'll be the first to cling onto my back and be carried around the house at a fast gallop by a pretend horse, who makes whinnying sounds.

Gail Willard, her husband Dick and their children are my temporary family; I'm the nanny, living in a converted coal bin in their cellar, while my parents are on sabbatical in Florida. Dad has driven his beloved VW up from Florida and is leaving it for me to use, should I need to. For the past seven months Dad and Mom have been in Gainesville, where Dad has been studying physics at the university and writing a paper. Soon they'll relocate to spend the second half of the year in London; Dad will teach and study there at Kings College. He plans to fly to England to meet my mother who is already there. Mom and Dad never fly in the same plane, in case, God forbid, it might crash and they would be killed. By always flying separately, they guarantee that one of them will be alive to take care of their children. My parents haven't noticed that my brother Paul and I are both adults, capable of taking care of ourselves.

After hugging my dad goodbye, eager to start the journey on which I've decided to embark, I call out to Gail "I'll see you in a couple of hours," lace up my leather nurses' shoes and take off running down the street. Rinty and Brigadoon, two neighborhood dogs who've hung around with me ever since junior high catch me at the corner, and by the time we reach the edge of the Fells Reservation, wilderness Indian land, a quarter-mile from the Willard home, a half-dozen or so dogs have joined me, tails wagging, grinning up at me to show their delight, all managing somehow to avoid entangling their legs in mine.

My dogs and I enter the woods where we are greeted by a sacred quiet. The dogs are silent; they too feel something reverent here. We stop, all of us, human and canine animal and listen to the stillness, and then we hear it: the low sad sound of a mourning dove, shimmering through the forest, bouncing from tree to tree so that it's nearly impossible to tell from where the mournful strain is coming. And, now we hear more music... a cardinal's melody and the primal staccato beat of the spring tree frogs rising up into the cool air from the recently thawed swamp, where, just two months ago, the children and I had skated.

Above us is the yellow-green fuzz of the beginnings of summer's canopy of leaves. Below us, on the forest floor lie last year's leaves; leaves for which the tree has no further use; leaves that, for six months, have lain flattened by winter's snow and ice; leaves that are now revealed, naked, in the unsightly process of decay and degeneration, crumbling apart into thin, umber, lacy skeletons, forgotten in the new rush of spring buds. In a few more weeks a delicate carpet of lilies of the valley, foamflowers and dogtooth violets will sprout miraculously from the brown litter of last years' dead growth.

The sides of this magnificent living cathedral, this holy palace, are sturdy trunks with wide branches that reach like arms held up in prayer, opening wider in adoration, up high and the even higher, right up against the sky. This is a place filled with miraculous life that blooms and blossoms forth from itself, unfolding from the inside out, not as a sculptor would impose form from the outside onto the formless clay, but as a divine internal force bringing forth form, from the inside, that reveals itself slowly and wondrously to the waiting world.

Now, we begin to run again, and with each footfall, with each beat of my heart, I feel a sense of peace. A calm fills me even as my lungs and heart begin to sing joyfully. I love to work hard like this. Some inner spirit draws me on and on, deep into the woods. It is here, running in the primordial forest that I feel most like myself. An all-encompassing love surrounds me. I run on and on, and that love washes over me like baptismal water.

I run until I can run no more, then I flop down on the earth's sacred body, and smell the sweet rich perfume of her nourishing soil. I roll over, open to the broad, blue sky that stretches out above me, and I drift into a reverie. I move my hand back and forth over my face, opening and closing my palm and wonder: *"How can my thoughts activate the nerves in my hand? How do I intend something? How are the impulses of activity in my nerves seen subjectively by me as color, shape and form? And who is this me, who sees, intends, perceives, thinks, and feels?"* To me this is a mystery of immense proportions, as wondrous as and overwhelming as existence itself.

5

......

Scrunch, scrunch, scrunch. It's later that evening, I've finished my run and am back at Gail's, where, from inside the coal bin, I hear the sound of John's construction boots outside on the gravel driveway.

"If you're looking for Cinderella, she's down in the coal bin," Gail chirps out. A moment later the back door opens and John ducks his head as he enters. "Heh! What 'ya doin?" His gruff voice has a note of protection and jealousy.

"Painting."

John flops down onto the day bed that serves as my couch during the day and would be my bed at night except that I've taken to sleeping outside in the backyard under the stars. He looks over at my latest painting then at the space around him. "This looks like a cave," he observes, "with cave paintings," and he sweeps his hand back and forth in the air, like a docent, referring to the mural of trees, flower and animals that I've painted on the walls.

"What are these?" he asks, picking up one of several clay sculptures.

"Heads of people I see on the subway when I go back and forth to the Museum School."

"This one looks like President Johnson."

"It is President Johnson."

"I'm betting he wasn't on the subway."

"Wise guy." I bop him on the head with a feather pillow.

"And what's this?" He picks up the top book from a stack on the table that doubles as my desk. "Descartes? He touches the next book, and then each one in the pile. Anatomical drawing? Fundamental Physics? Biology?"

John turns his attention to the furnace in the corner and asks suspiciously: "Bobby Lou, what is all the bedding draped on the furnace?"

"My bedroll."

"Why is it on the furnace?"

"It got wet last night."

"Was there a leak in here?"

I smile sweetly and answer: "No, it rained and I haven't yet mastered the art of tucking the tarp over and around me."

"What do you mean? Were you outside?"

"Yeah, I always sleep outside."

John stares at me incredulously. "Even in the rain?"

"Rain, snow, summer's heat."

"What on earth for?"

I feel exposed and vulnerable, being examined this way, as if hundreds of little ants are running over me. I want so much to share my love of the earth with John in a way that he will understand. "Because I love the earth," I begin. "I want to experience it in all it seasons… We're here on this planet for some inexplicable reason, for a very short period of time, and I, for one, want to make the most of it. When I'm outside I fall asleep looking up into the mystery of the infinite universe. Outside I feel the nourishing spring rain, the brutal winter cold, the crisp tang of autumn, and now I feel the rebirth of life. But I just didn't get the tarp quite right last night... usually I'm dry, warm and cozy."

John's mystified look is replaced by a grin that softens and opens his face from ear to ear, stubbly chin to strong, unlined forehead. "Come here," he coos, pulling me close, "You're the funniest person I've ever known."

We start to wrestle and play on the couch, and just as we begin kissing the kids rumble down the cellar stairs, the dogs burst in the back door and we're suddenly inundated in a heap of laughing, wagging bodies.

……

"How about we stop at Chick's Roast Beef?" John hollers over his shoulder. The wind catches his words and they tumble about, flying past my ears, I can barely hear over the roar of the motorcycle engine. It's a few weeks after the marathon, and John and I have headed out of town to the coast, to Gloucester.

A half an hour later we pull up in front of the one of the ubiquitous, shiny, metal railroad dining cars, one of hundreds of similar diners sitting anchored to the ground in towns and villages through out the country. The smell of fish permeates this particular hamlet, a classic old fishing port.

The diner's nearly empty save for two fishermen hunched over at the counter, scooping clam chowder through their salt and pepper beards. We walk to the two stools farthest from the door and that's when John notices the newspaper strewn along the counter top, the bold headline font proclaiming: "War Protesters Burn Draft Cards!" And in that short time, John's attitude changes, the day has darkened and, as we step up and slide on the stools, he hisses at me under his breath, "This damn war! What a waste of lives, money, everything. Every fiber of my being says it's wrong. Once I graduate I'll be eligible for the draft." His words just hang there, ominously.

"Oh John, what will you do?"

"I don't know. Go to jail. I don't know. But I do know that I refuse to fight in this immoral war."

We each order a slice of custard pie and a cup of coffee. "Half coffee and lots of cream." I request. "I can't drink this stuff, but I like to see the galaxy form when I pour in the cream."

Then we hear it: spat out like someone trying to dislodge phlegm from their throat, "Bunch of hippies, draft dodgers." It comes from one of the fishermen, who never glances up from his bowl of chowder. He gestures towards the newspaper.

"Yeah, those pups don't know what a real war is." Like his companion, the fisherman acknowledges no one with his eyes, only the bowl in front of him.

"The Soviet Union and China, they'd take Vietnam in the a minute if we weren't there. Those damn communists. They're everywhere. They'll take over the world if we don't fight."

"They tell us we're fighting to free the South Vietnamese," one of the fishermen grumbles, "but we're really there for the tin and oil. That's what I think.... "

"You know if we leave there'll be blood bath. The Cambodians will invade."

"Sure, I know that. But do these hippie draft dodgers? Do they even care?" He whacks the newspaper with his hand.

John and I get up and move to a table by the window but the damage has been done. His hand shakes as he lifts his fork.

I struggle to understand and to know what is really true. War horrifies me and I believe there must be a better way to resolve conflicts, but how? Wal, my dear friend, is in the Navy somewhere in the Pacific. My father ardently believes that this war is to protect the Vietnamese and to save the world from the threat of a Communist totalitarian global empire. What is true?

I know that, right now, John and I have to finish quickly and be on our way. "Let's get out of here and go for a run," I say.

Twenty minutes later we park the cycle on the edge of Dog Town Common and he complains, "Oh boy, I shouldn't have eaten so much pie."

"Me either," I groan as we start running up the rocky trail on the wild granite outcropping.

"Until I met you, I hadn't run a step since high school. You're really whipping me into shape," John grins. The scene at the diner has dissolved, for the time being, into the background.

"Good."

"Tell me again how you got involved in this insanity?" His words are staccato; he's already breathing hard.

"I loved to run as a kid. I'd see a green field and I'd feel so much joy at its beauty that I'd just have to tear across it at top speed. Everyone else stopped running after high school... but I never stopped." The trail is getting steeper, and it's becoming harder for me to talk. "And then I met.. Will.... He ran.. cross-country at Tufts... the only way I ... got to see him... was to run.... after him.. when he trained."

"Do you ever hear from him?"

"No."

"Good."

Now we run in silence. From behind me I hear John's breathing. I glance around at his face, so serious as he focuses on every step. His brown hair is dampening as it falls over his forehead, and in those few brief moments before I look ahead again, I feel a sudden jolt of love for this handsome, square-faced man with his broad shoulders and elegant hands. He isn't as glamorous and unattainable as Will, but he's solid and good.

Soon we emerge from the underbrush at Whale's Jaw, a towering granite boulder left by the last retreating glacier nine thousand years before. John clambers up and I follow. We straddle the top, feeling the rough granite on our legs and hands. We look out at the landscape below. The wind blows against the places where our skin is bare. I shiver. To the north is Essex Bay and beyond that is Ipswich Bay, two cold dark blue lines along the horizon. John puts his arm around me as we huddle together against the chill.

"I'll tell you a secret, if you tell me one, " I flirt coquettishly with John and snuggle closer.

"OK. Shoot."

"I'm going to run the Boston Marathon," I grin up at him, thinking that I might as well have told him I was pregnant.

"You're what! You're nuts, Bobby Lou. Certifiable. This is proof. Twenty-six miles three hundred and eighty-five yards. No way."

"John, please don't tell anyone. If my parents knew they'd have me locked up for sure."

Silence, only the wind has a comment as it swirls around us. Finally I ask: "OK, what's your secret?"

"I can't compete with that."

"This isn't a competition."

Silence again and then: "OK, true confessions. I ... uh.. I uh... I think about you everyday... and..."

He draws me closer. A flood of warmth envelopes me, a mixture of embarrassment, fear, love and desire.

We are silent again for several minutes.

Finally, John asks: "How can I help?"

"Help what?"

"Help you run the Marathon."

I'm surprised at his enthusiasm. "We could measure off distances with your cycle and you could drop me off and I could run home, each time further and further, you know?"

"Yeah Bobby Lou, we could do that."

My journey has begun. Do I dare hope that I won't be alone?

Chapter 3: Why Create All This Wonder and Glory?

That evening I work on my sculpture of President Johnson. I sprinkle the sienna brown clay with water to soften it. I like the way it smells like earth. For thousands of years women have used the clay of the earth to fashion pots, plates, bowls, and, no doubt, to sculpture.

Studying the photos in the newspaper, I work the clay. As I work a peaceful feeling descends around me. The words stop. The lamplight gently falls on my hands and on the clay. I hear the subtle sounds of the household: the gurgle and clamor of water flowing through metal pipes, the creak of wooden floor, the shouts of the children, and the murmur of the TV. Outside I hear the sounds of the woods in the back yard the pulsing beat of the tree frogs, a primal sound, the promise of new life, eternally reborn again and again for millions and millions of years.

The sound of the wind in the trees is different now. Gone is the wild eerie whine and terrible roar of winter's gales tearing at the bare branches. Now the wind is gentle and soothing as it caresses the newly burgeoning maple florets and fragile new leaves, which even in the dark are pushing through their confining bud cases and growing out into their first night.

Feeling tired, I wrap the clay in moist towels. I carry my bedroll out into the soft velvety darkness and look up in wonder at the stars that sparkle across the sky, dancing behind the dark limbs of the maple tree. As I carefully make my bed, covering it with a tarp, folding the edges under, and snuggle down inside, a feeling of contentment fills me.

Suddenly I am aware of being out in the Universe here. Its mystery surrounds and fills me. I feel the earth beneath my back, the comfort and huge heaviness of it. I feel a loving presence out here in the dark. It is the creative force and power of all this wonder and glory. I'm not sure who or what God is, but here in this drab suburban back yard I find myself immersed in the majesty and beauty of the entire universe.

How did all this wonder and glory get here and why?

I adjust my binoculars and look deep into space. I feel the immensity of the universe stretching away into infinite space.

Why bother will all this? Why bother to create all these burning stars? Just the creative effort to make one photon is beyond belief and here are uncountable numbers of photons, and atoms of all sorts. Who or what would have the intelligence necessary to design all this and what would have the power to bring it into existence?

I want to experience all this to the fullest, while I can.

I shut my eyes and instead of seeing an empty blackness, I see the most exquisite patterns made of tiny pixels of different colored light. The ever-changing patterns well up from some internal source more complex and beautiful than oriental rugs, one after the other, blue featherlike patterns breaking into sweeping shades of ochre and orange, while pale green fringes like delicate lacework slowly form along the sides. The beauty of these designs is magnificent. How I wish I could paint them, but whenever I try, they change, and my crude brush strokes cannot capture the intricate delicacy of these sublime patterns. Beauty within and beauty without, so much beauty is given to me. A sense of wonder and gratitude fills me as I lie in the dark in my cozy bedroll in the Willards' unpretentious back yard, where the swing, made of a flat wooden board hitched to two ropes tied to a high tree branch, waits for tomorrow's children.

......

The next day I get up early and begin training for the Boston Marathon. I have no idea how to train, no running clothes, no running shoes. I run in nurses' shoes and a black tank top bathing suit over which I pull some shorts and a cotton shirt.

"I suppose I just go further each day," I muse out loud to my canine friends whose furry bodies press against my legs.

I enter the forest. The air is quiet and moist, cold on my bare face and hands. The smells of the primal woodland are dank, filled with the musky scent of old decaying leaves.

I feel the soft dirt of the trail under my feet and hear the padding of my own feet mingled with the sounds of canine paws. I lean forward. My body picks up the rhythm of my arms and legs moving. My heart beats, my lungs expand and contract. The rush of cool fresh air in followed by the rush of warm air out is a song my body sings.

Around me swirl the intricate ever-changing forms and patterns of the late April woodland. The brown-barked trunks of the burgeoning trees stand like sentinels protecting the tiny, emergent new life. The silent trees herald the spring, touching the sky with their fingertips. The wind rushes by my ears when I run making a flam, flam, flam sound. An invisible body of air wraps coolly around my own body bringing news of other places, of lands to the south already green, warm and moist. Delicate beige, mauve, purple, ochre and ecru tints blend together in an array of exquisite forms, which flip by my eyes like a movie film, somehow relaxing and healing my mind.

I have made this secret discovery: that running in the woods with the dogs restores me, relieves all the stresses of suburban life, and fills me with a sense of freedom and happiness.

I'm now twenty-one years old, and I've been running in the woods like this for the last ten years alone, solitary, secretly. I'm rediscovering something here that has been all but lost in modern society. I'm reconnecting with ancient roots, to a time when women were goddesses and ran through the woods with their hunting dogs, a time when the wonders of the earth were new and their causes mysterious. I'm recovering from a thousand years of civilization and reconnecting with an ancient human potential, some primal unity of mind, body and spirit, lost in modern society.

But today is different.

Yesterday I was just running for the sake of running, and for the peace it brings and the time it allows for thinking. Today I have a purpose, a goal. It is the first time in my life that I've decided on my own on a long term goal—something that I want to accomplish for myself—something that I will work on bit by bit until I accomplish.

I think back to March of 1964 when I first heard of the Boston Marathon.

"You who love to run, have never heard of the Boston Marathon?" Pa Usher had been surprised.

I shook my head.

The light had shone through the tall windows falling on the breakfast table, lighting up the glassware with what felt to me like love. I felt a sense of peace here in this kitchen, with the Ushers, as if I'd escaped back in time to a place where the hustle of modern life fell away and only the peace of green things growing was left.

"Every April on Patriots Day they run twenty-six miles from Hopkinton to Boston."

"Twenty-six miles, without stopping?" I was incredulous. "How do they keep going so long?"

"Go out at see it. It's open to anyone in the world. As far as I know it's the only race like it anywhere. I used to watch it as a boy..."

"Coffee?" Momsey asked.

And that had led to my father and me going to see the Marathon, an event that has changed my life.

A granite ledge dripping with recently melted snow juts up to the right. Primitive green moss and lichen cling to it, while the bended heads of newly emerging fern fronds begin to show in the sunny sheltered nooks of its crevasses. I breathe deeply of the moist earthy scent and feel a tingle of excitement wash through me.

Today I will run all the way to the fire tower. This is my short-term goal. As I push up the hill I feel tired. My legs are straining. I'm not sure if I can do it. Breathing hard I feel my arms pumping and aching. I'm tempted to stop. Who will know after all; I'm all alone? ... I will know. If I'm going to run twenty-six point two miles, I have to train all the way to the end. Finally I reach the top. I catch my breath and feel a triumphant sense of accomplishment.

I jog slowly down the other side into a small valley.

Bending low, I feel the scratch of brittle twigs against my side. Finding a dry patch of leaves, I lie face down and inhale the scent of old dusty leaves and pungent earth. I watch in amazement the private lives of hundreds of insects, newly hatched, scuttle about under the overturned leaves. There is curious intimacy in the small places of the woods, the crevassed bark of an ancient oak tree, the moist corners of woodland puddles. The sunlight creeps softly into each cranny caressing, touching the waiting bits of living plants, with its invisible hands, giving them the light they need to grow.

The earth is an ancient, miraculous place where life flourishes ever new. Pouring down from above and bursting forth from within, resplendent in the trees and bushes, far flung across the sky, some wordless Loving Presence comes to me in these quiet moments.

After a few minutes the dogs gather around me, wagging their tails and grinning at me, their pink tongues lolling out as they pant. I smell their wet fur, and see their furry bodies as masses of brown, white and gold. They nose me with wet black noses and gaze at me with loving, shiny brown eyes, as if to say, "Get up! Get up! Come on the day is young, there are hours ahead of us and miles of trails to explore."

"OK, OK," I grunt, jumping up, restless to run again. How quickly the wetness inside my clothes cools, when I stop running. My leather nurses' shoes are covered with mud. My white socks are brown with grime; my shorts and shirt are spattered with dirt. I run with no trails to guide me, ducking under low hanging hemlock branches, smelling the sweet, tangy turpentine scent of pine. I feel the soft brush of their tiny flat green needles across my arms and face; I touch their thick, heavy, broad trunks with my bare hands. I break off a green lacy twig and chew on it, savoring the spicy fresh flavor, feeling for a moment like a deer.

I clamber up over the rock ledges to the top, and run along the crevassed granite looking out over the tops of bare, lavender and taupe trees that branch up, like nerves, in forked, dendritic patterns. I feel the rhythm of my body picking up speed and the tingling of each and every cell as blood courses happily along its branching veins and arteries. When I run free and happy like this in the woods I discover a deeper truer core to my own being. This is me, wild and free, running through the woods with the neighborhood dogs.

Chapter 4: Home in My Cave

Home again in my cave, I feel a sense of satisfaction and security. Above I hear the muffled scuffle of shoes and outside I hear again the sad, mournful, sound of the mourning dove, a sweet sound that reverberates with the poignancy of the passage of time. I snap on the desk light and observe the pool of yellowy light that plays over the grained wood. My biology book lies open. On the corner of the desk is a pile of philosophy books including a paperback book of essays by Sartre, Soren Kierkegaard's *Sickness Unto Death*, a Book by Karen Horney, a hardbound copy of Descartes works, a book on calculus, my physics book by Jay Orear, with its dog-eared, scribbled on, well-read pages, Einstein's small paperback on Relativity, the musical score for Bach's Mass in b minor, and assorted other text books.

The rectangular window is full of flowerpots and enthusiastically growing geraniums. I glance out the window to the backyard, a muddy area, worn from children's games, next to the garage, and a wooded area behind that.

In the far corner of my room is a set of shelves with a dozen clay sketches of heads, and the bust of President Johnson. The bust is draped with wet cloth to keep the clay moist and workable. On the walls I'm painting murals of deep magical forests, with thriving plants and mysterious animals. On the floor lie some paintings of geraniums and a painting that I'm doing for my father, of an apple and a candle. Tubes of paint of different colors, ultramarine, phalo blue, emerald green, medium yellow, cobalt, burnt sienna, ochre, crimson lie side by side on the floor, where the afternoon sun touches each of them in turn as the earth turns. Propped against the back wall are some abstract paintings of what look like complex oriental rug forms mixed with biological shapes. These are my feeble attempts to capture my closed eyed visions.

Then through the half opened inner door, as my eyes adapt to the dark, I see the furnace with my sleeping roll draped over it. I wonder if it is dry yet from last night.

I think back to September 1963, when I first moved in with the Willards. When I first started sleeping outside, I'd look out at the moon shining behind the dark veil of scudding clouds that, as they passed, revealed the silvery disc. The stars and brilliant planets glittered through the bare branches of trees. I'd feel the air blow across the face of the earth and touch my own face as I'd lie looking out into the heavens. I'd feel a primal thrill of knowing that I am alive on this magical planet and part of all this wonder.

I watched the leaves turn yellow, orange, then red. I felt the way they felt as they let go and fell down in random array and lie flat on the ground, waiting to become next year's soil. I rejoiced in the flooding, healing, cleansing autumn rains that came in November, beating down on barren racks of trees, and testing my ability to make a water tight sleep roll. In the winter the soft snow fell onto my upturned face and silently covered me, as I lie warm inside my sleeping roll. The winds of March and the rains of April brought the new hope of spring. And, now delicate new living green grows on the tips of every twig. I feel alive when I sleep outside in the wondrous, living realm of nature.

But I want to know more. I want to experience more fully this great loving source of all creation. What is it? Even as a toddler I'd felt this all-present love around me, especially when I was with Nana, my father's mother. I still remember the way she held me in her arms and showed me the wonder of the catbird, who ate raisins out of her hand. She would walk with me in her gardens and show me the beauties of the tulips, begonias, snapdragons, the Scottish heather, the wild blueberry bushes, from which we picked the luscious fruit, and the sweet raspberries, hidden in the damp place along the stone wall that Grampy had built.

I'd felt that same love pouring down in the sunshine that had shimmered, translucent green, through the leaves of the towering chestnut tree in our backyard in Watertown, the first home I remember. My dad would take me on his lap and tell me the story of Beethoven's Pastoral Symphony. The world was inhabited by an invisible love that was everywhere just behind what I could see, hear, touch, feel and taste.

My sense of being surrounded by some sort of huge invisible love did not fit with any of the stories I was being read about religion, and yet as I grew, my love for nature grew and so did my sense of some sort of Presence of Love everywhere, just behind what I could see. My running was a direct result of this sense of love. My running was a way to express my feelings of delight in being alive. When as a toddler I'd taken my first steps I was thrilled with this new-found ability to move. I'd move my legs, and lo the entire world around me would move. My mother despaired of ever making me hold still. I'd wriggle away and whoosh, I'd be gone, skimming along as fast as my legs could move across the great expanse of green growing grass.

By the time I reached junior high school I'd discovered that running and thinking went well together. I'd take off up into the woods again and again, day after day, and as I ran I would think. My friend, Richard, took to stopping by my house on the way to school and we would walk together discussing such topics as "Is there a purpose to life?" "What is the soul?" "Where were we before we were born?" "Is there a God?" After school I'd go up into the woods, and think about these matters long and hard as I ran. I'd also work through any problems I'd encountered during the day, and any injustices I'd incurred at home at the hands of my loving parents. Running made all the stresses of the day disappear.

I kept my woodland retreat and expanded my range, running further and further, exploring new trails. I also began to think about science and philosophy more seriously. I remember my sense of amazement when my father had taken me to the museum of Science.

"Come, I want you to see this," he'd said mysteriously.

We had entered an open room with a very high ceiling and sand scattered on the floor, as if it were a child's sand box. In the very center of the room hung a metal container with a funnel on its bottom, suspended from a long wire that was attached to a ball bearing in the ceiling.

"Foucault's Pendulum… Help me fill the bob," my Dad had said bending over and scooping up sand with one of the several scoops lying about. We filled the bob with sand and brushed the excess sand off the floor.

"Now," said my Dad, grabbing the bob. "We walk it back to the corner and let it go."

I watched as the pendulum bob moved back and forth, spraying out a line of sand onto the floor.

I looked at my dad as if to say, "OK, What's so special about this?"

"Just keep watching he said."

After a while the most amazing thing began to happen: the pendulum began to change its course. Gradually as we watched, the angle of the bob's trajectory began to shift. We could see how the sand trace left by the bob no longer went from corner to corner of the room but gradually made a larger and larger angle with its original trace. The bob was still swinging back and forth, but the angle of its trace was changing.

"What do you suppose is causing that?" my Dad asked me.

I looked up at the ceiling and could see nothing that would cause the wire to shift. I wondered if as the bob became lighter that would cause its trajectory to change, but that made no sense.

"Maybe the room is somehow changing," I mumbled.

"Close, close," my Dad smiled.

"Then the room is changing?" I surmised, thinking it might be on some kind of rotating device like a large lazy Susan.

"Not just the room... What is the room attached to?"

"The room is attached to the building.... and the building is attached to the earth... and the earth is..………….. rotating."

Suddenly my mind flew off into space and I looked down at the room in which my father and I stood, and I saw the pendulum moving back and forth along the same course as the earth turned under it. A shot of excitement and happiness bubbled through my solar plexus. That is amazing! I could see that the bob somehow was in constant communication with the entire universe and was orienting itself towards the whole universe, even as the earth turned under it.

Afterwards as my father and I walked together through the halls I felt the entire universe arrayed around us. There were stars above our heads and stars below our feet and stars on sides of us. There were dark places between the stars that somehow had some kind of existence like dark jello. We were not just walking up Massachusetts Avenue. We were walking through the stars and, like the pendulum, I began to orient myself not just to the local scene, but to the entire universe.

This orientation has stayed with me ever since. This is why I love to sleep out in the stars at night, where I feel close to the miraculous creator of all this sublime wonder. I'd felt this everywhere I went, even sometimes in study hall at school, where I'd watch the sunlight pour down through the high cafeteria windows and the shadows creep across the tables. I'd feel the same awe I might feel in a church.

That same year, 1956, my mother's father died. We had called him, Grandpop. He was a tall bald man with an intermittent stutter who had worked in Washington D.C. and was passionate about politics. Every dinner table conversation was a debate and regurgitation of the latest happening in the Capitol. He loved American musicals and used to dance around awkwardly as he played a record of Oklahoma, on his state-of-the-art victrola. A photograph on the bureau in their upstairs bedroom suite showed him as a handsome young man standing next to a fulsome beauty, a large-boned, strong woman with a steady direct gaze, my grandmother, Grandmom, taken in that unimaginable time before I was born, when she was young.

Grandpop was a writer. The clackety click sounds of his professional typewriter issued incessantly from his upstairs study, where, because of a sacroiliac dislocation, he stood up to type. He wrote many plays and books, mostly about politics, the protagonist being an idealistic young man fighting corruption and scandal. He never published, and let himself be supported by his devoted, wealthy wife.

His death had seemed unreal to me. He had lain in his upstairs bed dying of pancreatic cancer while Grandmom cared for him for many months. At the funeral I'd pressed close to Nana nuzzling into her black wool overcoat for comfort as the February air chilled us. Little did I realize that this was only the beginning of the dying. I had begun to see that death as well as life was part of a universal pageant that extended from the tiniest atom to the far reaches of the cosmos.

In the summer of 1956, my parents sent me to a camp in Vermont. As a child I'd loved horses. And that love continued into adolescence. Though homesick at first, I soon grew to love this horseback riding camp and its director, Audrey. Here I could ride horses, canoe, sail, hike, water-ski, play tennis and run across the grassy hills and through the wild forests.

Every Sunday we would hold vespers out on the hill, where the horse pasture was. Audrey would speak about life, spirit, love and friendship in a way that would have us all in tears. Overhead the stars and the night wind seemed to be part of the universal love that filled the world. We would sing together, as we learned and grew, never thinking of endings, until the last campfire of the summer, which was like a death, a tragic ending filled with crying campers. Life's poignancy and brevity was being forced upon me, juxtaposed with this huge vast love that I felt everywhere.

During the winters I worked to save up enough money to go to camp. And in the summers I gloried in new-found friends and in my growing spiritual connection with life and with nature.

When in Miss Bailey's English Class, in ninth grade I'd first read John Muir's writings, I recognized him as a kindred soul, just as I had Thoreau and Emerson, who wrote in the vein of the New England Transcendentalists. Muir felt the same kind of religious or spiritual awe as I felt in nature. He felt the presence of the Divine Creator expressed in every rock, stone, plant and animal, just as I did. But I felt it on the subway too and with the people I love. Sometimes I'd feel this same gigantic, invisible love fill our living room where my mother and father would sit in armchairs and my brother Paul and I would sit on the couch or sprawl on the floor, listening to music and reading. I heard it in the music of Bach. I heard it when my father would play Beethoven's Moonlight Sonata on our family piano and fill the house with music.

In high school, as I learned more about science, my wonder at the miracle of this incredible creation grew. I'd marvel that there were atoms and that the atoms were such that they built up in octaves, with increasing numbers of protons and neutrons in the nuclei and increasing numbers of electrons in the shells surrounding the nuclei. It seemed to me astounding that the world should be created so that this was so. What could have ever thought up such a system? And why? Or if nothing thought it up, how did all these atoms get here, and why the way they are and not some other way? I studied biology and thought about what life is. What really is life? My discoveries amazed me and filled me with awe.

In physics class, at the Tufts School of Special Studies, where I studied from the fall of 1961 to the spring of 1964, I marveled at the wonder of gravity and spent many hours throwing rocks up and watching the perfect parabola unfold. I thought about gravity and mass. Why is the inertial mass always equal to the gravitational mass? I thought about elementary particles. Could there really be so many of them? Could there be a smallest particle? What would it be like? I thought about the constant speed of light and marveled that light traveled at the fastest speed possible. How could all this wonder have got here and why is it the way it is and not some other way?

Chapter 5: Route Thirty-Eight

It is impossible to separate my running from my love of life. My running is simply an extension of my life and of my celebration of the fundamental mystery of life. And yet as I grew towards adulthood, I realized that something was seriously wrong with the lifestyle that the fifties had planned for me. It was a kind of impersonal life that I was supposed to live that was cut off, severed from, the intrinsic reality of my own personal life. It was a kind of social charade I would be required to play, a role prescribed by society, at the expense and the sacrifice of my authentic self. The sense became more urgent as I grew that I could not live the life that society had planned for me as a woman and that I would have to either escape, or change society into something where I, and those like me, could live without having to sacrifice their real selves.

Now that I am training for Boston my running has taken on a new dimension, an inchoate motion towards an integration of my running, as an expression of life and nature, with the human world, for at last I've found people who run, people who feel the same way as I do about life. I am impelled by some internal passion to run with them in a celebration of this vision of what it means to be a human animal on this earth, moving across the surface of the earth on foot, breathing the air of the earth. I want to share my running with others. I want everyone to feel the same sense of joy of life, and happiness that I feel when I run. That running is a competition hardly crosses my mind. Of course I want to run as fast and as strong as I can and to finish as well in the race as I can, but I don't think of myself as running against the other runners, rather I want to run *with* them, to participate in that river of moving runners that has inspired me with such irresistible power.

It is now May 1964 and the world is in bloom, perfumed by the sweet scent of apple blossoms. Like a green dragon, the land has put on new scales and breathes with new life. It exhales its cool breath of fog from its mouth, the swamps. It sprouts green grass, like fur, from its body, the hills. And it covers its nakedness with verdant, veined leaves.

John and I are headed out Route Thirty-Eight on his cycle, measuring off eight miles.

"It's amazing when you think the atmosphere is only twenty miles high," I observe, when at last we stop. "Less than the distance of the marathon."

"Eight miles is a long way. Are you sure you can do it?"

"No. I'm not sure at all. That's why I want to try..."

"I hate to leave you here by yourself, just arbitrarily like this..."

"It's not arbitrary, it's exactly eight miles to the Willards' house..."

"OK. I'll meet you there."

I dismount from the back of the cycle and stand on the side of the road.

"See ya later," John calls over his shoulder as he roars off. I hold my breath until the exhaust fumes dissipate.

With John gone, a sudden alone feeling comes over me here in a place I've never been before, I feel like a stray dog or cat, cast off by an ungrateful owner, having to make its way in a strange place. But of course that is ridiculous. I shake off the thought. I miss John. I miss the dogs. I'm not use to running without the dogs, outside of my magical woodland kingdom. I'm not used to running along streets and sidewalks, dodging cars, smelling the toxic fumes of exhaust, having people stare at me. I yearn for the quiet and privacy and beauty of my woodland retreat.

The sidewalk is hard under my feet, not like the soft, comforting elastic feel of turf. The sunlight harshly glitters on the metallic finish of cars and trucks. The air rumbles with the sounds of internal combustion engines. Slowly I start, putting one foot in front of the other, doggedly trotting along the side of the road, finding gravel and sand to run on when possible.

Eight miles! I wonder if my body will make it or if I will collapse or have a heart attack or a stroke. I'm going into new territory, expanding my limits, not knowing the results. On and on I trot feeling like a wild animal who has strayed off the trail.

I'd first run cross-country with Will, whom I'd met the fall of 1962. Will and I had met in the Tufts University Library. One day as I was studying physics, he had sauntered in and draped his suede jacket over the chair next to me. I liked his chiseled face, gentle brown eyes and sinewy body.

"Hey would you like to come with me and play the chimes?" he'd asked.

We had clambered up the stairs of the chapel bell tower.

"Where's the music?" I'd asked, thrilled by the bird's view of campus that stretched out breathlessly below.

"There's no music," he had replied.

I looked confused.

"We make it up."

This guy was a little weird, but I liked him.

The keyboard was a contraption of wooden levers and looked to me sort of like a loom. He took the bass and I took the treble and together we covered the campus with the most amazing sounds ever to issue forth from a bell tower.

Several days later we met again in the physic building and decided to explore. Up and up we clambered the stairs until we came to a small door. Here was someone capable of getting into as much trouble as I… My mother would just *love* this….

We cracked open the door and discovered a room, replete with a disintegrating arm chair, a stool that looked out over a built in desk, through small windows out over Somerville to Boston.

The attic became our hideout and here we met after classes.

One day he arrived carrying a bag of some grayish brown stuff, which he plopped down on the desk in front of me, like a caveman bringing home the evening kill.

"Clay!" he exclaimed.

We sat and modeled figures for the rest of the afternoon. Over the next months I made dozens of clay heads of people I saw on the subway.

When Wal first told me that he ran long distance I had been amazed that anyone could run for five miles without stopping. It was soon clear that if I wanted to see Wal I would have to run, since that is all he seemed to do. At first, I'd puffed and moaned, struggling to keep up with him. He would loop around and catch me. But gradually he would make smaller and smaller loops and eventually I was keeping up with him. I remember the first time I'd run all the way from my house in Winchester to the physics building. I worked hard on my courses: physics, Spanish, calculus, biology and philosophy.

In the spring of 1963 Will had graduated. We had met again in Nova Scotia in the summer of 1963. I'd taken the Bluenose ferry over from Bar Harbor and had been camping and hiking in the pristine forests, when suddenly a car screeched to a stop and out jumped Will. We walked along the road and camped at night in the forests together. We followed the shore around to Digby. There we'd taken the ferry back to the mainland and hitched a ride to Boston with a trucker. I knew that he and I were friends, like brother and sister. It was not a romantic relationship. And yet I felt a strange kind of passionate love for him. I learned later that he had joined the Navy and that was the last I'd seen of him.

Now as I run, following Route Thirty-Eight, I remember how Will and I had explored Boston and the suburbs together on foot. I wonder what he would think of my plans to run Boston?

Then the thought of John flickers through my head. It's been almost a year since we met.

I remember back to the time John and I first met:

I'd gone to Rockport to visit Grampy after Wal had left. It was the summer of 1963, six years after Nana's death.

"Be careful on the rocks, sweetheart," Grampy had called out after me.

"OK Grampy!" I shouted as I walked through Nana's gardens down to the shore of Sandy Bay and eased myself over the seaweed covered granite rocks, into the water, cold even in July.

Lost in a reverie, I paddled through this serene, quiet underwater world. I rounded the rocky promontory and moved slowly into the cove. Rockfish tickled my arms and legs as they nosed about for food. Underwater, barnacles opened their two white shells and waved their tiny blue fingers back and forth catching microscopic sandwiches for lunch. Mahogany mussels clung to the rocks. Conical periwinkles pensively perambulated with the utmost slowness, on their self produced streets of slime, as if their little world were all there were, and they were the most important things in it. Iridescent seaweeds, blue, green and gold, swayed sensuously and a mottled crab scuttled sideways, I broke through the surface for a breath. The frigid temperature was slowing my muscles down.

Guitar music and singing voices across the cove attracted my attention. Two young men sat on the opposite shore. Curious, I paddled into the Seaward Cove. Strains of Bob Dylan reached my ears. "How many seas must the wild duck swim before she can rest in the sand? And how many years must someone exist before they call him a man? And how many deaths will it take before we know that too many people have died?…"

Grabbing the seaweed in my fists, I pulled myself up on a submerged boulder in the middle of the cove and lie warming myself in the sun. I watched the yellowish brown seaweed, with its gelatinous floatation sacs, undulate back and forth with each sighing rise and fall of the water, like breathing.

"Hey! Hey!"

I looked up. One of the men on the rock was calling. I squinted.

"Hey!" he called again. "Come on over!"

I squirmed off the seaweed and swam over. The young man reached a hand down and I grabbed him, wrist to wrist and he pulled me, dripping out of the water onto the rocks. I looked into his pale, square face and blue eyes. He looked like a pilgrim. Some spark of recognition kindled between us. We stood face to face, grinning at each other, not knowing what to say. I was almost naked, in my black tank-top bathing suit as I stood shivering and turning blue with cold. He flung a towel around my shoulders.

"I'm John," he said.

That was the beginning.

John and I had met again in September walking up Fenwick Ave. As it turned out we were both headed for the Usher's house. I'd felt a twinge of jealousy as I suspected he was going to see Leslie, the younger sister of my friend, Debby.

The Usher's big yellow farmhouse had been a haven for me during high school. The familiar earthy smell of the back room, the dark comfortable feel of the old house engulfed us as we entered. The high ceiling of the kitchen gave a sense of spaciousness to the cluttered room. Light from the tall glass-paned window played over the oval wooden table that was covered with dishes, letters falling into the butter dish, cups, plates, a scattered newspaper. Lucky, the fat black and brown shorthaired hound greeted us, wriggling her body as she wagged her tail.

Momsey Usher was at the sink, washing dishes by hand in the old white enamel pan, wearing rubber gloves. Pa was sitting at the head of the table with the window behind him though which sunlight flooded the room, juxtaposing the sensation of a church, lit from on high, with the domestic everyday life. I felt a kind of loving presence here too. Momsey turned and greeted us, her dark eyes glistening, her dark hair pulled back in a tight bun.

"Coffee?" she smiled, grabbing an old chipped, speckled blue enamel pot off the converted woodstove, that now sported a gas burner and a row of white enamel handles through which the silent blue flame could be regulated.

"So you two know each other?" Pa exclaimed.

The sunlight caught the edge of the cut glass cream pitcher and sent a shower of rainbow colors over the walls and floor. I knew that Momsey's aged, white-haired mother and failing father lived upstairs and that she was caring, not only for her three children and husband, but also for her parents. She looked tired, her eyes sunken into dark circles. She poured us a round of coffee and quickly drank a cup herself. This was the first place I'd ever drunk coffee. I didn't like the taste. It was bitter and I didn't like the swimming over stimulated, dizzy feeling that it left me with.

Momsey, a grammarian, would have corrected me, had she read my thought. "'Not left me with'... she would have said. It should be, 'With which it left me.'" I would have smiled uneasily and felt awkward.

John and I had begun to see each other. We would take our sketchpads and walk around town sketching things. I admired the bold, quick way he used the felt tipped pen to sketch the rectangular array of buildings in downtown Winchester. My delicate line drawings seemed weak and inconsequential in comparison and I felt embarrassed at my laborious, slow drawing. I sketched a profile of him, which I shyly gave to him. He loved all things architectural and we would make grand tours on his cycle to see every Richardson building within a radius of fifty miles.

We would sprawl on the floor by the fire in the Willard's living room fireplace and watch the hot, bright, orange and yellow flames flicker and roar like an ancient demi-life devouring the logs.

"Flam, flam, flam! The wind in the fire sounds like the wind in your ears when you run," I observed. We drew closer together and felt the heat of the fire consume us.

Then one day in early January 1964, Gail had reached out into the frigid air, lifted the metal cover of the front porch mailbox and sorted through the letters. John would write from Yale. Every few days I'd receive a letter, and would spend hours writing a reply.

"Here's another letter from that no good man of yours," Gail would kid me and throw the letter into my lap as I sat curled on the couch in the living room where a lively fire burned in the fireplace.

I ripped open the letter and read. "He wants me to come down to New Haven,"

"It's about time!" Gail was relentless.

My face was pressed against the hard cold window of the late afternoon train from Boston to New Haven. The train pulled into the New Haven station and I disembarked.

It was dark as I looked for John's thick figure on the station platform. There he was! I felt an uprising excitement and spurt of something inside me.

Snow was swirling down in lazy whirlpools.

With the hot roar of John's cycle under us, the air cut around us. On our manufactured, traveling tornado, we weaved in and out of night traffic. I delighted in the perfection of the night. The car lights in the other lane coming towards us looked like two, side-by-side strings of shiny white diamonds. The tail-lights in our lane looked like two parallel rivers of red rubies receding. The freedom of speeding like this on the open road was intoxicating. The inestimable wealth of all these diamonds and rubies made the riches of Solomon pale. Sparkles of melting snow landed on our faces sending happy, patterned arrays of sensory delight up thousands of neurons to our warm brains, which reposed in the safety and shelter of our unhelmeted heads. Overhead the stars were hid by lowering clouds of snow. How beautiful it all was!

We stopped for a hamburger. Coming in out of the cold into the restaurant, we felt the warm, dense habitat of humanity filled with warmly clothed human bodies, people's faces, eyes, hands, voices, the greasy, satisfying smell of meat cooking and onions frying. John could see my face but not his own and I could see John's face but not my own. We talked and were silent in a swirl of confusion and delight.

We could have been Neanderthals, dressed in furs and leather, clustered in a winter cave, roasting a communal wooly mammoth. Out of the corner of my eye I caught the headlines: "Westmoreland Appointed." Lieutenant General William Westmoreland is appointed deputy commander of Military assistance Command in Vietnam. Over fifteen thousand American 'advisors' were then in Vietnam and we had sent over half a billion dollars to Vietnam that year.

Outside, in the quietly accumulating blanket of snow, in the darkness, the huge trees of the inner courtyard stood silently as they had during the time that generations of students have passed through these halls. Gas lamps lit our way. Snow, swirling in the conical glow of each light, laughed and danced.

John packed a snowball together and threw it at me. I packed one together and threw it at him. We bent over, working together, and rolled a small snowball across the snowy ground. The snowball accumulated layer after layer of sticky snow and became bigger and bigger. We wound around in irregular circles missing trees, pushing harder as the enlarging ball became heavier and heavier. The fine art of snowman construction was one in which we children of the north were well versed.

The snow felt cold and sticky as it soaked through our gloves. We trimmed our snowman with bits of stick and bark and poked in two stones for eyes. We laughed and then wrestled in the snow. John crouched on his hands and knees and bulldozed me off my feet lifting me up on his shoulders as he stood up. I liked the feel of his body, the way he lifted me as if I were a leaf.

John's dorm room was a wonder of modern technology. A bicycle wheel hung suspended from his ceiling, and from it were strung an array of objects in a mobile. His bed was built up over his desk, close to the ceiling. His desk was lodged in the cubbyhole under the bed. His walls were plastered with posters that he had printed in the print room.

I had felt strange, illicit, being in the deserted corridors of an all male University, in which women over night in the dorm was strictly forbidden. That weekend everyone was away skiing or elsewhere.

"Want to see my time-lapse photography?" he asked.

"Sure."

There on the screen unfolded images of buds of tulips opening into flowers, animated, growing, moving, flowering and then dying, passing away, fading, petals falling, until only the bare brown stalk was left. That is us, he was saying. I didn't want to look.

I felt awkward, exposed, watery sitting on his armchair with his draped jeans socks and old shirts. I tried to appear as if I felt entirely at ease in this new environment; that it was the most natural thing in the world. Girls in these times are supposed to be demur, discreet, passive, innocent and pure, angels and Madonnas, above all earthly functions. Had I not been brought up on fairy tales? Snow White, Cinderella, and Beauty and the Beast. The heroine was above the fray, living in a castle, ethereally beautiful, the object of romantic adoration. Had I not been schooled in the divine business of marriage? Nice girls didn't do it until they were married. And pregnancy was an ever-formidable danger, which could de-rail a life and ruin a reputation.

As a little girl of four I had declared to both parents that I was going to find someone just like my Daddy to marry, and I'd draped myself with window curtains for a wedding dress, worn my mother's heels and played marriage with my little girl friends. I felt loyal to the love I had for my father. I felt that to have sex with a man outside of marriage and parental approval would be a betrayal of the worse sort.

And indeed I did feel that marriage was not just a relationship of convenience or economics or social convention, but that it must be based on true love. This true love was spiritual; it partook of the divine mystery of all creation in which I was continuously imbedded. Feeling so acutely as I did the sacredness, even of trees, the wind and small bits of sand how could I not feel the sacredness of a union from which was to spring forth children, perhaps the greatest miracle of all.

And there before me was a human being. I, who was in love with the universe of stars, the night wind and the moon, was now face to face with a person whom I was beginning to love, shyly. I felt weak and strangely disconnected, a stranger to myself, removed somehow from the reality of the present moment. I, who was often so engrossed in the present moment as to completely lose track of time and location, I, who could feel the insides of a trembling pattern of sunlight dissolve into light, felt strangely removed from this warm human being sitting next to me, with his arm wrapped damply around my waist.

I froze. Suddenly all the feelings I had had privately, when exposed, there on the table, in the bright penetrating light, evaporated and I was left absolutely empty. All the tenderness I'd felt reading his letters and laboriously answering each line, the feelings of hot desire, the thrill in my solar plexus, the up rush of love, all vanished and I was left sitting next to this person as if a stranger, as if an actor in a play, playing a rehearsed part, under the harsh stage light suspended from a bicycle wheel on a strange ceiling. I felt suddenly homesick for my parents, for my childhood.

I could see only the outside of this person. I could see his large head and feel his heat. I could look into his blue eyes but I could not fathom his thoughts. I could not know what he was thinking or feeling unless he told me, which he did not. He pressed his lips against mine and I could smell his smell. He reached his hand inside my blouse and touched me, as I'd never been touched before, which sent electrical signals racing through my body, and filled me with boiling hot water. I felt reckless. The strangeness of it all.

He fumbled with his belt buckle and with the buttons on my shirt. It occurred to me that I should help. I didn't want to appear aggressive or unladylike and was dimly aware that nice girls weren't supposed to do this. But it seemed so innocent, awkward, childlike, being undressed, undressing someone. I'd always liked little boys and felt sort of globally attracted to them.

But there we were undressing each other like children under the hot glaring light hanging from the bicycle wheel on the ceiling. He got his pants off, as if he were going to the bathroom, and then clambered up the superstructure onto the elevated bed and pulled me up after him. There we went under the covers and took off the rest of our clothes, dropping them onto the floor where they hit with cloth thuds and stayed heaped together like that until morning.

He reached over and pulled the light off with a string. It was a relief to be out of the glaring light and I cozied in with him, feeling the warm, soft smoothness of his skin. I felt safe, the way I felt when I'd wormed in between my Nana and Grampy in their big double bed as a child. It was the warmest coziest safest place I'd ever known. And this reminded me of that. It felt like home. I couldn't imagine what the big moral fuss had been about. What could be more innocent and natural than to climb into bed with someone you love?

We hugged and held each other and kissed some more. It felt like being a child again, this thing that only adults do. We just held each other like this, our arms around each other's warm soft bodies. I felt warm, vulnerable, and safe. I felt as though I was home in a way I'd never known. A feeling of great tenderness and gratefulness towards this person in my arms, who held me close to him, filled me to the brim.

That horrible inner hardness, which I'd erected in those long years against the coldness and lovelessness, since my Nana's death, the disappointment and terrible hurt of my love for Lenny, began to crumble and tears rushed up behind my eyes and dribbled hotly down my face and over his arm. He, feeling my tears, looked into my face and kissed my cheek and wiped the hair out of my eyes.

We lay like that in each other's arms.

I yearned for a spiritual relationship that was also a physical and sexual relationship of soul, but I had no idea how to find or how to create it.

The times were already changing and I was caught between the old ways and the new ways. I was in my actions and thoughts participating in creating the new ways, and yearning for something more.

......

The next day dawned gray, still and cold. Morning light shone dimly in the window. We were in bed under the covers looking at each other and touching each other's faces tenderly. It was warm, soft and dark in our little cocoon and we were in no hurry to get out and touch the cold floor with our bare feet.

We walked arm and arm slowly across a gray frozen the bitter cold of the January beach. The snow looked sad, empty, desolate and alone now that it had stopped dancing. In the distance were some buildings. A few desultory gulls poked around the shoreline.

"Let me show you the merry-go-round," John exclaimed. We had made our way over the piles of small rocks and across the cold sand and climbed up on the merry-go-round. John did a handstand on one of the horses. I rode, in my wool skirt, astride the frozen painted horse.

That had been five months ago. I assumed in my innocence that that meant that we were engaged, and yet I had strong feelings that I wanted more than the traditional marriage role that a woman was to play. I had a life's work. The only trouble is that I wasn't sure what it was. I loved John, and I loved the way we were together, but I didn't see how that could ever work in a marriage, at least not the traditional marriage like what our parents had. I wanted something different, but there was nothing different then.

Now as I run along Route Thirty-Eight through Woburn I feel strangely alien. No one else runs in these days. For a woman to run is so far outside the norm that it is off the charts and outside the chart room. I don't fit in and I feel it. Only the vision of the Boston Marathon keeps me at it. I'm in love with that race and I want to run in it. I know nothing of the formal world of athletics, all I know is that I'm supposed to run that race. It is part of my destiny. Amazingly I never question it. I just plod on along the edge of Route Thirty-Eight completely out of place and out of time, entirely alone, doggedly running the eight miles that John and I have measured out.

Slower and slower and slower I run, until just barely jogging, I force my way up the last hill to Sargent Road. I am stubborn. I won't walk. I will run every last step.

At the Willard's front porch I stop. The dogs surround me, pressing close to me, looking up at me with loving brown eyes. Wearily I pat them. Brigadoon brings a stick, wanting to play, but I'm too tired. The dogs look disappointed as I pull myself up the stairs and disappear into the house.

"Well…. It's about time!" John drawls, "What took you so long?" He takes another sip of beer. He is sitting with his feet up in the TV room with Dick watching the Saturday afternoon game.

I bop him with a feather pillow and crash exhausted beside him.

Chapter 6: Nana

A veined, pulsing, scarlet swatch clings to the surface of the gigantic yellow-orange yolk under the bright warm glow of the microscope lamp. An embryonic heart is pumping red blood into capillaries that grasp the yolk with tiny branching fingers.

I marvel at this: The chick heart, knowing how to form itself, pulses rhythmically, here on this round yolk. How does it know what it is meant to do and how it is meant to be?

"How does it do this? How does the heart know how to form like this?" I breathe.

Dr. Payne a vivacious young man in his thirties leans over me. He wants to test out a new curriculum ... of plunging the student directly into experimental work.

Dr. Payne's work saving whales has earned him international acclaim. Last winter, he, his wife and four children camped out in Patagonia in an effort to record and understand whale songs. It was summer there. I'd seen a film of this venture and heard the recorded eerily beautiful ancient songs of whales. I'd met his wife and children who live out on a little farm west of Concord.

A sense of awe fills me as I watch under the microscope. A chick embryo is forming here by itself, sucking nourishment from the round golden yolk, which glistens like the sun in its planetary immensity enlarged under the microscope.

"How does it know how to do that?" I repeat to Dr. Payne.

"The living system is a complexity of biochemical reactions, the hope is one day to reduce the mechanics of biology to the mechanics of physics, to explain the living system in terms of physical laws," he replies,

"Oh," I say with a sinking feeling.

"You don't agree?" he queries.

"No," I say shyly.

"What do you think life is then if not a living machine?"

"I'm not sure, but I don't think it can be reduced to the laws of mechanics as are now understood," I respond hesitantly.

Over the next weeks I study for my biology and calculus final exams, and two nights a week I take the bus and trolley into Boston to the Museum of Fine Arts School where I am studying drawing. The subway roars as it races along the underground tunnels, shrieking as its iron wheels careen around the corner at Park Street.

I watch the tunnel lights flash by in the darkness and think of Relativity Theory. How amazing it is that distances seem to shorten and time seems to stretch out when one is moving at high speeds.... much higher than a subway. I imagine that I'm out in space traveling at near the velocity of light. The masses of the material objects that I am passing seem to be getting heavier at these speeds. But the strange thing is that for each observer, who is on a uniformly moving coordinate system, a rocket ship for example, the distances, times and masses on the other's persons ship appear to be getting shorter, longer and heavier, whereas his or her own distances, times and masses seem to be staying the same.

And just as weird, light appears always to be moving with constant speed in vacuo, no matter how fast I am traveling towards or away from it. Why could this be? What does this say about the universe? How did the universe get to be this way and not some other way? If there is a Creator, how did the Creator create this and why? If there is no Creator, how did it come into existence with this elaborate design, functioning so magnificently in all its detail, with such seeming intelligence?

I'm jarred out of my thoughts by the shriek of brakes and clatter of people disembarking.

At Huntington Station the transit emerges from the tunnel and I get off, carrying my drawing pad under my arm. I walk across the Museum lawn past the bronze sculpture of the Native American on horseback. He sits astride easily, with his head thrown back gazing upward, with his arms down and out to the side. He is opening himself to the sky and at night to the universe in a kind of prayer. Not a supplicating, bowing prayer, but a direct communion with the Great Spirit, the Creator of all this splendor.

May's gentleness takes me by surprise. For so many months my journeys to the Museum school have been in the dark night of winter. I'd trudged across the frozen lawn, as if across the snow covered tundra, feeling the sting and bite of frigid air, snow, and freezing rain. My Indian equestrian friend would be gazing up into the dark universe where, on clear nights, Orion and his dog would shine brightly and the Pleiades would sparkle. He now gazes up into the warm evening sky and the colorful remnants of the sunset.

The scent of turpentine greets me as I enter the long low building that houses the School. I walk along the cement corridors gazing at the drawings that other students have done, feeling inadequate, wondering if I'll ever be able to draw that well.

My class is gathering. Students sit in folding chairs in a semicircle around a raised wooden platform where the model will pose. This week's model is a woman of immense proportions who sits covered with a robe on a chair chatting with several students and the teacher. When the class starts the model stands up and disrobes. I feel a sense of awe at the power and beauty of the human figure. Her immense pink body bulges with curves. Her breasts are round and full, her belly rotund and her stout legs are strong. The room is quiet except for the skritch skritch sound of charcoal on newsprint and the occasional comment of the teacher as he strolls around the room critiquing our work. The overhead lights radiate heat over us. I sit, stunned at the force of this huge, nude body sitting so calmly before me, unable to draw a line.

After class it is late. The city is dark as I board the subway. I watch the people leftover from the day, and note the variety of facial types, people with long noses and curving brows, people with short stubby noses and abruptly rising foreheads, people with blue eyes or brown eyes, hazel and green eyes, people with dark hair, short hair, long hair, blonde hair, brown hair, people with dark skin, light skin and all shades of skin in between. Oriental people, European people, African people, each face is different and unique. I memorize different faces so that tomorrow I can sketch them in clay.

At Sullivan Square I change to a bus. As I wait on the platform a middle aged short man approaches me.

"Hey honey, want to get laid?"

"Laid? You mean like an egg?" This is the first time I've heard the expression.

"You know… have sex," he mutters with what seems to be an expression of disbelief at my ignorance and embarrassment at having to spell it out.

"No thanks," I say and move to the other end of the platform. He ambles off pathetically into the night.

The bus pulls up. I sit in the glaring light and look out the window at the night whizzing by. Finally the bus disgorges me in West Medford and I step out into the dark, quiet night. I glance up at the stars and walk along the road that leads to the Fells. Entering the night forest, I walk along a dim bridle path that is a short cut home. I know the path well and have no trouble finding my way in the dark. I'm in familiar territory again; the peaceful darkness of it surrounds me.

The rustle of night breezes through the trees sounds soothing after the harsh glare and clamor of the city. The scent of damp woods and newly formed oxygen revives me. I look behind me to make sure I'm not being followed and I'm alert to any signs of nasty men who might be lurking in the woods. I'm confident of my ability to outrun anyone who might be a threat and I know the woods so well that someone would be hard pressed to find me.

Soon I emerge in familiar streets. I leap up the Willard's front stairs two at a time and quietly open the door.

The living room lights are on and Gail is curled up in her favorite blue upholstered chair trying not to look as if she is waiting up for me.

"Hey, wandering spirit," she laughs. "Have some hot chocolate." A fire crackles in the fireplace. May can be chilly after dark. The grandmother clock rings eleven o'clock. We sit and talk into the night. Gail tells me about her life growing up, her judgmental mother and henpecked father. She regales me with tales of her four years studying mathematics at

Radcliff, and how when she met Dick she knew that he was the one.... her regrets at giving up mathematics, but the joys of motherhood more than make up for it, she maintains.

I tell her about my family and parents and about my Nana, who saved my life when I had whooping cough as a child. I tell her about Nana's gardens and the catbird that ate raisins out of her hand. I describe the wondrous beauty of her flowers and the golden light of love that filled her kitchen.

Being in Nana's gardens was like being in the Garden of Eden. Her love healed me, and saved me. She infused in me a divine sense of things, a feeling of pure love. I tell Gail how Nana had taught me to read and to write long before school started.

"What happened to your Nana?" Gail asks gently

"She... She..." Suddenly I cannot speak for my throat and eyes are unexpectedly filled with remembered grief. I cannot tell Gail how it was when Nana died. I sit dumbly gazing into the fire while the memory of Nana's small frail body, lying alone in the bed where I had snuggled down between Nana and Grampy as a child, overwhelms me.

Nana had lain there weakly responding to Grampy who sat helplessly by her side holding her tiny fragile hand. My little brother, Paul, and I were called in to say goodbye. Nana reached up and took my hand. Her hand, usually so warm was cold to the touch. She looked at me and smiled softly. I gazed at her soft crevassed face. It was February. I wanted to give her something... a present.

All my childish, fourteen year old, mind could think of was to draw her a picture of a horse in the snow outside with my feet, by trampling the snow. When the gift was complete, Grampy and my Dad helped her to lean forward and look out the bedroom window. I looked up at her and waved. She looked at me and waved back. That was the last time I ever saw her. The tragic vision of her small, sweet face in the window waving good-bye to me is forever etched on my mind.

By March 1957 she was in the hospital. I remember the sinking, unreal sensation I had as I walked along the shiny linoleum floors of the corridor. I caught a glimpse of her hospital bed through the door, but I knew that the white heap of sheets and tubes was no longer my beloved Nana.

I remember that day — raw and cold with a wild, ragged wind. Paul and I were sent outside to play and we huddled in the lee of a granite boulder on a barren hill near the Addison Gilbert Hospital and dabbled aimlessly with sticks in a half frozen puddle. We spent the day there on the foreboding, rocky ledge, near the ancient cemetery. At last at dusk we heard my Dad whistle the first four notes of Beethoven's Fifth Symphony. It was our family call. We slid down the boulder.

"Your Grandmother has died," he said gruffly. I felt a sinking, dark, numb feeling in the center of my being as though the floor had disappeared underneath me and I was falling down into an endless black pit.

We piled into the cold car and drove home without another word. As we pulled into our driveway, Paul and I, in our grief, were squabbling about something.

My Dad wheeled around and in his own pain, spat at me, "You evil child. Have you no respect for your Grandmother!"

I felt my insides curdle and something go blank inside me. On disembarking from the car I looked up, as I always did, at the stars, my friends, to get my bearings in the universe, and the stars, which had been clear, crystal pin-pricks of light, were all blurred.

I felt as if I were filled with hot burning sawdust. For days I went through the motions of doing what I was supposed to be doing in school, but inside something had died. I'd go up in the woods with the dogs and run and run and run until I could run no more. Then I'd lie still and listen.

Gradually I began to notice things around me again. A tremulous light played along the open corridors between towering white pines, touching the soft, brown fallen needles that carpeted the forest floor. I smelled the sweet scent of tangy pine. I looked up through the whorling branches at the fragments of blue sky, like stained glass in a cathedral. I saw the intricate patterns light on the massive reddish trunks and branches, which sprouted delicate, tiny, green pine needles.

A familiar sense of being surrounded by and infused by some invisible all-present love penetrated me again, and I felt that Nana was there, speaking to me in the quivering dapples of sunlight and in the quiet whispers of the afternoon breeze, saying as she once did, "I love you." And in my soul I felt rising that old familiar feeling, "I love you too."

"You've never really allowed yourself to grieve her death, have you?" Gail touches my arm.

I shake my head, "No." But I cannot speak.

Chapter 7: Springtime At the Wu's

"Oh look!" an earthworm!" Lisa exclaims.

Pungent earth scent fills me with a kind of primal happiness, the happiness of things growing and new life. Winter is over and now we are caressed by the sweet warm winds of spring. The entire earth is reborn.

Gail and I are outside in the garden with the kids. I am heaping the fragrent brown earth into rounded mounds where I'm planting peas and corn, tomatoes and squash.

Gail is fixing the fence.

I pour out some seeds into Lisa's small-outstretched palm.

"Why are plants green?" Lisa's eager up turned face asks me.

"It's because of the chlorophyll," I say stopping to tie Lisa's shoe.

'What's that?"

"Its a photo-pigment that takes the energy in the sun light and turns it into biochemical energy, which it uses to make sugar out of carbon dioxide in the air and water."

"Sugar that we eat?"

"Yep. Exactly the same."

"Is that where sugar comes from?"

"Yep."

"What makes the water and that other stuff into sugar?"

"The energy of the sun."

"Mom..." To Gail who is coming over, "Do you know where sugar comes from? From dioxslide and water and sunlight in plants."

"That's exciting, Lisa." ... She turns to me, "What have you been teaching these innocent children?" She looks at me with her mischievous grin.

"Look Mom, an earthworm." Lisa pulls a long worm out of the dirt and holds it in her hand.

Looking closely at the worm, Gail observes, "Now there's a face only a mother could love."

"Earthworm mothers are also fathers," I say.

"Now, that's going too far," Gail muses.

"Really. They're hermaphroditic."

"I'm a mathematician, not a biologist."

"Each worm is both male and female."

"Now, there's and idea. Why didn't we think of that! Think of all the trouble that would save!" Gail surmises.

"No they still need each other. They each mate each other. Head to tail," I explain.

"Oh that's even better! Each one is has double the fun!" Gail is waxing poetic.

"You are incorrigible." I grin at her.

"I hope so! Spring is the time for sex! Sex is wonderful! Without sex there would be no life and life is wonderful!" She throws up her hands and laughs.

"I jump up and grab Gail's and Lisa's hands. We make a ring and dance around the garden, shouting, "Sex is wonderful Sex is great. If it weren't for sex we wouldn't ......existicate!"

The old biddy next door peers out of her window and slams it shut with a disgusted look. Gail and I burst into peals of laughter.

"Oh dear. Now we've done it," Gail feigns remorse.

"What have you done?" John arrives, waltzing down the driveway.

"We were just singing," Gail and I say at the same time.

"I know. The whole neighborhood could hear it," John grins.

"We liked it," we say.

"I liked it too. I thought maybe there was something I could do to help!"

We all laugh uproariously.

"I've come to abduct Bobby Lou for the weekend."

"Oh really! What fun! I'll go pack," I run off and come back a moment later. "Will I need my sleeping bag?"

"No. We have a place."

We roar down the Connecticut Thruway on his cycle.

Professor's Wu's house is in the country outside New Haven. It is hand-built, with ladders going up the walls, many levels and wonderful spaces, with light flooding in from skylights above. Outside is an orchard in bloom and a pond with ducks.

"There you are. Come sit down. Wing will bring some tea." Professor Wu is a diminutive man, with graying hair, elegant in each deliberate motion he makes with his perfect, small hands.

We sit around a quaint handmade table. Everything in the house is small, just as they are. John has to bend over to get through the doors.

"We built it ourselves.... the four girls, Ming and myself. We set limits to define how we would build it."

"Limits?" John asks.

"Art is limitation. Each form of art is characterized and defined by its limits. Without limits there would be no art. In pencil drawing the artist is limited to representing through a one-dimensional line on a two-dimensional paper devoid of hue. He is limited... He

35

intentionally limits himself in order to create his art. In painting there is color, hue and brightness but only two dimensions. In sculpture there are three dimensions but no hue, and so on."

John and I nod.

"When we built this house we first chose our limits. The first limit was that we would build it by hand ourselves using no machine tools, only hand tools. The second limit was that we would use only second-hand materials."

"Fascinating," John says.

"We found this door at the dump." He points to a carved wooden door behind him. "This table we were given by friends. These timbers were from an old warehouse that burned."

"What a great idea," John and I look around in amazement.

"At first we built the kitchen and one room where we all lived. As the girls grew we added on bedrooms." He points to ladders going up the walls to cozy bedrooms.

"It's a wonderful house," I say.

"Bobby Lou is an artist," John ventures.

"The artist is someone who is more sensitive to nature, more aware of the subtle reality than others, sometimes so sensitive and aware that it is hard to live in the world," Professor Wu says bowing his head slightly and looking up at me from under his neat, thin, dark eyebrows.

"I was telling Bobby Lou that her work is better than most of the things I've seen in the museum...The modern things. A sculpture that looks like a huge turd another one that looks like a pile of girders."

"That isn't art. It is a social commentary on banality. It comments on meaninglessness rather than expressing meaning," Professor Wu pontificates.

"For me, art is spirit. It is the spirit coming through into the world," I venture.

"Yes! Great Art is always about the spiritually transcendent aspect of experience," Professor Wu agrees.

Wing comes in with the tea.

"This is Wing our eldest and this is Ping, Ling and Jing." Three lovely small girls come in shyly. They bow.

"Hello," John and I say.

"My wife, Ming, is cooking. She is still awkward with American ways having been brought up in China in the old ways."

Ming emerges with steaming bowls of Chinese delicacies. She and the girls place the food on the table and disappear.

"Oh, please ask them to join us. We wouldn't feel right having them in the kitchen while we eat," I say.

Professor Wu motions to Wing who is at the door. She comes in; he speaks with her softly. She disappears and a few moments later they all appear from the kitchen and sit down.

"This is delicious. What is it?" I say to Mrs. Wu.

In a thick Chinese accent, Mrs. Wu says, "This is Chinese vegetable soup."

"We grow all of our own vegetables and pickle them for the winter," Prof. Wu elucidates.

After the meal Ming and the daughters clear the table the men retire to the den to drink Chinese wine and smoke. I'm confused where to go. Do I stay with John, as I want, or do I segregate according to gender, which is evidently the custom but makes me feel bad inside?

"In marriage the wife must submit herself to her husband. She is the inside. He is the outside. She is the root. He is the tree. The wife is the servant of the man. It is the way nature intends it to be," I hear Professor Wu saying as he and John walk off with their rice wine to his library.

I sit at the table fiddling with my chopsticks. Then I pick up my plate and take it into the kitchen.

The kitchen is full of light from skylights. It is an indoor garden, full of growing vegetables. A fishpond, with carp swimming, reverberates with the sound of water in a fountain. Plants hang from the ceiling and fill every corner. The place is like an oasis, with shelves full of jars of canned vegetables. It's Ming's world. It feels safe, protected, removed from the outside world, full of children and green growing things. I wonder if I could settle into a place like this, as into a big feather bed, making my small world beautiful as she has. It is peaceful... but utterly confined.

"In Chinese the woman take care of the inside world, the children, the food, the home. Man take care of the outside world and brings the money to the woman." Ming smiles shyly.

"I always said if I get married it would be to my best friend," I say.

I look out the door at the men in the library having a philosophical discussion and drinking. I watch as Ming arranges little cakes on a tray, walks in mincing steps to the men, bows and withdraws back to the kitchen and her dishes. A kind of fear fills me… a fear that I could too easily be seduced into living in a beautiful cage and never feel the wind beneath my outstretched wings, never be who I am meant to be.

Later in the afternoon, John and I are stretched out in bed in a charming cottage made out of natural wood, like a gazebo, with two floors and a ladder up the wall to a balcony.

"I'm so happy!" John lies on the bed on his back with his hands folded behind his head. You were right. "It is the Garden of Eden. There never was a Fall. You said it's all right here waiting for us if only we open our eyes and see it."

I touch John. "Original innocence. We don't have to lose it," I whisper. "The earth is a garden of love."

"If you let it be." John rolls towards me.

"If we care for the earth and create beautiful gardens all around us and within us," I murmur.

We begin to rub noses and kiss gently. The melodious chirruping syrupy Mocking bird's song washes over us. Flowers bloom profusely around and over the cottage perfuming the air with sublime quietude and well-being.

He nuzzles me and pulls me towards him, stops and leans back with his arms folded up, his elbows bent and his hands behind his head, satisfied. "I want a place just like this, with a fish pond and a wife who dances around the kitchen happily making delicious soup for our family!" he proclaims.

He stretches his arm around me and looks at me adoringly and begins to undress me slipping his warm hand onto my blouse, which he unbuttons. I reach up and undo his shirt buttons and belt buckle.

Chapter 8: Big Plans

"What is it?" Gail asks.

I am sitting at her kitchen table eating a peanut butter and banana sandwich, staring into space. I shrug.

"Something's the matter." She puts on the teakettle and sits down beside me.

"I just don't know what to do about John," I lament.

"Why? What's happening?"

I shrug again.

"You two are a great couple," Gail ventures.

"Yes. I love John. That's not the problem."

"What is the problem then?"

"I just don't know what to do about marriage."

"Why? Has he asked you to marry?"

"No."

"Then what's the problem?"

I sigh.

"It's just that I'm confused."

"About what?"

"Marriage."

The teapot whistles and Gail gets up turns off the burner, and pours hot water into our cups. I watch the water turn reddish brown as the tea diffuses out.

"I think I want to marry a man I love and have children, but that's not all I want to do."

"What else do you want?"

"Well…. I'm not sure… I've never seen what I want…I don't want to be married the way my mother is… living like a captive… supported…. but also trapped… I don't want to just be a housewife taking care of some man's house… of John's house…

"Now we are friends and equals and I love that…. but if we were to get married our relationship would change… He would have all the male prerogatives and I'd be a second class citizen, deprived of my rights and my independence…. supported perhaps… but having to give up myself…" I wander on in a confused monologue. "I want children… but I also want something else."

"What?"

There is a long pause while I stir the cream into my tea and gaze at the galaxy wondering why tea galaxies are never as dramatic as coffee galaxies. It must have something to do with the temperature of the water or the consistency and density of the tea or coffee…

"This probably sounds weird.... but I keep feeling that there is something I'm supposed to be doing.... Some life's work... or something I'm meant to do.... but I don't know what it is... and the way things are set up... I'll never even get a chance to find out... and that makes me very sad...."

Gail puts her hand on my arm. "I know what you mean." A shadow passes over her round face. Her dancing blue eyes darken for a moment. She brushes a wisp of her light brown, wavy hair off her forehead and looks down.

"So what are you going to do?"

"I don't know. This probably sounds crazy... but I want to take a trip...."

"Where?"

"Across the country."

"How?"

"In my father's VW van."

"What?"

"I want time to think. I want to follow this... this sounds nuts... I want to follow this love of the earth that I feel... Ever since I can remember I've felt surrounded by this kind of giant invisible loving thing that is just behind what we see and touch and feel... This kind of creative force of the Universe. When I'm with people I love I feel it. When I'm in nature I feel it. It is everywhere... but to be able to hear what it is telling me.... I need to listen to it in a quiet place where it is very strong.... I want to experience the earth... this planet and to feel the entire continent, to explore... I thought I'd go see Debby and her new baby in Wyoming..."

"All alone?"

"I won't be alone... I'm going to get a puppy.

… that is if it's OK with you to have a dog here."

"Of course it is. The kids will love it. But, what about John?"

"He can come too, if he wants."

That evening I scan the paper for puppies for sale. I know just what I want—a white malamute puppy. An ad jumps out at me for pups descended from Yukon King. Quickly I make the phone call and head off in my father's VW van.

As I lean over the gate in the corner of the kitchen where the bitch is nursing five furry pups, a pinkish white pup looks up at me and I feel a spurt of something right in my solar plexus.

"That one," I say, pointing.

The woman lifts up the squirming bundle of fur and holds it up to ascertain gender. "Female," she announces. I can't tell if she thinks this is good or bad. "They're ready to be weaned… in fact we're already feeding them solid food."

"Perfect," I say, counting out the cash.

I wrap her in a soft blanket that I have brought with me and settle her in a cardboard box on the floor of the passenger's side of the van and drive home. The world seems to glow with an especially warm and friendly light.

When I open the Willard's front door and set the box in the living room floor the three kids squeal with delight. We spend the rest of the evening crawling around on our hand and knees with the pup.

"What is her name?" Gail asks.

"Moot," I reply, "because she is a malamute and she is a moot point." I know my parents would be horrified if they knew I had bought a puppy. My dad is devastatingly allergic to dogs, cats, horses, soap, nuts and many other things.... But what my parents don't know, is that I have no intentions of ever living at home with them again. I am going to stay with the Willard's, until I get married… if I ever do… which right now is the furthest thing from my mind.

Chapter 9: Parting

It is June and I'm studying for final exams. Moot has grown even in a month.

"Knock, Knock...." I look up from my Calculus book.

John's familiar face peers around the corner as he ducks under the door lintel of my coal bin cave.

"Come on! Let's go!" he urges.

"Where?"

"Swimming."

I glance at Moot sleeping in her bed, and step out into the night.

He leads off into the darkness and I follow.

We enter the night forest and pause to listen to the sounds and the silence. Carefully I lead him along the trails I know so well, through the pinewoods, to the lake. Frogs fall quiet as we pass. Far above, arches the entire universe, its velvety darkness ornamented with sparkling jewels, which tonight seem even more brilliant and glowing than usual.

John's hand feels strong and soft in mine as we walk together to the edge of the lake. The water laps quietly. A breeze stirs the leaves on the birch trees. The wind ripples the face of the water and blows through our hair. The moon shimmers on the languid liquid. Frogs croak and salamanders speak with the tongues of ancient languages.

We bend down, peal our clothes off, and leave them in careless heaps. Face to face in the moonlight we stand glowing naked white in the darkness. The sublimity of the moment opens us up to the universe above. John's large warm hand enfolds my smaller delicate hand. I glance at his masculine body and down at my own feminine body. We test the water with our toes and wade in.

We stretch out, feeling the cool liquid envelope us like jello. I feel John's loving hand along my back and curved buttocks, as though he is carving me from stone. We swim out into the middle, roll over on our backs and lie suspended, looking out at the dark universe. I think of slimy creatures swimming beneath us and push the thought out of my mind. It is their pond after all, and to them we must seem like slimy, strange creatures.

"It feels as though the entire universe is a pond and we are floating in it, doesn't it?" I observe.

Being like this naked in Nature, floating in the universe we know that the love we feel for each other is the love out of which the entire Creation is manifesting. This is a sacred moment. We are immersed in the holy waters of the planet earth. We are made of the elements that have been forged in the cores of ancient supernovas. Like the stars, we are untold billions of eons old and we are ever new.

An amphibian trills and a bullfrog croaks its deep guttural call. Is it looking for its mate? John swims next to me laying his body along side me. I lean back and feel his magic hands caress me. I run my fingers along his rippling back and across his chest. We are part of the whole, as natural as the trees and the dirt.

······

After several more weeks of hard studying and taking final exams, I have a few weeks to rest before I leave for my job at Camp Hammond on Cape Cod. John is finishing up his finals and beginning his summer job working building a house in Essex.

For the month of July I am to take care of fourteen seven-year-old girls, and to teach them arts, crafts and swimming. With mixed feelings I pack my trunk and duffle bag, roll up my sleeping bag, stuff my knapsack with clothes and load up the VW. Finally with Moot supervising from the passenger's seat, I head off to Plymouth, the place where the Mayflower, carrying a company that included my ancestors, William Brewster and Richard Warren, landed in 1620. Elder Brewster, as he was called, drafted the Mayflower Compact that set out the way in which they would govern themselves by a council and vote and in so doing provided the foundation for the nation that was to follow.

 A few days after camp begins, on July second, President Johnson signs into legislation the Civil Rights Act of 1964. I remember how Dick had laughed as we had watched the House of Representatives debate the Bill, back in February.

"Oh great," he had spouted sarcastically. "Now that intrepid Senator Smith has added 'Women' to the list, making it illegal to discriminate on the basis of sex." The entire House had broken into laughter. Gail and I had been steaming.

"What's so funny about that?" Gail had spouted.

But now the entire bill, sex and all is being signed into law. This will have far reaching implications for everyone.

Every day that he has off, John comes down to camp Hammond on his cycle and we run and play in the dunes. One day, motoring back from one of our adventures, we stop at a cafe for a bite to eat. I've been dreading telling him about my need to take this spiritual journey west, but finally I gather my courage.

His response is predictable and swift.

"You're what?" John exclaims angrily. "You're not going out West! This is nuts." He bangs his fist on the table.

"But I have to go..." I protest. "Why don't you come with me?"

"I have to work this summer. I can't just go off on a three thousand mile trip in a VW camper!"

"Why don't you just take August off? Think how much fun it will be."

"This is nuts. You're nuts. What on earth possesses you to take off on a trip like this?"

"I love the land. I want to see how land looks that has never been touched by man..."

"And you think that is what you'll find?"

"If I go far enough..."

"It's all strip-malls and highways just like here..."

"I want to see Deb's new baby...."

"That isn't reason enough. I don't want you to go."

"I don't want to hurt your feelings. I just need to do this... I'm following something... Some spirit of the earth... I want to find out what creates all this. I want to experience it more. The creative power of life... the Creative Power of all existence.... This sense of Love I have in everything...."

"Now I know you're nuts."

"Why does everyone tell me I'm nuts when ever I do something they don't want me to do?"

"I don't mean to be mean, but there's a kind of innocence about you that is in one sense very profound and in another sense is just plain stupid. You could be hurt out there. It's dangerous. Where are you going to sleep?"

"I'll camp out.... Sleep under the stars."

"Absolutely not. What if someone attacks you?"

"That's silly."

"No I won't allow this. You absolutely cannot go period. If your parents were here they'd never let you go... "

"It's not as though I'm leaving or we're breaking up or something. I'm just going to take a little journey. It would be as though you went on a business trip to Europe for four weeks. It wouldn't end our relationship. We will still write and call and be together in our hearts. Then when I return we'll celebrate! ... I love you... I just need some time to follow this...."

"You love me, but not enough to actually be with me." John is hurt and angry.

How can I explain to him how important this is to me. I am following the love, the mystery of the universe that I feel in everything, behind everything, the creative power out of which all we see is born. It is here, but what is it? I want to know it, face to face.

Should I give up this calling, which from the outside makes no sense? Should I just settle down and marry John and be a housewife like my mother? I am torn.

By the end of July we've arrived at an uneasy truce whereby I'll go across the country as long as I can be back in four weeks. He's not happy about it, but he'll be working anyway.... he finally concludes.

Three days after the end of camp Hammond, I load up the VW camper and Moot and I drive out of the drive waving good-bye to Gail and the kids. With a pang, I'm already looking forward to the moment I'll return.

"Let's go for a swim... in the Pacific," I say to Moot, feeling a rush of excitement.

As we drive off, the familiar landmarks look small and strained, as if in a dream. We drive out towards the limits of where I have ever been before, beginning our three thousand mile journey.

A few moments later John arrives.

"Too late," Gail sympathizes. "She just left. But she'll be back, and then she'll be ready to be with you. This is her solo flight. She has to find something in herself, before she is ready for the next step in life."

John walks down the driveway into my coal bin and sits dejectedly at my desk where he reads my "Precepts:"

Precepts

Love your land for you are part of it.

Love the earth for it nourishes you.

Love all living things for they suffer and are joyful with you.

Give thanks for your dally food. Eat only enough to sustain yourself.

Know the plant that offered itself to you and the animal that was killed for you. Know that life is assimilation.

Praise the sun in the morning and in the evening for it is the energy source of the earth-life.

Kill nothing except with reverence. Refrain from killing any man.

Evil is your hurting another person. Do not partake of this.

Self-distain is profaning your God. Do not partake of this.

Do not hurry, but acknowledge all things as you come upon them.

Seek not to avoid death in business, for he will not be so easily detained. Seek rather to know him as the basis of self-knowledge.

Accept him and you shall not fear him.

Sing of your work.

Let each man love his wife and each women love her husband.

Let there be respect and honor. Let each man know his wife's giving, and each woman know her husband's giving. Let the husband work so that his wife may live, and the woman work so that the husband may be joyful in his living.

Let each through the other love humanity better.

Do not let jealousy in your heart. Be kind and understanding.

By Bobby Lou Gibb 1964

Chapter 10: The Journey

Daisies dance in the center strip. Wind pushes against the flat front of the camper and rushes by the side windows with a roar. Ahead, the road squeezes up from a point on the horizon, widening to a broad flat sheet of tar, punctuated with the same white dotted lines my brother and I, as children, had watched out of the back window of the family car.

The supple, green stalks of grass sway with the moving wind as the coastal plain of Massachusetts gives way to the softly rounded Berkshire Hills.

Turning off on a damp rutted dirt road, I pull to the side, park and disembark with Moot who looks up at me as she does and smiles with a toothy grin. I hug her and she wags her tail and leads off into the brush, with me following closely. These woods are wilder than the woods I'm used to, with deer and bear, woodchucks, birds of all sorts, and yet it is quiet. The forest is a huge mysterious living creature. I feel curiously vulnerable.

August, and already the light is changing. I can feel autumn coming even though it is hot and the cicada bugs sound like electrical short circuits buzzing. The light is slanted and orangey yellow, illuminating the forest floor, touching each and every tiny piece of soil, each quivering leaf, the vibrant green moss and the feathery, lacy, green ferns. Insects sing; mosquitoes hover trying to make a landing on my hot, young skin and to help themselves to dinner. Deerflies bombard me, stingers poised for action. Picking up speed on the open dirt path, I outrun them, like a horse.

Above me, the canopy of green leaves wheels by. The flickering light and shade decorate the patterned trunks of immense, thick trees, which rise fifty to seventy feet into the air, heaving their bulking, massive weight up towards the sun and sky. The dank sweet smells of leaves and damp earth tease my nose.

I run uphill, through the endless tree trunks, which are clothed in gray-brown bark. The huge trees build themselves upward, despite the irresistible pull of gravity. I push against the weight of the earth. My body tingles. I breathe harder. I breathe the air that has traveled around the globe without boundaries—the air that nourishes the whole world.

I stop and scoop up water out of a stream and splash it over my head. Rainbows of colored light emanate from the quivering silvery globules. I pull its clean, clear sweetness into my mouth, feeling it run down my throat. "Thank you for this. Thank you for this, whoever, whatever you are that has provided all this, and who has created this beautiful earth."

Moot lies down in the stream panting. She and I are creatures of the wild. I notice how the stream in which she lolls, takes on its own form, heaping up into semi-stable dynamic forms, open systems, which, like living systems, are in continuous flux. The interaction of the flowing water with the rocks causes the water to take on an outward form that persists, even though the actual molecules that make up that form are continually flowing through it.

As I sit watching the stream I fall into a meditation.

I am looking for something. I am following something. What is it? For many years I've thought about life and the universe, science, religion and God. As a child I attended Sunday school and I learned that God is a supernatural being, in the form of an elderly man, who created and rules the universe. He lives in the sky and is invisible. He is like a King, a patriarch. Like my Dad, he watches over you and protects you, but he can also judge you and punish you. He created the world in six days and rested on the seventh day.

I love the passage in Genesis: " In the beginning God created the heaven and the earth.

"And the earth was without form, and void; and darkness was upon the face of the deep. And the Spirit of God moved upon the face of the waters.

"And God said, Let there be light: and there was light."

The profound majesty of this passage had caught my imagination from a very early age, but as I grew and learned more, I began to wonder how this God could have created the world and then later destroyed all life on earth and punished his children. How there could be so much fighting and hatred in the world? I began to feel a discrepancy between the God of Love that I felt around me and within me, and the descriptions of God as a man-like, invisible figure, who could hurt people as well as create them.

Yet my feeling, as a child, had persisted that there was a human-like, supernatural, man-like God who had created nature, just the way that men create houses and buildings. I was taught that there were three things: the empty void, passive clay-like matter out of which everything is made, and God, a supernatural deity who actively makes things out of the clay. How else could anything have form? I felt God to be at the head of a committee of powerful men who controlled everything that happened, and created everything that was made, not only houses and skyscrapers, but also nature—even the atoms.

As I learned more about science, I marveled at the intricacy and beauty of this creation, and I began to question my naïve beliefs. I had taken the world to be just as it appeared to me to be, a naively realistic view, in which the colored, solid, locatable objects existed out there in the external world just as I saw them. Somehow an image of these objects was transmitted to my brain through my nerves and this was perception. But something was missing? What was I not seeing?

Form, I had been taught, was caused by an external force, which existed in an insubstantial spiritual way around and between matter. God formed matter into the forms of nature. This forming process was similar to the way in which a potter would form a pot from inert formless clay. Indeed this was the way God created man and woman, from clay, or in the other version, God created Adam and then created woman from Adam's rib.

In science, form was taken for granted and the question was never asked: How did all this get here in the first place? The search was for the smallest particle, as if by finding the smallest particle one would then understand how all the complex forms had arisen. But I could see that understanding the brick would not necessarily lead one to an understanding of the house made from the bricks. Yet the question was never asked: Made by what or whom? It was assumed by atheists that matter simply existed, and it was assumed by believers that God had formed matter into forms.

Yet from the earliest age I had felt surrounded by an invisible kind of love, which I thought must be God. But as I grew my ideas of what this God was began to change. I began to question the assumptions of our culture that there were two distinct separate substances: matter and spirit. I began to wonder whether there was a unitary substance. I began to question the assumption that this is primarily a material world made of solid hard bits of things that exist out there. I began to wonder what role our own perceptions have in our conceptions of nature and of God.

I was seeking a synthesis of the concepts that I inherited: the concept that split nature from God, setting God above nature as an absolute ruler; the concept of man as a fallen creature; the concept of a material world; the concept of a separate top-down authority over a fallen natural world; the concept that the male was superior to the female and was supposed to rule over her; the concept of a supernatural deity. I was asking profound questions and was deeply troubled by the inconsistencies and divisions in the beliefs that I had inherited. My direct sense of being connected with the all-loving Divine Source no longer fit with the beliefs that I had inherited from my culture and I yearned for a deeper understanding.

Now, I have set out on this journey with the purpose of having uninterrupted time to think and with the hope of following this feeling of love that I have to its Source. Who or what is this Divine Creator? How does it or did it Create the world? What is the fundamental nature of the world? How do we perceive? How does it all make sense?

In thinking about biological systems I had begun to see a circularity. I had begun to see that the active force of nature was coming from within and was not externally imposed.

Like a living creature, the forest changes, as the birds and day-creatures rest, the chloroplasts in the moist leaves slow down their photon-induced activity, and the nocturnal creatures start to stir.

It strikes me with sudden clarity, as it has many times before, that no human being put these woods here. The forests are not like the farms, which people make or the cities which people build; the forests build themselves, like the moss I'd seen so long ago, building itself in this curious circular paradoxical way. All living forms build themselves into themselves. I feel within the living forest the glory of the creative power of all existence.

As the light evaporates out of the evening sky, and pink strands of clouds weave through the western trees, I bathe in the cold brook, which runs near my campsite. I change into my evening sweat pants and sweat shirt, which feel cozy and warm, soft inside.

I pour Moot's dog food into her dish and cut up some vegetables and a hunk of cheese for myself. I'm tired and ready to sleep, so I carry my sleeping bag and ground cloth off into the protective brush some distance from the VW, where I make a little nest of pine boughs and cover myself with more pine boughs laid gently over me.

Moot lies next to me and I put my arm around her and feel the peace that lying on the earth always brings to me. The mother earth takes away all the weariness and cares of the world and holds me in her loving arms, as my Nana once did. I feel my Nana here in the living forests close to the Nature she loved so much

Chapter 11: Language Without Words

The next morning, I eat breakfast in a truck stop cafe at the border between Massachusetts and New York. I study the reflections inside my spoon. The waitress, whose face and figure appear upside down and momentarily elongated in my spoon as she approaches, brings my coffee and takes my order. Men at counter talk in the low, gruff way that men do.

"Coffee?" the waitress asks setting the cup down on my paper place mat.

"Yes, please," I say glancing up into the weary face of a middle-aged woman. I imagine what her life must be like. She probably has raised a family of children, an amazing feat, and now works to bring in a little cash and to get out of the house for a while. For a moment I feel like her, as if her life is my life. I know how I would feel living here in this town, being a waitress.

She pours a steaming cup. I pour in the rich cream and watch the galaxy form. I watch the light play inside the cup as the moving swirls of cream silently form a spiral vortex. I think of how this small galaxy in my cup is connected with the Milky Way galaxy in which we live. At these moments of intimacy, I am seeing as a child, still on my Nana's lap transfixed with the wonder of everything.

"How does it do that? How does it know how to do that?" I muse. "It does it itself... How?"

I listen to the men at the counter talk.

Peering into his cup, the trucker turns to the man next to him, "Hey, did you see the way Mickey Mantle hit that homer in Chicago?"

"Damn near broke the bat," his friend agrees. "It was his four hundredth and ninety fourth home run.... wonder how much longer he'll be playing.."

The waitress brings me a plate full of scrambled eggs.

"Thanks," I say.

"So.... my husband and I are saving to get place in Florida," she continues her conversation with the other waitress.

"Yeah, my money's on the Yankees...." the conversation on the other side of me resumes.

After gobbling a plate of scrambled eggs and home-fries, I head on west following the secondary roads, and looking for good places to run.

The beguiling farm country of New York State unrolls by the open windy windows. The country becomes more mountainous as I drive south and west into the foothills of the Appalachians

I spend hours running in new places, glorying in the freedom of it. *Vast clouds move and roll themselves across the sky on towering columns of invisible air. The earth, huge and ponderous, turns itself over and over. The wind blows itself. The deep forests grow all by themselves. All this wondrous nature is unfolding itself all around me. What creates and maintains all this wonder and glory?*

At night I curl up in my bedroll. The sounds of a million insects and little trilling amphibians sing me a celestial lullaby. Far above, the vast array of intergalactic space stretches out in uncountable infinities on every side, deep, soft and safe. I nestle into the comforting darkness with Moot snuggled in beside me. A feeling is quietly growing inside me of the sublime beauty of the reality of it all.

Where and how did all of this begin? How does it continue?

Each day as I run I am becoming overwhelmed by the sheer wordless reality of existence itself.

There are no words out here, only wind, earth, and sky.

An intense sense of belonging to all this overpowers me. I am alive, and in love with everything. The sweet scent of the dank, deep woods fills my nostrils. The glorious dome of the blue sky above is my roof. All is moved by an unseen hand, flowering forth from an unseen body, intricately designed by an unseen mind, and yet, wholly itself, moving itself, unfolding itself. In the same way, I am moving myself and glorying in the feeling of racing headlong down the steep side of a mountain and pausing to look at a sunset at night.

All of this moves itself!

No one makes it go! No one moves it!

The trees grow. The birds sing. The clouds move. The sun shines. The earth turns. Nature moves itself in some grand, vast, highly-coordinated, intricately-related, intelligent way. How? Why? How did it get here? What designed Nature to be able to form itself like this? And if nothing designed it, how did it get here?

Moot sits on the seat beside me looking out the front window. Her soft white furry ears are pricked up like antennae, taking in all the sounds. Every once and a while she leans over and nuzzles the side of my face with her ears down, and wags the tip of her tail. I wrap my right arm around her for a moment.

In Pennsylvania I pull off the road and park by a field of cows.

Leaning against the side of the van, I pull on my wet muddy nurses' shoes. Moot watches me.

As I dance along a ridge in the Appalachian Mountains, glorying in the gnarled, knotted roots, the moist, mossy banks, the sensuously rounded mountains, I feel the wonder again and again, rippling through me, the delight that this wordless wonder all exists.

Each living thing seems so exquisitely aware of itself. It speaks to me in a language beyond words. The shape of the maple leaf, broad and flat, is like a letter of the alphabet. Each plant is a hieroglyph of some ancient language, each knowing exactly how to form itself.

51

How does it know what form to take? How does all of this evolve? The huge vastness of it all hovers near in every leaf and buoyant flower as if to say, "We are. Here we are. We are alive!"

Tonight I make camp on the outskirts of a farmer's field. The stars are particularly bright tonight and glitter with an energy I've rarely seen.

Chapter 12: Life Itself

The next day, I continue west, approaching Pittsburgh in the distance. The small jiggle under the car has turned into a gut-wrenching clamor. I pull into a gas station. The noise is so bad I can hardly hear the attendant as he gives me directions to the VW repair shop in Pittsburgh.

I wrinkle my nose against the acrid fumes. An efficient, broad-shouldered German man with close cropped, graying brown hair, speaks with an accent as he looks over my van, efficiently scribbling something on a work order and handing it to me to sign.

"Bad news, the engine is seized up. If you want to drive this car, you'll have to replace it," he pronounces.

Luckily I've brought my biology books and the June 1964 issue of Scientific American with me.

I settle into the waiting room in a plastic covered chair with Moot lying on the cool cement floor, panting. The doors are open and it's hot. I open my favorite Scientific American issue, which is all about the newly discovered DNA structure and the way the cell functions. I read for hours. Moot is asleep on the floor next to the remains of a hamburger bun and wrapper and a plastic container of water. Outside sounds of rain splattering down and distant thunder.

The living cell took two billion years to evolve. What an incredible miracle this is! How did it do such a thing? What possessed it to even try? What created, or creates, a world like this: A world in which a living cell can evolve?

How do cells grow? How do cells divide? How do cells communicate? They do it all themselves, autonomously!

......

I remember how I'd thought about life in ninth grade and how I'd made the most amazing discovery.

Mr. Curtis, our biology teacher, had said that no one knew what made life living. This question had rattled around in my head for days. Finally, at the end of one of my runs I sat down on the edge of a field and I thought. "I will not leave this place until I figure this out."

I had noticed a small translucent green moss plant, which caught the after noon sun. I lay down beside it, cradling my head in my arms concentrating on it.

I felt the moss. I felt how it was pulling water out of the earth with its roots. I felt how its green filaments were catching photons of light from the sun, with its chloroplasts, and using that energy to make sugar.

I put my face next to the moss, then I stretched out full length and lay on my stomach with my head in my hands, elbows propped on the soft earth looking at the delicate beauty of the moss and I thought harder than I'd ever thought before.

"What makes you alive? How are you different from a stone?" I imagined myself within the moss, inside its delicate structure, inside a single cell. I could see that it was a complex system of complex molecules all organized and ordered... but organized and ordered by what?

What was this moss doing? There were no little green men running around organizing it and building it. It was not as if it were a machine and someone had designed and built it.

"Is there something inside it which is living and it confers this property of livingness on the cell?" I wondered. "What could it be? When something dies, does that thing leave?"

"If it itself is not living, but something inside it is what makes it living, then what makes that inside thing living? Is there something inside the inside thing that makes it living? Where does it stop? At some point there has to be something that is just living, that is living in itself.

What is this 'living'? Just saying there is a ghost or soul that inhabits the machine and makes it live, doesn't explain life, because it doesn't answer the question of what sort of thing this undetectable, immeasurable ghost is, or what makes the ghost alive or how it could possibly transfer its life to the whole organism. If some one part of the organism were living, like the hermit crab inside the shell, then the question still would be, what makes that one part living in and of itself?

I could see that life wasn't some invisible thing inhabiting the system, nor was it part of the system. Rather, life, livingness, had to be a property of the whole system working together. The living cell lived because of its internal functioning as a whole, not because of something else, which inhabited it or some part of it, which conferred life to it.

But what was this thing that it did as a whole that made it living? What was creating this activity? I could find nothing like a motor that was hitched up to a piston, which was creating the motion of something else. The chromosomes weren't making the mitochondria move. All the processes were going on autonomously within the cell as a whole. The whole cell was doing it somehow and each of its parts participated in the processes.

And what were these processes? The processes were organized molecular activities, complex molecules reacting to form other molecules and long complex chains of chemical reactions. These molecules were catalyzing other reactions, all held together by membranes, which were themselves being organized and built out of other complex lipids and protein molecules.

There was no doubt that it was the whole of the cell that was living.... but how? The parts of the cell by themselves weren't living but all together the thing had life. How was that possible? I felt my mind warping as it tried to grasp this concept, tried to understand something new, tried to think its way through this riddle.

"What is organizing it? How does the cell and its molecules know how to do all this?"

Finally, exhausted by this effort, I fell back and rolled onto my back and looked up at the sky. The dogs, sensing a motion, stood up and pressed around me, nosing me, "Can we go now? Have we had enough of this senseless lying about?"

My mind went absolutely blank and I despaired of ever solving this puzzle, of ever understanding what life was. I drifted off into a kind of dazed sleep.

After sometime, I came to, with a peculiar excited tingling sensation in the top of my rib cage. I felt something nonverbal, some wordless set of relationships had put themselves together in my brain, and then bubbled up into the part of my brain where there were words.

I sat there some more. The thought was so fragile I was afraid if I moved it would vanish.

Yes, it was coming clearer now. It was like watching a photograph developing from a faint image, getting stronger and stronger until I could make out what it was.

I ran through it again, *"The living system is not static like the rock. OK, I see that. The living system is a continual interplay of internal processes. OK, I see that. In some sense it is the processes that make it living. OK... And then what?*

"What is it doing?"

It is taking the carbon dioxide of the air, the energy of the sun, the minerals of the soil, and water into itself.

I imagined this happening at the molecular level. I could go inside the cell and see the little molecules dancing....

And... And... The living system is taking these ingested molecules dissociating and rearranging them and using them to... to.... to what? To build itself."

"To build itself. To Build It Self. TO BUILD ITSELF!"

"Ah Ha!

"That's what life is doing. It is building itself. It is taking the molecules and energy of its environment and it is bringing them into itself and rearranging them into itself!!

"But what is itself?

"Itself is just the sum total of all this activity of this living system, which is constantly building itself in this highly organized way ... into itself. There is a circularity to it, in which what is being built is also what is building. And, that's what life is!"

Here as I sit reading Scientific American I see the secret of how living organisms remember how to build themselves! I see that contrary to popular belief, the DNA does not control the cell like some king. Rather, the cell uses the DNA to remember how to build the molecules out of which it constructs itself and through which it regulates itself.

The whole cell works together in highly coordinated complex activities, regulating itself, and building itself... forming itself, through its activity as a whole and through the activities of each of its parts. Here again is this curious self-activity, self-organizing, self-structuring that I'd seen in the moss and in the woods at home.

This paradoxically recursive phenomenon strikes me as something ignored by both science and religion. In a mechanical system, what is made and what is doing the making are separate, and the one acts to make the other. But in nature, especially in living systems there is this curious reflexivity, where what is organized is what is doing the organizing, what is formed is what is doing the forming, what is acted upon is what is acting.

How is this possible? It is as if the living system knows how to do everything it does and goes about doing it in a methodical way. What kind of knowing is this? What kind of universe would it have to be in order for self-forming systems to arise?

I lapse into deep thought.

If, in a mechanical system, something other than the system designs and builds it, but in nature these systems are designing and building themselves, then this self-building must involve the processes of interaction. How is this possible? It seems to me that by insisting on nature being a machine-like mechanism, scientists are subliminally requiring there to be an external designer builder, which has traditionally been God. But is this true?

Is this what God is, an external or supernatural designer builder of nature? Does nature need such a designer builder or can it design and build itself, and if so, what then is God? Even if it can design and build itself, how does nature come to exist in such a way so as to be able to design and to build itself? Just saying it can design and build itself, if it can, doesn't explain how it exists in the first place or how it finds itself with the ability to design and to build itself, if it can.

This self-forming ability of nature reminds me of the way the rock knows how to follow the trajectory of a parabola, as I'd learned in my physics course at Tufts. The rock interacts with the earth and that interaction causes both participants to change their motions. The molecules in a living cell interact with each other the through these interactions create new compounds, new processes and new dynamic structures.

In nature there seems to be this kind of self-formative intelligence, not as something in addition to or separate from that which interacts, but as an intrinsic property, or ability, of interaction, which arises simply from the shape, activity, form and ability of the interacting components to interact in the ways they do in various circumstances. The projectile is able to follow its own interactive trajectory in relationship to the earth, which is embedded in the whole universe.

Once the idea of self-forming systems had occurred to me, I began to see them everywhere in nature, not only in living systems but also in chemical and physical systems. In nature there are no little green men running around building things and making things move. In nature all this motion and formation is being accomplished by actions and interactions of the parts of the systems themselves.

But that still leaves the question of what designed the world so that DNA could vary itself to produce new life forms? It does it itself, as the organism interacts with its environment. I see that, but what designed it to be able to do it itself? What intrinsic power does it have to allow it to form itself from the inside out?

Here is the very creative force of the universe at work right before my eyes in every cell. The more I learn about science the closer I am to this Creative Power of all existence. But what is this Creative Power I'm seeing, which acts from the inside out?

......

"Your car's done," the receptionist interrupts my thoughts.

"Oh great. How much?"

"One hundred and thirty-five dollars,"

Wow, that makes a big dent in my four hundred dollars, which is all I have left of my camp earnings. I count out the bills and fold up the statement yellow copy. This leaves me with only two hundred and sixty-five dollars to get all the way to California and back.

The bright neon lights make jiggling patterns, on the windshield and on the water on the street, which are beautiful to me. If I have been given a gift, it is the gift of seeing beauty. Everything is beautiful, the patterns of rain on the window, the reflections of lights on the pavement, people's faces, the cracks on the pavement, dust in the road. All speaks to me of an unseen power, which creates, with astounding care and love, the tiniest detail. The living cell has evolved itself as part of this. But how?

I drive into the nighttime suburbs. The rain has stopped. It is late by the time I find a small dirt road and drive off into absolute blackness. I have no idea where I am but I pull over to the side find a flat place to lie down and fall into a deep sleep.

Chapter 13: Afternoon Pond

The green pastures and neat farms of Pennsylvania give way to the ragged hills of West Virginia.

"Yeah! West Virginia," I shout as we pass the sign on the border. Moot wags her tail and puts her paw on my arm.

I make camp in West Virginia beside a pond.

Steaming, fetid pools of algae reek of life and death; pond lilies build themselves in eight-sided symmetry, the delicate, breathtaking beauty of their pure white internal chamber, like a tiny church, with praying hands folded, purple, pubescent, unabashedly sexy. Gaudy stamens hang thick with semen, in the heat of late afternoon, waiting, desiring, wanting only to be consumed, and in that consumption to bind into new life, to become together what neither can separately be: Consummated— a life and death wish.

The wild, invisible air embraces me, caresses my body, touches my bare legs and arms and face with its windy fingers, and engulfs me with its voluminous body. It loves me in the very fact of its being; it nourishes me with every breath I take, and I respond with love.

An intuition comes flooding through my mind and suffuses itself into my being again. The Creator is not a separate head. The creator is not off somewhere else. The Creator is fully present. That which designs and builds the objects and phenomena of nature is not separate from, but is infused all through nature. It is not a top down hierarchy, a master slave, king subject, mechanic machine relationship between the Creator and the world, but is rather a reflexive relationship, where what is designed is infused somehow with what is designing it, and what is built is infused somehow with what is building it.

How else can living systems have arisen as self-builders? Self-building implies an intrinsic reflexive act of building itself. This is, to me, a most astounding miracle. All of nature partakes of this quality.

A sense of awe and wonder floods me as I begin to realize the implications of this mystery revealed. This is different from anything I have ever known, different from everything I have ever been taught. In science, nature is seen as a giant machine. In science nature simply exists, and the question is never asked how or why. Science is consumed with understanding the intricacies of the machine, refusing to make speculations as to the reason why that machine exists or how it got here. Science makes no assumptions about the existence of a creator or a creative force, much less of an anthropomorphic deity, which can act to create such a wonder. Religion, too, assumes that nature is a machine, and, being a machine, it must need a mechanic to design and build it.

Reality is much more astounding and miraculous than any of our small human models have led us to believe.

I have not understood Nature in all its immensity before. My very understanding and image of the Creator is changing; it is becoming much more immense and more immediately present than I have ever imagined. The entire natural world feels like Nana's garden, imbued with this same love, a love that flows from the Creator and spreads in wonder and glory, through all creation. What then is the true nature of the Creative Power of the Universe?

I run on, and on lost in thought, consumed with the experience of the moment. I dance down the hill like a rivulet sparkling in the sun, joyfully celebrating all existence. This is why I run. Running is for me the doorway to the Divine Nature of all being.

......

I recline in an afternoon pond.

Moot, once white is now black. Fury legs and nose, mud-happy, smiling dog, her wise, yellow wolf eyes are laughing.

Luminous ripples move steadily across the pool, expanding methodically with constant speed. I focus on the image of trees, clouds and blue sky reflecting in the mirror surface, and, holding that image in my eye, I focus again on the fragmented, brown bottom, the old sticks and leaves, muffled over with filaments of mossy, gooey, dirty algae, which hang in soft beards, wiggling, like worms, in the subtle currents, where among sediments, sedulously settling, segmented nymphs, flatworms, and eyeless slimy things live.

I stretch out my smooth, tan body feeling the cool wetness against my bare skin. I lie here on my back watching the landscape of my body move rhythmically up and down as I breathe, in the same way I watch the rest of the pond breathe.

My internal ecology is as far from my own conscious creation and control as the ecology of the leeches, who nose about in the decaying, encrusted dying leaves at the bottom of the pond.

My body knows how to take care of itself, how to breath, how to form and build itself, how to keep the billions of cells all working together. My larger self knows how to do it, without the knowledge, conscious intent or even the consent, of the small me that I think I am. This is most extravagant.

Why bother with all this? What is doing this? What is this sense of holiness that I am following?

There is a Presence to it, which is everywhere and in everything, once you see it. Something holy, something full of love, brimming with divine mystery, even in this tepid, dirty pond.... something that feels like a vast, all-present, transcendent Love, but it is a different understanding than I've ever had before.... perhaps I need more words or new words.... or no words at all...

How can life build itself?

Life is a special kind of system, which occurs in nature, which is capable of taking the molecules and energy of its environment and reconstructing them into itself. And yet until it does so, it doesn't exist to do so.

How can a living system exist in order to build itself until it has already built itself? This paradoxical thought gives me a peculiar sensation. It is a disorienting thought, one that has no place in the preexisting structures of my mind. It is a thought that threatens to force me to change my preconceptions, to grow, and therefore it is a scary thought; yet, some how it is true.

I watch a neon blue dragonfly, perched on the end of a dead tree branch that sticks up out of the water, cleaning itself like a cat. I think about how it has evolved wings, and how it recapitulates its evolution in its metamorphosis from nymph to dragonfly. How can such a thing happen? A crawling creature like a segmented worm sprouts wings, not only wings but the entire neuromuscular apparatus that makes flying possible. It cannot be just an accident. It cannot be a mistake; living organisms must at least have the built-in ability to vary their phenotypes by varying the way their genotypes are expressed and ultimately varying those genotypes themselves, under certain circumstances, even if such varying is brought about by the organisms' reactions to external conditions and has a randomicity to it.

All life is related on the molecular level. All living systems have genes made out to the same amino acid base pairs. All living systems have similar metabolic pathways. The closer any two species are genetically, the more recently they have diverged evolutionarily. These primitive creatures in the pond are my illustrious ancestors. I could hang their photographs on my library wall along with my grand parents. Even the trees, shimmering in the afternoon breeze overhead, dappling the silent sunlight, share the same genes and biochemical organizations. What greater miracle than the wonder of evolution! What greater expression of love than the inter relatedness of the family of living creatures?

I am in a sacred place.

Weightless light plays through the rippling heavy green leaves. Transcendent light, traveling through the universe at the fastest known speed, reflects here insubstantially. The wonder remains intact. Not explained away with a myth or story or belief, but directly experienced, in all its mystery. How sweet to savor the mystery itself, the humility of realizing how much I do not know, the sense of awe it inspires.

Here in this forgotten, fecund pond, resting under water, with all my relatives, I can feel the sweep of the emergence of self-building life over the past four billion years, I can feel it as the manifestation of the divine mystery. I can see the extraordinary in every ordinary thing. I lie back and take a deep breath.

I am flooded with love as I watch how the delicate line of interface between water and air trembles in response to the wind and I watch how lovingly each pattern of light is meticulously reflected by the smooth, relaxed surface of the water. I wonder at the abundance of water on the earth. Surely this is the holy water of the earth, abundantly and freely given, poured forth in an expression of divine love, which provides for all creatures, each part of it responding to each other part with perfect love.

Here I rest in the self-spawning bosom of the fruitful earth and find perfect peace. I look up in wonder, and feel the companionship of all these intricate self-builders, brimming with the excitement of becoming themselves again and again. These all are as familiar to me as myself. I am looking into my own face. I am all this, and it is me.

Thank you for this gift of life. Thank you for letting me experience this life here on earth full of its own splendor and glory. Thank you, whatever You are; brimming with this tough, tender love.

I reach out and touch the water gently, lovingly with my fingers and it responds with perfectly concentric overlapping rings, which expand regularly across the pond, transferring its motion to the tiny bits of dust and leaves against the dark, moist edges, overhung with roots and dank, secret chambers hidden under the banks where still more self builders live, lurking.

Suddenly it strikes me that that at which I am looking is looking back at me. Strange thought. Trees don't have eyes. Water doesn't have eyes. Frogs, yes, they no doubt have seen me and that is why they are keeping quiet. The dragonfly perched on the twig sees me, perhaps not knowing what I am, but never the less seeing. I realize that at this moment I am immersed in a vast ocean of consciousness, which arises not just within me, but all around me.

Each leaf, each twig, each animal, each form of nature, even the delicate ripples, the air, even, if I could see them, the atoms and molecules, and certainly light itself... all of it seems to glow with a sense of itself, not a perception such as I have with my complex brain... but a sense, somehow, embodied in its very form, of its own existence as it is.

Lazily, I fold and unfold my hand, swishing the water, feeling the pull of the liquid. I watch the ripples spread out across the pond catching delicate edges of light as they move. What is it that I'm actually thinking to make my hand move? What is a thought?

"How is it that thoughts can become physical motion?" I don't know how my thoughts can possibly activate my nerves and cause my hand to physically move.

What is consciousness and how can it arise?

Chapter 14: Who Am I?

From Wheeling West Virginia I call Uncle Fred and Aunt Lois. Then, Moot and I drive across the fertile green rolling farmland of Ohio. I watch the "Burma Shave" signs flip by. After filling a pan of water for Moot in a ladies room at a truck stop on Route Sixty-Six outside of Dayton Ohio, I splash water on my face, brush my teeth, and smooth my hair.

I sit eating a plate of scrambled eggs and writing to John.

"Coffee?" asks the waitress.

"Thanks."

I watch the creamy galaxy form itself in my cup and marvel.

Deep, dank, pungent earth underlies all of Ohio and Indiana. The smell of it tickles your nose when you run. The sweet smell of green grass, oats, and corn makes you want to laugh.

Early in the evening I turn up Fred's and Lois's driveway in Indianapolis. The door opens and the family pours out onto the front lawn.

"Fred! Lois!" I throw my arms around Lois.

The kids, Peter and Lindsay jump on my back, shouting "Horse, Horse."

"Bobby Lou! How are you! You look great! I haven't seen you for an age." Lois exclaims in her warm low voice.

Appearing right behind Lois. Fred says, "Robert! Hey you don't look half bad for a week on the road." He has always kidded me by calling me "Robert."

"Hey you guys look great!"

"Horse! Horse!" the kids shout.

I whiny and snort and canter around with a kid or two on my back.

Do you still have the ships bells?" I ask

We spend several days together. The kids help me paint a colorful mural on the piece of canvas that is fixed on top of the VW van. My Dad put the canvas there to help keep it cool inside, never thinking that someday it would become a mural. After a few days, I feel the tug of my journey beckoning on ahead of me. I drive west across Illinois.

As I cross the Mississippi River at Hannibal, Missouri, the flat, wide water moves under me, slowly like the skin of a snake. I sense an inner shift. As subtly as the currents change, I stop moving away from something and I start moving toward something.

The land is flatter and bigger as we leave Missouri and enter into Kansas. We find a farm, with fulsome fields of corn and a tidy little white house that looks like a good place to rest for the night. I walk up and knock on the door.

The farmer is a woman. She invites me in to supper. She is there alone with her paralyzed son, who is about eight years old. We talk into the night. Her husband left her because she would not institutionalize the boy. God is with her everyday, she says. I feel so much love inside this house I can almost touch it. The boy glows with a kind of love and so does the mother. Once again, I find everywhere I look, in what is taken to be ordinary lives, I find extraordinary people, living with extraordinary courage, beauty and love.

The woman asks me if I need money. I confess that replacing the engine in Pittsburgh has left me a bit short. She reckons that the fences need painting and that if I want to stay and paint the fences she could pay me a little something. She offers me a bed in the house, but I tell her I love to sleep outside under the stars. She understands what I am saying. "We all find God in our own ways," she says with a sweet smile that for a moment reminds me of Nana. I feel touched by being so understood and accepted.

At night as I lie back on the earth, Moot draped over me, her chin resting on my chest, I look up into the soft night out into the infinite heavens and hear the singing of the wind in the grass around me. I feel brimming over with this love that I am following, a sense of well-being here where the human, the divine and nature are joined into one harmonious whole.

The earth is turning beneath me and I look up and out searching the infinite universe with my eyes for some answer. "This is who I am."

I listen to the crickets chirping and buzzing in the singing grass around me as if a huge orchestra is playing out here under the stars, the near insects play a lower pitch and less frequent, the more distant ones higher and faster. Hearing the tiny fragile buzz of a mosquito, I pull my hair over my face as mosquito netting and snuggle down so only my eyes are showing, eyes with which I see the glory of the night etched across the sky. I feel a joyful tingling in every cell of my body as I realize that the same life that permeates the universe is in me. Moot stirs in her sleep and yelps as she chases something in a dream.

......

The next day I set out on my morning run along a dirt road behind the farm house. The land is slightly rolling and the roads are laid out straight. I love the openness of this place and find myself thinking as I run. Running and thinking go well together. For hours there is no telephone and nothing else to do but enjoy the beauty of the day and think.

"What is consciousness, then?" I find myself thinking. *Is there a consciousness in everything? Is there only one type of consciousness and everything tunes into that, in some way? Is the entire cosmos as a whole conscious? Does each type of thing have its own consciousness? Are only animals with nervous systems conscious? Are only humans conscious? Are only some types of system conscious?*

63

I doubt if a refrigerator feels cold to itself. I'd be very surprised if a car has some kind of subjective experience. But what about a rock or a tree? What about an atom or a photon of light? Could it have some sort of subjective experience, some sort of inner experience of itself?

How could I ever tell, since there would be no way of getting inside that other system to detect its consciousness? Science cannot detect consciousness because consciousness is not an extended thing with location, mass or energy. Most religious doctrine considers consciousness as a kind of insubstantial spirit that inhabits an otherwise material world. But neither of these views is satisfactory to me.

I am conscious and that means I am awake, and sensately aware of my surroundings. I can also be unconscious, or I can be asleep. When I am unconscious is there part of me, way inside, that is still aware of itself? When I'm asleep I'm not aware of my surroundings but I am aware of my dreams. Whoever "I" am. Who is this "I" who is aware and who decides to move my muscles? Who is this "I" who has decided to run the Boston Marathon and who decided to run this morning and who keeps my arms and legs moving and my breathing and heart beat in synchrony?

What is this ability to be aware of itself? And who or what has this ability? What is a subjective experience, and who or what has it?

Descartes has said that I think therefore I am, but it seems to me rather that all I can say is that, in so far as I think I exist, I am that thinking.

On and on I run feeling the morning air warming in the sun. Moot trots on ahead, then stops to sniff the bushes. Moot, I have no doubt, is conscious. Her sensate world may be different from mine, but still there is no doubt to me that she has a subjective experience of her surroundings, and so do other mammals, and birds, snakes, and even insects. Is this ability to subjectively perceive inherent in nervous systems?

I'd seen that there is a self-formative intelligence inherent in nature and in natural systems, and that it is not separate from the thing itself. It is not like an insubstantial, invisible, weightless, separate intelligence entering into a system; rather the system itself is the embodiment of the intrinsic, dynamic, self-formative ability of nature. *The ability of parts to come together as dynamic wholes is, I think, fundamental to the nature of the universe itself. But how? How did the universe get this way?*

Suddenly I see again that there's a difference between self-experiencing intelligence and self-forming intelligence. A living organism forms itself through its own internal interactions and its interactions with its environment as a whole. The system is in some sense the interactions of its parts. But this does not necessarily mean that it has a subjective experience of its internal interactions or of its interaction as a whole with its environment. There are two things: Self-Formation and Self-Experience. I might say self-formative intelligence and self-experiencing intelligence are quite distinct, though related. And neither of them are 'things' at all. What sort of phenomenon is subjective experience?

I breathe in the sweetness of morning, the pungent scent of cows, the delicate perfume of cut grass, the dusty scent of the road.

If naturally occurring whole systems have subjective experiences of some sort, not identical to the way animals with nervous systems have them, and certainly not identical to the way human being have them, but still, some sort of subjectivity of experience, then this opens the possibility that the whole of nature, in its intrinsic being has, or is, some sort of subjective experience, that is, a kind of mind. But what is mind? Is not mind just the inner workings of a brain? But how does a brain, which is a material, physical object, made out of atoms and molecules, have subjective experience? Is mind or consciousness or subjective experience just the processes of brain or of other physical mechanisms? But what, then, would give these processes the ability to be aware of themselves?

The white lacey tops of Queen Anne's lace mingle with the reddish lavender clumps of clover. Nature's divine garden is here on earth, abundantly pouring forth its goodness into the world.

So, in fact, there are two different questions: How do natural systems self form? And, what is subjective experience?

Would the whole of existence have this ability to experience its processes subjectively? What is the whole of existence, anyway, and what is its fundamental nature?

I spend a few days on the farm painting fences to earn enough money to continue my journey. Then after saying good-bye, I push on in a northwestwardly direction.

Chapter 15: Nebraska

No Outside

Gently undulating, vivid green fields and the immense blue sky of Nebraska welcome us. A line of huge puffy white clouds reaches from horizon to horizon. The wind moves sensuously through the grass like invisible hands turning the green to silver as each individual blade turns its underside up for a moment. I'm driving along the edge of a cornfield, which has been carefully planted in dark green rows that flip by me like soldiers marching.

I'm so overcome with the beauty of this place that, in the early afternoon, I pull off onto a dirt road by sun-glimmering linden trees. I spend two hours running across the prairie with Moot. I breathe in the sweetness of the grass and the musky scent of warm earth. The grass in some places is as high as I am.

As I run I watch the patterns on the road and the blue sky above. I look up into the immense trees that quiver in the wind, resplendent with light. The ragged heart-shaped leaves turn over from silver to green and back again. The vast rolling fields of grain sensuously snake in huge willowy swathes as the wind winds across the wide, whispering plains. I look up and see, reflected in all creation, the very face of the Creator. But what is this Creator, this Creative Power of the universe, which is embodied in each and every piece of it, however small?

When the sun glows larger in the west and seems to waiver with the ascending dampness of evening, I get a feeling that means it is time to settle for the night. I see a dirt road winding out between fenced fields of thick green corn and something inside says, "Yes, that one."

I turn off with a feeling I am heading home. If there is a farmhouse, I drive up and ask if I can camp out behind the field. If not, I pull off in a sheltered place and settle in for the night. Pouring out some dog food for Moot, I gaze out across the line of shaggy trees to the deepening sky beyond and then cut up some fruit with my knife. Pungent cheese on bread is my simple meal. I feel the rising cool air breathing out of hollows. The music of birds hidden in the forest, mingling with the sighing of evening trees, makes a smile well up inside me.

I am happy and free in a way I've never known before.

As night deepens I make a nest of grass, lie down and pull the rough woven Navajo blanket I'd found in my grandmother's attic up over me. All the fatigue of the day falls away, as if the earth calms me with her magic invisible caring hands. The earth, huge, vast and comfortable under my back feels again like my Nana's lap when I was a child.

The wind makes swishing sounds in the grass as the stalks bend and vibrate in perfect harmony. Crickets buzz and tick. Further away trees sigh and heave as the wind passes through their heavy, dark green leaves. My heart thrills to the music of the earth singing herself to sleep. Far above, subtle stars quiver and disappear when I look at them. Deep blue evaporates from the day sky revealing volumes of darkness. Specks of burning light appear as the stars flicker on. It takes my breath away as I realize this unutterably beautiful earth is my home. A milky swath, looking like a celestial road that arches overhead, is really the disc of my own galaxy.

I am perfectly at home in the vastness of my own galaxy. I am part of all this wonder. I am in it, with nothing separating me from the furthermost reaches of the universe. I am safe here, a tiny speck of warmth nestled in all this vastness. I listen to my heart rhythmically thumping, its rhythm blending with the rhythm of the crickets and cicadas. I know that my life is woven strongly into the fabric of all this life. Deep within me arises the sense that I don't have the remotest idea why or how all this is here. A strange and wonderful feeling begins in my chest and throbs like ecstasy through my whole body.

When I lie on the earth like this, I am filled with a sweet sense of belonging. I feel the earth beneath me, huge and planetary, I feel its weight. I feel my tiny weight held to its huge weight as if we are two magnets, a very large one and a very small one, both made of the same elements arranged in different ways. I think of the elements in my body being formed in the cores of supernovas billions of years ago. The carbon in our atoms is the same as the carbon in this grass. Lying directly on the earth fills me with simple peace.

Far flung arms of wheeling galaxies, whispering sounds of wind touching tall stems of grass rustling, sing songs of night. As night deepens more and more stars and galaxies come into view.

"How far does it go on?" I wonder out loud to Moot, who shoves her furry white nose into my face and presses her body up to mine.

Suddenly, the realization ripples through my body:

This that I am seeing, spread out in all its magnificent splendor before me, never ends.

The Cosmos has no outside edge, no outer boundary.

An object with no outer boundary! What can this actually be like? Every other object of our experience has a boundary, which limits it, defines it, sets it apart, but here is something with no outer boundary. It's one thing to say it; it's another thing to know it, to directly experience it, to feel the reality of it.

I lie awake feeling this mystery coursing through my being in waves of fear and joy. My mind strains to comprehend such a thing: an object with no outside surface. No matter how far I go, there is still as much of it ahead of me as behind me.

I lie here awake, hanging off the bottom of the earth, like a water droplet hanging under a fence rail, looking down into infinite space and time, feeling the reality of this universe with no outside. It is impossible to get outside it, for as soon as you do, you are in it again.

Since you exist, you are part of everything that exists, so as soon as you step outside of all existence, if you could, you would still be in it; it would expand to include you again.

Every time I try to think of an object with no outside my mind breaks down. I've always thought of the universe as kind of a big ball, which tapers off gradually into nothing, floating... floating... in what? In space? There is no space outside of it and no time outside of it, nor any object, or any motion. And what if there was a big bang? If there was a bang, there must have been something there to bang, and where did that come from? What does it expand into? Nothing. There is no space or time for it to expand into. Existence creates space and time within it, or rather space and time are just the way we order events, so the events define the distances and times, which we think we are measuring.

Outside of Existence, there is absolutely nothing. There is not even nothing, because if nothing exists in anyway then it too is part of it. Nor is there anything before it or will there be any time after it, because there is no time before it or after it. So there is no temporal or spatial outside to Existence.

There is no outside surface to all that exists. An object with no outside surface... It is almost impossible to think.... It is impossible to think.

I sigh. Moot sighs too and lays her white furry head on my stomach.

Something else is going on, something much more subtle and profound, ... But what? These thoughts flip though my mind, stretching it in ways it has never stretched before.

Chapter 16: Debby

I am up, on the road, before sunrise excited by this gut level realization of a self-moving, self-building universe with no outside. The sun is coming up in the rear view mirror. I peel a banana with my teeth as I drive, munching it, feeling its smooth texture and sweetness in my mouth.

"Think of it Moot! This has no end," I mutter, "The Universe has no outside."

I pause and look out across the prairie that is wheeling by, the close objects flipping quickly by the window while the distant objects move more slowly, staying with us as we move and then falling by the wayside. "It may be that this universe we think we see is one of many universes, just as our galaxy is one of many galaxies, but at some point you can consider all that exists in any way, however it exists, whether it is a thought or a physical object and you can consider the universe of all that exists in anyway, even the potential to exist in so far as it exists, is part of all that exists. Then taken as a whole this set defines all that exists and nothing can exist outside of it. If something does exist outside of it then it is included in the universe of all that exists, and so it is in it.

"Of course, since you define the Universe as all that is, you can just as well call the All-That-Is, 'The Universe of all Existences,' or the 'Cosmos.' Whatever you call it, you define it as all that exists. You could call it...the 'Meta-Universe of All Existence, including all universes and all possible universes past and present and future.'

"And when you are talking about 'Everything,' you're including even 'Nothing.'

"There can be nothing outside the Cosmos of all Existence, not even Nothing." Moot cocks her head and listens attentively, as I babble on. We roll across the plains hungrily looking for a truck stop where there will be comforting people, food, waitresses, music, voices, smiles — human things.

After a good breakfast of scrambled eggs, toast, coffee with galaxies, and grape jelly, and a wash in the ladies room, we are on the road again.

"Are those clouds? Or are those the Rocky Mountains?" I wonder out loud.

A half an hour later I shout, "Those are the Rocky Mountains!" Moot wags her tail and laps my right ear with her pink tongue. For an hour the mountains get larger and larger. The camper is straining, puttering slowly along the breakdown lane as huge semi-trucks roar by us.

"The Rocky Mountains! The Self Moving Universe, which has no end! Isn't it amazing!" Moot puts her head on my shoulder and sighs. I wonder if it is all conscious in some way?

The rectangular cement and glass buildings of Denver jut into the thin mountain air. I stop briefly to take a look at the Art Institute and push on to get in a run and make camp before nightfall.

The sky is deep, dark, translucent blue. Light and dry, the air is intoxicating. On and on I run through ancient Douglas firs; their immense reddish trunks spiral upward, whorling with dark, green, lacy needles that sprout profusely from rough barked branches, which turn like the spokes of great wheels as I run by. In a tumble of forms and scents, the beating of my heart mingles with the rhythm of my breathing. My legs push strongly against the weight of the heavy mountain beneath me. I feel like a wild wolf.

Happily exhausted, Moot and I find an upland meadow filled with wild flowers, surrounded by mountain peaks. I lie back in the grass and look around me. Everything glows with the afternoon sun. Here in this meadow I am getting closer to whatever it is that is leading me on this fantastic journey. As night closes in, the world wraps itself in soft darkness. I snuggle into my sleeping bag. In the distance a wildcat screams. I have never heard such a wild eerie sound. But with Moot beside me I feel secure.

......

The next day dawns bright and clear. I lie in the sun warming up from the cold of the night. Moot is running in circles chasing mice in the grass, which is wet with cold droplets of dew. I get up, stretch, shake out my sleeping roll and run around with Moot, trying to warm up.

To warm up I run in a large circle jumping small bushes as if I were a horse on a jump course. I feel the thrust as I take off into the air. I'm flying, like the Pegasus, the mythological winged horse that fascinated me as a child. I clear the first bush, and the second bush, turn to make the corner and take off in a leap over the next bush, which is a bit taller. I launch into the air and realize at the top of the arc, that on the other side of the bush is a huge dark hole, a perfectly round circumference about five feet across with nothing inside it except an absolute blackness of enormous depth.

I'm headed for certain death in the darkest hole I've ever seen. Moot sees the hole too and stops. Instinctively I try to change my trajectory in mid air. I throw my entire weight to the right and extend my arms and legs. I land hard on my right shoulder with my legs dangling in the hole. I grab hold of Moot who digs in and pulls me back.

I lie on the ground for a moment realizing how close I came to perishing without a trace. My heart is beating hard. I roll away from the hole and get up. Then curious to see how deep it is, I approach warily. Squatting down, I throw some pebbles into the cavern. I wait and wait and never hear the pebbles hit bottom. How precarious and precious is this life and how quickly and without warning it can disappear at any moment, when you least expect it.

"Oh Mooty," I exclaim throwing my arms around her white furry neck. "It must be a drill hole of some kind…. But why in the name of heaven didn't they cover it up?"

After breakfast at a truck stop, which bustles with friendly waitresses who joke with tired truckers hunched over their morning coffees, Moot and I head north into Wyoming, where Debby, who has married a logger, is living up in the mountains in a trailer camp with a new baby. For a moment my mind wanders back to the sunlit Ushers' kitchen and the time when Debby's father first told me about the Boston Marathon.

Encampment is a town made up entirely of trailers. People have built gardens, additions, barns and machine shops all around their trailers, which have settled into the land like pumpkins in a field. Debby throws open the door of her yellow trailer, her brown hair pulled back with a kerchief, a baby slung over her right hip as if it had grown there. She looks at me with those hazel eyes I know so well.

She grins, "Come on in, you all."

"Hey, kiddo you've got your self a real place and a real kid."

"It's real all right," she says. We laugh.

The morning light plays across the wooden breakfast table, stacked with letters, notes and memorabilia.

"This table looks exactly like your mother's kitchen," I say, "Everything falling into the butter dish."

"I know," she laughs, "I didn't manage to leave everything behind."

"So how's it going? How's your trip?"

"Great," I say.

She pulls her baby onto her lap and looks down at him. He reaches out his tiny hand and grabs her finger. I feel something in my insides move, some little spurt of something. A rectangle of sunlight, dancing with a haze of dust, moves across the floor, up the leg of the table and onto the baby's face. The tiny room with fake wood walls is filled to the brim with a kind of dusty golden love.

"So, when are you going to settle down?" She teases.

"Something is pulling me inside." I say, "Do you know what I mean? It's as though something is trying to tell me something. It's inside me and it's outside too, pulling me like a magnet. I want to know the truth of everything. But it's more than that too... I want to feel something.

"Something is drawing me to some revelation. I don't know what it is. It's like a quest. My life is a quest. This big friendly thing, which is inside me and is everywhere all around me keeps showing me things, teaching me things. I feel love. But not just for one person. But this great overwhelming love for everything everywhere. I don't know what it is but I feel happy when I'm following it and not happy when I'm not."

"I know what you mean. My mother used to talk to me of such things. Living out here in the mountains you feel that. It's a Presence of some kind."

71

"Sort of like that," I say getting up and beginning to wash the dishes that are stacked in the sink. As I wash, I look out the window and think: What if this were my life? What if I were married and living in a trailer raising a kid? Even though I want children, for me, right now, it would seem like dying. I have something else to do, but I don't even know what it is.

We spend more than a week, unable to tear ourselves apart, walking in the mountains and talking.

Finally it is time for us to go. Moot jumps into the camper. We say our good-byes and head off towards a range of mountains in western Wyoming.

"What creates all this wonder and glory?" I muse out loud to Moot, who puts her paw on my arm.

"Whatever it is... I am following It."

Chapter 17: Wyoming

Face to Face

After several hours of driving I turn off the highway and follow a small paved road up and up and up into a vast pristine wilderness. The air here is so thin, clear and transparent that the fragile blue sky is almost black.

I pull over, park in a small clearing and open the door of the van slowly. A few moments' walk leads me to a view of the most magnificent mountains I have ever seen. Deb had told me about this.

The Presence is so huge here in this holy place that I can feel its weight around me. The joy I feel is not the light, airy ecstasy that impels me to run at top speed across a green shimmering field and twirl and leap. This joy is a deeper tone, a more sublime chord, a chord from Bach's Toccata and Fugue sounding the most profound depths of the organ.... the first chord of Bach's Mass in B Minor.

I walk slowly, absorbing each perfect detail of the place where no one has tread, and where each fir needle lies exactly as it falls.

The veil is thin here.

Moot and I climb for half and hour through the great dry conifer forests all the way to the edge of the tree line, where the trees give out onto a vast barren rock. Fragmented chunks of the planet's crust jut up irregularly as if heaved up from the bowels of the earth in some primordial, cataclysmic birth. What had been the floor of a warm primeval sea, florid with plant and animal life, mollusk shells embedded in uncountable trillions of tons of sandstone, has been crumpled like so much paper by the upheaval of the granite substrate and the basalt magma beneath it.

I gaze out across the valley at the rough, cracked, ragged, upthrusted mountains. The perfect silence is vast. A single hawk soars. The silence is heavy. I stand here transfixed by the awful emptiness of the place. It is so empty that it is full.

The place is filled with something so vast, so sublime, so terrible and powerful that my insides constrict with fear and awe. I can feel the Creative Power of the universe here, physically present. But where? There is no thing, no person, no image, no separate entity, yet the overwhelming sense of the physical being of a Divine Presence is coming from everywhere.

The presence of the Divine Being is of an awe-inspiring Personness, a mighty force, the creative force of the entire universe, manifesting here on earth. The Creator is in these mountains. It is the same Divine Being who had been in the sunlight dappling through the forests, now transformed from the graceful presence of living things to the immense power of barren rock in cataclysmic upheaval.

I can almost reach through to the other side of the veil and touch the Creator... and ... the Divine Creator can reach through and touch me, not just touch me but pull me through.

I feel a sudden glimmer of fear. The small self who I think I am, Bobby Lou, could vanish and I could merge back with this Primordial Being, which I feel here, as the reality of all that exists.

The Divine Being is here not just as a spirit inhabiting an otherwise material, physical world. The Creative Power is physically presence.

The fear inside me is becoming panic but I am fighting it. I want to see what this is.

I feel as if I could disappear entirely if I continue on this line of thinking. The immediate sensate experience of the bare fact of unadorned, primal existence coupled with the overwhelming immediate physical presence of the very Creator of that existence is everywhere.

I am suddenly terrified that it will pull me over the edge of the cliff, and I reach out to clutch a bush, terrified, not that I will fall, but that I will jump, that I will want to fly, impelled by some ungovernable demiurge to become one with this power.

I stand riveted to the spot and inside me the sense of terror slowly gives way to exultation. An ecstasy like nothing I have ever known wells up inside of me and meets the joy of the entire universe. What I most want is to become one with this overwhelming Love, this Divine Source of my existence. This ... Existence is what I most truly am.

All memory is erased and I am only in the present moment that continues on and on and has always been for infinities of time, before time and after time. All the familiar landmarks disappear. I have no idea how I got here or how to get back. I want only to merge with this thing and to feel forever this unending Love and Peace. I want to soar to fly, to lift up into the very being of the Divine Creative Power. This is the same joy that has always been with me only intensified millions of times. The orange rays of the afternoon sun reach out from under dark, welling-up clouds.

I realize that the Creator is here in the raw, untamable wildness, not just as an invisible, weightless spirit inhabiting a material physical world, but as that very physicality itself.

Suddenly I see again that what I see, touch and feel are my perceptions of my interactions with what is really here. My thoughts are my conceptions of what is really here. What is really here I can never know directly through my senses. I know only my perceptions and conceptions of what is really here. What it really is is beyond all words, beyond all perceptions, beyond all concepts. What I see as matter, mind, spirit, motion, thought, color, are only my perceptions and conceptions of my interactions with it.

What then is really here?

Then the most extraordinary thought occurs to me. The sensation rocks me to my very core:

All that really exists, beyond my conceptions and perceptions of it, is the Ultimate Creative Power of all existence. The Creator of all existence is fully present everywhere, all the time; it is all that really exists and it is not separate from that which is created.

What really exists beyond my conceptions and perceptions of it is the Divine Creative Power of all existence and that is what I am feeling; that's what I've always been feeling. It is coming from everywhere because it is everywhere. It is the real existence of everything that exists. Could this be?

Chapter 18: Nevada

Marathon Mountain

"What is the Divine Creator?" Burning with this question, I drive southwest from the Wyoming Rocky Mountains through the corner of Utah, through Salt Lake City noting its lovely clean look, down across the Great Basin, into Nevada. The dramatic sculptured pillars and canyons of Utah give way to the mountain ranges of Nevada, peaked and blue, with immense open valleys running between them. I stop briefly in Ely for gas and food.

The vastness of the country fills me with joy. I keep pulling over to the side of the road, leaping out of the car, calling to Moot, and running out across the huge open grassy upland valleys, whirling my arms up into the air, leaping and twirling around in celebration. I can imagine this entire valley lifting out of some primeval sea. An oceanic immensity still lingers.

I am blindly following an urge I can hardly define. It is a spirit, which had come to me in the patches of sunlight on my crib. It is the beauty of the sunlight filtering through the leaves of the chestnut tree in Watertown. It is the love that had flowed through my Nana and the wonder of the catbird eating out of her hand. And it is here in these mountains, a huge vast loving Presence, the same Presence that's everywhere, once you realize it.

That night I drive way off the road into the mountains. The sign had said, "Next Services 100 miles."

Moot and I make camp at the top of a hill. A sense of peace unlike anything I have ever known fills me. The sunset spreads a thousand miles across the sky, flaming orange turns to yellow, then pink, purple and deep mauve. One by one the stars emerge from the blue black sea of space until the entire sky is blazing with tiny crystals of light. The earth turns majestically beneath me, brimming with life, ancient and planetary. There are more stars than I have ever seen.

As I throw my head back and look out into infinite space. The universe with its billions of galaxies and stars takes my breath away. I feel the reality of its existence pressing into me and me into it. I reach out and touch it. The Cosmos that stretches out to furthermost reaches of existence is right here before me. This that I am touching here now is the same existence that reaches on forever, the same existence in which great galaxies swarm, and unimaginable numbers of stars sparkle. There are more stars than dark places.

How did all this come to be? Why all this vast tapestry of being made with such care, why not one vast emptiness? Why all this wonder? And why this way and not some other? It is incomprehensible to me that it should exist.

Why bother with all this wonder and glory and activity? Why go to all the trouble of making uncountable numbers of stars, and even more uncountable numbers of photons? Why build up more and more complex atoms in the blazing hot cores of stars? Why build up atomic structure in octaves of electron shells? Why in this way and not some other way? Wouldn't the creative effort just to make one atom or one photon be unimaginably difficult in itself? Why so many? Why such abundance? Why not just one big void?

Then the thought occurs to me: *If there is a Creator of all that exists, or if as I'd seen in Wyoming, the Creator is all that exists, what created the Creator?*

If something created the Creator, then that which created the Creator would be the Ultimate Creator. And then, what would have created that Ultimate Creator? Another Creator? This would lead to an infinite regress with each creator being created by a larger more powerful creator. This couldn't be true.

I look out into the universe searching for an answer.

If there is a Creator, or, if the Creative Power of all existence is what really exists beyond our ability to conceive and to perceive.... then what creates, or what created, the Creator? How did the Creator get here?

If something else created it, then it wouldn't be the Ultimate Creator. If it exists without being created, there would exist something that it didn't create.... namely itself and so it would not be the Creator of all that exists. And if it is just here, then how? How could something just be here? What could that mean?

If there were a huge void of nothing before existence, where did the void come from? There could not have been a void from which all existence came into existence, because that void would have to exist in some way, and that void would have had to contain the potential for something to exist, and that is something that exists. Where did the potential to exist come from? Something would have had to create that, and what created that?

What is really here must be very different from the way I think it is. It something unimaginably different from what anyone thinks!

I feel I am up against the very limits of my brain to think. This is a riddle of immense proportions. Here, at last, I am at last face to face with the Creative Power of the Universe. This is what I've come to find. I see it here before me and I feel it all around and within me, but what is this Creative Power of the Universe?

The space between the stars is filled up with something that exists. It appears to me that the same thing that is creating the moss is creating the whole universe and that it hadn't just happened once; it is in the continuous process of happening.

How does all this get here and why?

Suddenly I feel a tiny fragile bubble of wordless thought forming itself inside me. It bubbles up, making my knees tremble even before it becomes words:

"If there is an Ultimate Creator, It must create Itself."

A Creator that creates Itself? A creative power of existence that creates itself?

If there is an ultimate Creator, an ultimate creative power of all that exists, it must create itself. I have never heard of such a thing. This is even more paradoxical than life creating itself, because life creates itself by rearranging things that already exist, but here is something that is, not only creating all existence, but is also creating itself.

This is the most astounding thought I've ever had.

It is a complete paradox. Could this be so? Could the Ultimate Creator create itself?

How can It act to create itself until it exists?

It is ……... something impossible to think... something beyond anything imaginable.

No it couldn't be. It's just too unbelievable. And yet it is tearing my mind apart from the inside.

A feeling of intense love overwhelms me as I stand here. What if all that really exists is the Divine Self- Creator creating itself into existence? The universe I think I see, the universe I conceive, is just my perceptions and conceptions of my interactions with what is here.

Can this possibly be true? Can it be true that the Self-Creator is all that really exists and that It is creating Itself into being? I cannot know what really exists. I know only my conceptions and perceptions of my interactions with it. But what if what really exists, beyond my ability to know it, is the Divine Self-Creator and it is continuosly creating itself into existence as the Divine Self-Creating Cosmos before my very eyes, and even as my very eyes, my brain, my mind and even my thoughts?

I stand gazing out into the universe feeling overcome with its immensity and the miracle of its existence. The Divinely Self-Creating Cosmos exists in a way of which I have not yet conceived; in a way that no one suspects, in a way that we finite beings can only approximate with our models. It is a mystery beyond anything I have ever known, and yet I feel certain that what really exists out there beyond my perceptions and conceptions is the Divinely Self-Creating Cosmos of All That Exists creating itself into existence at all times and places beyond time and space. That which creates and sustains all existence is beyond anything that we humans have yet imagined, at least beyond anything I had yet imagined… The thought fills me with wonder. All that really exists is the Divine Self-Creator, continuously creating itself into existence as all that truly exists.

With a sense of intense excitement, mingled with sublime peace, I lie down, pull my blankets over me, throw my arms around Moot, who is lying next to me, and drift off to sleep feeling the infinite love and eternal intelligence of this universal Self-Creative Mystery and Power all around and within me.

Second Day

The next day I awake refreshed and rested, filled with a sense of joyful excitement.

All-That-Exists is the Divine Self-Creator, creating Itself into existence. It sounds so preposterous. And yet each time I come into the present moment and ask, how does all this get here? And I answer: It is the Divine Self-Creator creating itself into being, right here and now. I feel a surge of happiness and love inside me.

After a breakfast of cheese and fruit, I stand up and stretch. Far, far to the west, across a broad upland valley, a range of pale-blue mountains is just visible in the distance.

"Let's see if we can run to the top of those mountains!" I exclaim to Moot. We set out running slowly down into the broad valley, surrounded by the quiet, vast openness of the place. I listen to the sound of the wind in my ears, as if it is whispering some secret to me. I feel the wind blowing across the wide, wild plains, touching my face and skin. I hear the flam, flam, flam sound the wind makes in my ears when I run, the same sound the wind makes in the fire. A feeling of John rushes through me, the thought of us sitting by the Willards' fireplace, listening to the sound of the wind in the fire, flam, flam, flam, like the sound of wind in my ears when I run.

As I run, my mind is filled with the discovery I made last night that very possibly what really exists, just beyond my ability to perceive and to conceive, is the Divine Self-Creator creating itself into existence and that It is all that really exists. Of course I can never know since all I can ever know are my conceptions and perceptions of what is there, and yet if it is true, this would explain why I feel this ever-present love all around me, this sense of Divine Presence and intelligence. The Divine after all is defined as that which creates and sustains all existence.

I begin slowly, letting my body warm up, breathing the air, absorbing the pristine beauty of the primal landscape, brimming with love.

What I'm sensing is not a separate person or thing. What I'm feeling is the ultimate existence itself — that which exists beyond my capacity to perceive or to conceive it. And yet... since I too am its manifestation.... in my most intrinsic being, I too must be it... whatever it is. To me it feels like pure Love, a transcendent Love so vast that it is beyond my capacity to conceive of it.

But what is Love?

Love is a feeling that arises... when... when one feel intimated related.... What could be a more intimate relation that to recognize the source of one's own being, which turns out to be the source of every other being too. If love is an intimate relationship, then the entire universe, being intimately related, must in some sense partake of this Love, and the Self-Creator who manifests as the universe, the Self-Creator, which is all that really exists, has the most intimate relationship possible, with all existence…which is itself, and which I experience as pure love.

I think I see mountains and sky, but what is really here, behind what I think I see, is the Divine Self-Creator continuously creating Itself into existence.

I listen to the crunch of gravel under my feet. Here I am, on this earth, feeling wild and free as I run through these vast open spaces. The sacred earth turns Her face upwards to the heavens and feels the invisible hands of the wind. My ideas about God are changing.

The Creator is not a separate, supernatural, human-like deity,……. but can I still call the Self-Creator, "God," since a god is a separate human like supernatural deity and this that I'm sensing is much more vast, all present and paradoxical than a separate human-like deity? Although there is a personness to it……. All that truly exists is the Divine Self-Creative Power of Existence, continuously creating itself into being in the most perfectly natural way. It is both universal and intimately personal.

I feel disoriented from my old ideas and yet more oriented than ever to something much larger.

But, what if all that exists is just here by itself, not being created? What does that mean, 'here by itself'? It means that nothing created it. But what does it mean to create? To create is to bring into existence. To have been created means to have been brought into existence

To say that nothing created it means that nothing brought it into existence, which is to say that nothing caused it or causes it to exist. If nothing else caused it or causes it to exist, then either it is own cause, since by definition it is all that exists, or it has no cause at all, not even itself, which is to say that it has no reason to exist. But reason is a human concept, as is cause. To say that nothing has caused existence to exist is to say that the way in which the ultimate existence exists is outside of our human notions of cause and effect, or of reason... And yet it does exist... At least we take on faith that something exists... though we can never know directly. We know, at least, that our idea that something exists exists, or, at least, our experience of our idea that something exists exists, but we don't know in what way it exists, or if there is something out there that also exists.

But if something exists, which it does by definition or by experience, then wouldn't it, whatever it is, have had to either have been brought into existence or be in the process of being brought into existence and if not by something else, then by itself?

The pale, misty blue of the distant mountains darkens as I approach and the mountains look larger.

If existence brings itself into existence, then it itself is the Divine Creator by definition since the Divine Creator is defined as that which brings existence into existence.

But what if All-That-Is is just here, not having been brought into existence by anything else and not having been brought into existence by itself? How then did it get here? In what way does it exist if it has never been brought into existence? Is it possible for something to exist without having been brought into existence?

The process of bringing into existence implies the passage of time. But time does not exist prior to existence. So in the sense that time and existence are co-temporaneous, there never was a time when existence didn't exist because before existence existed there was no time and so, in this sense, existence has existed forever, that is, existence has always existed. But this still does not answer the question of how does it happen that existence exists in the first place?

I listen to the sound of my own breathing and watch Moot trotting beside me. "Good girl," I say reaching down and patting her white furry head. She grins up at me.

But OK suppose that all that really exists is... the Divine Self-Creator, by whatever name you want to call it, or whatever image you want to have of it, and it is creating itself into being. Then how does this Divine Self-Creator actually create the world... or rather create whatever corresponds to our image of the world? Not that something corresponds exactly to our image... but how does the Self-Creator act to create existence?

I ponder this lost in thought. I feel, from the inside, only the motion of my body running, my visual field filled with the subtle patterns of pale-blue mountains and intricate textures, ochre and earth. Moot trots along eagerly sometimes in front of me, sometimes behind me, often stopping to sniff the trails of animals.

The Divine Self-Creator doesn't have to... create existence ... It is already existence... not the existence I think I see... but the Existence that really is... The Divine Self-Creator creates existence simply and paradoxically by Being existence.

My mind is breaking down again. I watch the distant mountains darken from pale blue to a purplish brown. Moot stops to sniff something. The earth is turning and the air is warming under the hot sun.

This miraculous divine existence — that which really exists — must be bringing itself into existence in a way prior to and outside of time and space. It must be its own cause in some paradoxical way that transcends my ability to think it... Why? Because there is nothing else to bring it into existence,or to cause it, since it is all that exists, and all that exists is all that exists by definition.

If it simply exists without having been brought into existence by itself, without having been caused by itself or by anything other than itself, then what does that mean?

It means that it is either uncaused, or self-caused. But what does uncaused mean? It means it is outside the field of cause and effect, which are human concepts relating to how one series of events is connected to another, at least in our experience and perception. We reason from cause to effect and from effect to cause, which means we experiment with our environment in such away as to discover what conditions and events seem to control or to be associated with other conditions and events.

In terms of all existence, there is nothing outside of itself to which it can be related. All relationships occur within it, so in this sense to be uncaused is no different from being self caused, and that is to say that, if there is a cause, that cause must be within itself. But what if there is no cause at all?

What could that mean?

It must mean that it is outside the ability of human reason to grasp a sequence of events or conditions that precede Its existence in such a way that Its existence must follow, and of course this would be true because there was no time until it existed, and no time at which it did not exist. Nor is there any time outside of its existence. So if there is a cause, that cause must arise within it, and if there is no cause, then that simply means that there was no sequence of events or conditions that preceded it.

So that rather than being either or, it may be that to be self-caused and to be uncaused, while not being the same, are not mutually exclusive. It is uncaused in the sense that there was no condition or sequence of events that preceded it. But it is self-caused in the very nature of its existence, in so far as causation, which is a human concept, has any relevance to this ultimate existence at all... an existence that is beyond all human concepts and descriptions.

My mind is spinning.

Feeling dizzy, I stop thinking and come into the present moment. I feel the rhythm of my arms and legs, my breath and my heart. I feel the energy of the earth pouring through me. Out here, away from the humid green, protective canopy of the Eastern forests, it is more immediately obvious that the earth is a planet revolving slowly under the sun.

I feel the sun on my back and turn to glance at it. I think of the tiny sparkles of light I had seen last night as stars, which are still there, even though I can't see them because of the blue of the day planet. The sun too is a star, our star. I struggle to realize that this hot, huge, radiant globe, seen from afar looks just like one of those stars. Would anyone out there suspect that there is a planet circling this star on which life has evolved to such complexity that there are now animals who wonder about the universe?

After another hour or so of running, gauged by the turning of the earth under the sun and by the shortening of my shadow in front of me, I find myself at the foot of these mountains. The mountains are no longer pale-blue, or even purplish brown. The mountains are now chunks of brown rock. I begin the assent, dropping from time to time to use my hands to get up the steepest parts. Heat radiates from the warm rock. The sun passes its meridian; my shadow is a dark place directly underneath me.

Finally Moot and I stand on the top. A hot southwest wind blows, roaring in my ears, tugging at my clothes, washing my body with its body. As I look out over the valley behind us, and look to the west at yet another line of mountains, I feel light, and filled with exultation. Now the mountain on which we spent the night looks pale-blue on the eastern horizon.

Slowly I turn around letting my eyes take in this extraordinary scene, as primal as the early earth, rising up out of oceans to become dry land. I imagine how a warm inland sea once covered this land and how I would now be standing on an island, while all the valley below would have been under water. Fragments of calciferous shells of the inhabitants of those seas are still imbedded in this rock.

How ancient is the earth. How utterly peaceful it is in its eternal repose, which is filled with activity. A moment of geological time is a million years. I feel as old as these ancient rocks as if I have been here before, as if I'd always been here. I have been the warm inland sea, the sea creatures, the sand and the rocks warming in the sun. I step carefully going down the mountain. Slippery gravel makes the steep decent treacherous.

I stop and look out over the valley again. A herd of some sort of animal is moving across the valley. I wonder what they are? I hope they are friendly.

On reaching the bottom I pick up my pace again, seeing that my course will bring me in direct contact with the animals. Gradually I begin to make out what the animals are... Horses!

After a half hour or so of running I am so close that they stop grazing and look up at me in a line of long faces, barrel bodies and pricked up ears. I decide to run around them and set an oblique course. I'm confounded when they begin to follow me. Soon Moot and I are surrounded by the moving herd. We stop and they form a ring around us, heads facing in, to inspect us.

"OK guys," I begin unconvincingly. One of them stamps a foot and snorts. I lean over and pull up some grass as an offering. They are not impressed. Yet they are making no hostile moves and just seem to be examining us. Several of them move closer to get a good whiff. Moot growls and I put my hand on her ruff. We stand like that for what seems a very long time.

Finally, talking gently, I walk very slowly and carefully along side one of them, moving into the dangerous area of his hind hooves, but it is the only way I can get out of the closed circle.

To my surprise they turn and follow us. We pick up the pace and the herd strings out around us. After a while they lose interest and go back to grazing.

I return to the loose ends of my thoughts.

Whichever way I start I keep coming back to the same paradox. If existence creates itself then it itself is the divine creator, since we have defined the divine creator as that which creates and sustains existence... but it is not the material existence we think we see. What we see, touch and feel are the representations of our senses of our interactions with what is really there, which we can never know directly. Even our thoughts and our brains are it.

If there is a divine creator of all existence then it must create itself, since if it did not, then there would be part of existence that it did not create, namely itself, so it would not be the creator of all that exists, which would be a contradiction, since we have defined the divine creator as that which creates and sustains all of existence.

But what if there is no creator and everything just exists by itself? I have no idea what it might mean to "just be" in this absolute sense, but whatever the case, the most inclusive being, although beyond all human conceptions of cause and effect, must contain within itself its own cause and effect, or whatever corresponds to cause and effect in its terms, because it is all that is, and this means that even if it just is, that just-isness, is self contained, self existent and thus self creative in the sense that to self-create is to be in the continuous process of bringing itself into being, which describes a dynamic state of self existence. Moreover it must bring itself into being out of itself since there never was anything else besides itself. But this is the Divine Self-Creator.

I'd already see that there could not have existed a void before it, because in order to exist as a void the void would have to exist. Moreover, in order for that existent "non-existence" to become existence it would have had to change, and at the moment it changed something, either itself or something else, would have had to cause that change and that something would have had to have existed before existence, which is a contradiction.

Before anything changed there was no time. So in order for what we measure as time to persist, change has to persist. In fact, this dynamism must be part of its essential nature. But these are all human terms and human concepts. What it is in and of it self we can never really know.

I've been running the better part of the day and I am hot, tired and thirsty. My mind is having difficulty focusing.

I am very hungry.

At last I can make out the very small but familiar microbus standing just as I'd left it, stolidly.

Finally, as the Western sun sinks low filling the valley with slanted rays of thick orangey light, I reach my father's pale yellow VW microbus, which is faithfully waiting on the flat place at the top of the rise. I pour Moot a pan of water and drink out of the kitchen sink hose, splashing the cool liquid over me, washing off the dust of the day. I dry myself off and pull on my warm soft sweat suit for the night. Nights are cool in late August.

I try to ignore the unfinished thoughts that are rattling around in my famished brain as I light a fire and prepare supper. A good hot cup of tea settles me as I look up to view the spectacular sunset again.

I scrounge around for some dry sticks to feed the fire, breaking them with a sharp crack against my knee. I love living like this out in the open, simple and free. It never occurs to me to feel lonely with the entire universe as my constant companion and this all-surrounding love emanating from within all Nature.

Moot and I settle down to a meal of meat and potatoes with vegetables in a stew. As a special treat I serve her up stew over her dry dog food. The sky deepens to indigo as the stars twinkle into view. The diaphanous blue veils of day dissolve, revealing the immense theater of the universe.

I have seen that nature is manifesting itself from within with incredible intelligence, that in nature the head and the body are one. There isn't any external authority that is ordering nature to manifest the way it is manifesting. It is not a potter making a pot. It is the pot making itself from within…a self-building pot. All of nature is manifesting autonomously from within itself and yet the divine is fully present. We are immersed in and part of the creative power of the cosmos. I can reach up and touch it. It is inside of me; it is all around me.

I look out into the infinite depths of space and time and know, in some nonverbal way, that all that exists is the Divine Self-Creator and that it is creating Itself as All-That Exists before my very eyes, which are also Its creation. It is creating Itself in this paradoxical way that is outside of space and time. It is a miracle of astounding proportions, going on everywhere all the time. It is Being that is its own cause. It is everywhere and it is at all times. It is the true nature of all that really exists.

This is the Presence I've been following.

This is the Presence I'd felt even in the sunshine on the edge of my crib as an infant. This is the Love I'd felt in Nana's garden and shimmering down through the leaves of the chestnut tree, the love I felt in all creation and in every person. Yes. It is this Divine Self-Creative Power of Existence, which is continuously manifesting Itself as the reality behind all of what I experience, and is creating Itself into Being. This Divine Self-Creating Creator is All that really exists…

I feel in the very center of my being an exultation and joy such as I've never known before. The entire Cosmos is glowing with a transcendent Love that is beyond my comprehension and that embraces the infinity of all time and space and yet is the most intimate realization of my own being.

What had been background becomes foreground. What had been passive becomes active. What had been caused becomes cause. Everything takes on a power dignity, grace, meaning and sense of itself.

I pause and look around me at the wonder of it all. The vast, soft, dark universe, above me, glitters with stars. The edge of our own galaxy makes a broad milky swathe across the night sky. The wind brushes my face, blowing my hair, brushing the hair out of my face the way Nana used to, touching my hands and arms. I feel held in the hands of some universal love, the same love I'd felt in Nana's arms as a child.

"Oh Mooty, isn't it amazing…. It creates Itself into being in this miraculous way," I sigh as I reach out and stroke Moot's soft, furry, white head.

I lie down and fall into a deep sleep.

DiMa

The morning of the third day, the sky turns pink, then yellow and blue as the earth rolls over. The sun emerges from behind the eastern horizon, dripping orange as if from some vast interstellar sea. I spend the entire day on the mountain thinking and looking at everything with new eyes.

I sit touching the grass with my fingers. *This blade of grass, exquisitely green, quivering in the wind is, in its intrinsic nature, this Self-Creating Substance, this holy self-creating substance, creating itself as this blade of grass.*

Each thing is sacred.

Each thing is holy.

Each thing in its real identity is the Divine Self-Creator creating Itself into being.

This wind that caresses the grass, this dirt out of which the grass arises, this speck of sand, every molecule, this whole earth, and every human being are all divine, all holy, all existing together in perfect harmony. All are forms of this Self-Creative Being. All are in their real identity, this Self-Creative Being, which is continuously creating itself into existence everywhere at all times, creating even time and place.

The Divine Self-Creating Existence is not some separate thing, creating something other than itself from the outside. The Divine Self-Creating Being is what everything, in its real identity, is from the inside. What I think I see are only my perceptions and conceptions of it, what it really is is the Self-Creative Power of the entire cosmos creating itself into what everything I think I see is.

It is beyond all words and all description. The Divine Self-Creating Existence isn't just a material universe but it includes immaterial quantities like motion, organization, pattern, principle and natural law and thought. Reality is the Divine Self-Creator unfolding itself. It must create itself because there is nothing else to create it.

I begin to see the Divine Self-Creator everywhere hovering in the air, glinting in the sunlight. I can feel Her within me, the Self-Creating Miracle. I see that "Being," the ultimate noun, is a verb and that everywhere this Ultimate Substance is creating Itself out of Itself with a care and perfection that can only come from a Love beyond comprehension, from a transcendent caring so vast and so perfect that to realize it is to be transformed forever.

All that really exists is the Divine Self-Creating Miracle creating Itself into existence.

This Divine Self-Creativity creates all time and all space, everywhere simultaneously, not from some point or some place, but right here now at every point, at every place, at every time. It creates itself into what I perceive as matter and energy and motion, and into the relations of time and space. It creates all form out of itself. Each thing, each motion, is part of the self-creative self-activity of the whole.

Each form is a manifold of this Self-Creative Existence. Each individual thing expresses the dignity, grace, beauty and incomprehensible self-creativity of the whole.

Creation didn't happen once. It happens all the time. This is Creation, right here now in the eternity and infinity of this present moment. It is what Nature is, in its true identity. Creation is not a thing, but is rather the continuous process of self-creating.

It sees Itself with my eyes. It thinks Itself with my mind. It blows Itself as the wind. It sparkles Itself as light on the water, which is Itself rippling with joy at the touch of Itself as wind. All are forms of this one Self-Creative Beingness.

Thou grass, thou tree, thou sky, thou person, all manifesting this mysterious incomprehensible Self-Creative Oneness, this is the elusive enigmatic present moment out of which and into which reality unfolds.

Why does It create Itself? I do not know. No one knows. Why and how It creates Itself is the ultimate Mystery.

Every time I let myself realize that there is no outside to all that exists, I feel a pang of joy. I feel close to something very big and very dear. It becomes apparent that it is not a mechanical system like some big watch into which an external God injects himself in order to perform a miracle now and then. All of Nature is a miracle so vast as to be entirely unseen. There is nothing that is not sacred. All of Nature is this multitudinous, interconnected, self-creating Divine Miracle.

And what does It create Itself out of?

There is nothing besides Itself to create Itself out of. Therefore, this Divine Self-Creation creates Itself out of Itself.

What is it that creates all this?

There is nothing except Itself to create It. Therefore, It creates Itself. It creates even Its own ability to create.

And what does it create Itself into?

It creates Itself into Itself because there is nothing other than Itself.

It creates Itself out of Itself. It creates Its own Self-Creativity and it creates Itself into Itself. It's an effect that causes its own effect. It's a cause that is the effect of its own cause.

This is the Virgin giving birth to herself, the ultimate paradox, the Divine Mystery.

How can It act to create Itself until It exists? But how can It exist until It creates itself? How can It even create Its potential to create Itself until It exists? How does It do this?

A sweet golden love like warm honey infuses me and everything I see. Everywhere I look I see Her.

Once I see the reality of this Divine Self-Creating Miracle. I move into a state of mind where everything is miraculous. With joy, I feel it unfolding Itself, right before my eyes, as my eyes, which see it. It sees itself through my eyes, which are also it. I, myself, am Its unfolding. And so is every person.

How does this miraculous, incomprehensible Existence brimming with Its own Intelligence, unfold Itself from the inside out?

Life and all that I see glows with a wonder and a grandeur that I have never experienced before, a fullness, a meaning, an immediacy, a vividness, a love. Here is this sense of being held in the very hands of Love.

All that exists is the Divine Self-Creating Existence. What I see are the forms my perception creates within me, as I, who am It, interact with what is out there, which is It. What is really here is the Divine Self-Creating Matrice, the Self-Creatrix, which is all that really exists. It is beyond all cause and effect. It is the cause that is the effect of its own cause. It is the effect that is the cause of its own effect. It paradoxically creates Itself into being. It transcends all human duality, because It is everything and everywhere at once; It is all existence. Not the existence I think I see, but the existence that is really here. It is what our conceptions and perceptions really are. It is our consciousness and it is beyond our consciousness. It is what existence really is beyond our perceptions and conceptions of it, even this one.

This is the Ultimate Oneness of which all else are manifold. This is where being and principle are one, because both being and principle are but different manifests of Its One existence. This is where subject and object are one, because in Its paradoxical reflexivity, that which is the object of every action is also the subject of every action. In the Divine Self-Creator, cause and effect are one. That which thinks and that which is thought are one. All are but different expressions of the Original Self-Creating Oneness.

Every time I come to this point of realization I feel in the center of my being a deep pang of love, awe, and recognition.

This is what I have been looking for in these thousands of miles of wild places, this Divine Self-Creating Miracle, DiMa, the most sacred and holy mystery, which creates Itself in this paradoxical way behind what I think I see. This is why I feel it everywhere. Because it is everywhere, just behind my perceptions and conceptions, creating Itself into Being through this paradoxical act of self-creation. Although I can never know it, It is all I truly know, because who I really am is It becoming Itself as me.

I spend all day walking and sitting delighting in the perfection of existence. Moot follows me and sometimes I share my thoughts with her and she wags her tail and looks at me with her wise, yellow wolf eyes.

Tonight I build a fire and cook supper. Again the sunset spreads in orange streaks across the western sky silhouetting the range of distant mountains. The veils of day part and the glorious universe reveals itself.

I know this is our last night on the mountain. I wish I could stay here forever, and yet something is pulling me on, to what I don't know yet. I scratch Moot behind the ears and she grins, puts her paw on my arm and looks into my blue eyes with her yellow eyes.

Chapter 19: Golden Gate

The next morning dawns and reluctantly I pack. The blankets and tarp I'd draped over the van to dry are now warm in the sun and dry almost to crispness in the desert air.

I munch on an apple as I smooth over the ashes of the fire, dowse them with water and cover them with dirt. I want to leave the campsite better than I found it. Moot follows me around as I do each task.

There are signs on the border of California and inspection teams want to know if I have any fruits or vegetables. I surrender the remains of a bag of apples and, with a feeling of elation, cross the border into California.

Feelings of joy ripple through me as I drive though the wild and ragged Sierra Nevada Mountains. Cars and trucks honk behind me but I can't go any faster. I pull over to let them go by.

Arriving in Sacramento, I find it strange to see this vast urban area from the perspective of inter-galactic space and the Divine Self-Creator. I can't find a place to camp but finally find a motel that allows dogs.

The next day I drive on to San Francisco.

The Western sun glitters on the immense Pacific Ocean, making a shining path of light out across the face of the sea, which shimmers like molten gold.

As I drive across the Golden Gate Bridge, tears of joy stream down my face.

Following the road map, I find my way to Muir Woods. Groves of redwood trees grow in the valleys. We pull off the road and park the car. I have never witnessed a redwood tree before. The immense trunks of these trees grow hundreds of feet into the air, catching the sunlight on their reddish bark. Delicate lacy green needles shimmer at the ends of branches that whorl out from the central trunk. I feel, rising within me, a sense of love for these massive slumbering giants. Being in the grove is like being in a cathedral, deep, still and peaceful.

There is a Presence here, the Presence that has been here for centuries, for millennia, for eons... a Presence that is both spiritual and physical, that has existed since before Christianity, before Buddhism, before Islam, even before Hinduism. This Presence is all that exists and it belongs to no one religion, but is the ground of all religions. This is the Divine Self-Creator that has been here since the beginning of time and is here for all eternity. It belongs to everything, and gives Itself to everyone, free for the taking. It is the very ground of all being, and that is sacred ground.

......

Stinson Beach is longer and flatter than Muir Beach, and is open to the public. I walk out onto the sand, which feels cool and loose on my bare feet. Moot wanders off to a picnic down the beach. The thunderous surf of the Pacific crashes and bubbles. The rhythms of the Pacific are longer and slower than the rhythms the Atlantic Ocean that I have known for my whole life. The waves seem to take forever to form and between waves there is a long, long time while the next wave gathers itself together and rushes to the beach.

I dash to the ocean and dive in feeling a sense of ecstatic union with this vast ocean. Water pours over me, tons of water tearing and ripping my limbs in all directions. I dive for the bottom and wait for the wave to pass before surfacing.

My eyes open, from underneath, I see the golden sun rippling through the water, just like the picture in *My Book House* so long ago, the picture I'd seen as a three year old, knowing even then that someday I would find this green translucent cresting ocean wave and would dive into it.

Here it is and I am in love with it, with this ocean. Someday I will live here by this sea and I will swim every day in its glorious, purifying, healing waters.

I feel the pull of the water around my legs sucking the sand out from under my feet, dragging me strongly out to sea, and I struggle to regain my footing. Moot is now watching me carefully from shore. She doesn't like to swim, but she will, if she thinks I am in trouble; she will swim out to me and pull me in. She is a strong swimmer with her powerful shoulders and haunches.

"It's OK, Mooty," I shout as I struggle to shore.

I dance up and down the sand and then as the next breaker rolls in I plunge into it diving right through the top of it, breaking its foaming crest with my body, feeling its weight,

"Yahooo!" I shout.

Again and again I swim, leaping like a dolphin into the surf, yelling in my exuberance, flinging water up into a hundred rainbow colors with my arms and hands, watching the trembling liquid globules fall ever so perfectly, with such grace.

Then I turn and, feeling an inexpressible joy rising in me that makes my whole body sing as if I too am filled with sparkling light, I run down the length of the beach, leaping into the air, flinging my arms up into the sky, and twirling in midair. On and on I run breathing the sweet ocean air, feeling the tremble of the booming surf, hearing the sound of wind and sea in my ears, feeling life flood through me. I delight in the feeling of the invisible air moving around me and pressing its body against my body. Thank you for this air, which is everywhere so abundant and freely given, on which we all depend for every living breath.

Again and again I run up and down the beach sprinting until I can sprint no more, slowing to catch my breath, and then sprinting again, feeling my bare feet touch the flat wet sand as I fly along the water with the sky reflected below me. Moot follows me for the first laps and then wanders back to our pile of stuff on the sand where she sprawls her white furry body.

Every time I think of the mysterious Self-Creating Divine Mystery, paradoxically creating itself into Being, all around and within me, I feel a pang of love. It is like being in love with everything, but everything understood in a different way than I had understood before.

I plunge again into the sea and watch the oncoming wave.

As the wave approaches the shore it rises up slowly, keeping a steady pace forward. A darkening shadow begins to form on the face of it as it mounds up higher and begins to rise sharply to a peak. The oncoming face of the peak reflects the glimmering sunlight in great golden metallic swatches until the sand begins to drag the bottom of the wave. The crest looms higher and higher until it can no longer sustain its own weight. It crumbles, and falls, frothing white, pouring like a waterfall down its own oncoming face.

All is love; all creation, all existence is born of a love so vast and to be entirely unseen. I slow down and watch. The breaking wave hangs in the present moment like a pendant jewel of perfection.

Yet still it comes, proudly like a white horse tossing its mane, snorting its majesty, pawing the foam-flecked air. Onward it comes, churning in a magnificent crescendo of sound and tempestuous water, on it comes keeping the same steady pace even while its own insides are melting out of it. It flattens, like an old man withering, failing, falling.

On it comes until it is just a quiet dribble of itself peacefully sliding up the beach, reaching with its foam fingers, grabbing on to the sand, like a shipwrecked sailor who heaves on to the beach there to die, to breath its last and give itself to the flat warm sand.

But in this death, a new life is born in the anti-wave, which retreats back into the plunging froth of the next wave. Slipping silently under the incoming waves, it heads back out to sea bound to its own destiny, keeping its own pace charting its own course.

The present moment is the only time I truly exist and here I find this immense love out of which all of existence is creating itself continuously into being. This is the culmination of what I have been looking for. As the wave crashing on the beach comes to a trembling end and in that same ending begins its new journey back to from whence it came, so in the moment of final revelation I turn myself back to what I've left behind, knowing that Love is everywhere. Love is all there is.

The sun sets like the full orange yolk of an egg into the bristling top of a Monterey Cedar. The sun climbs slowly downward in irregular patches of fire, holding on to the uppermost branch until its feet are firmly on the lower branch, then descending again, lowering its flaming body with its gleaming orange hands, until its fiery feet find the next toehold.

Silently I sit with the wide sea before me, with the sun egg silently breaking and dripping like sticky yolk through the rough branches of the dark cedar.

And so he descends until there is but one glowing spark left smoldering between the dark pine needles, then that too is extinguished.

The sea reposes with her clear face open to the sky, rippling her body with each caress of the wind, reflecting from her wide eyes the sparkles of sunlight until they cease and she lies in peaceful peace beneath the life-bringing air, exhaling gently the evening mist. All is infinite peace, perpetual in its perfection, quiet, undisturbed, moving majestically through the Universe of stars and dark matter, moving through the void of eternal timeless bliss, the immensity of it unnoticed for the most part.

I have communed with the Spirit day after day after day and become one with It at night, immersed in the vast cosmos, itself abundant with an unimaginable number of galaxies, stars, planets and life forms, all the Holy System. It is the thought creating the thinker who thinks. I love that it can never be known but it is always known, that it can never be thought but it is thought itself, that it can never be seen, but it is the true existence of everything that is seen.

Cupping my hands I use some of our drinking water to wash off the salt, and, under the towel, slip off my wet bathing suit and slip on some warm sweat pants and a shirt and new socks, which I've washed and let dry in the back of the van.

I turn my back to the infinite, eternal ocean and set myself to making camp in the sand, wrestling with the tasks of scooping out a fireplace in the sand, hunting driftwood, piling it up so that the entire edifice will light with one match from tinder, kindling and logs strategically arranged to carry the self sustaining combustion of the match.

I set out food and prepare it. Reverently lighting the fire, I pause, as always, to note the fire, which is released from the wood in this magical ritual. I watch with childish wonder the way the hot, orange fire-tongues lap upward around the stacked wood caressing it before devouring it. I hold my hands up to the heat. Life is a sacred ritual, and when lived as such takes on a meaning and glory that fills me with perfect love. I listen to the sound that the wind in the fire makes, flam, flam, flam... like the sound of the wind in my ears when I run.

My clothes are drying, and a pot of soup is boiling. Three or four young people nearby are struggling to light a fire.

"Can we sit here? Our fire went out," a voice interrupts my reverie.

"Sure," I smile.

A group of kids my age, the guys completely shaved bald, and the girls with long silken hair that catches the sheen of the fire, sit down and cook hot dogs and marshmallows. I eat soup and Moot eats dog food.

"Where are you from?"

"Boston."

"Where's that?"

"In Massachusetts... in New England... On the Atlantic coast."

"That's a long way. What are you doing out here?"

Looking deeply into the fire, I say, "I wanted to see the country."

" Beer?" one of them asks, motioning a can in my direction.

"Weed?" one of them offers me a hand-rolled cigarette.

"No thanks," I shake my head. I'd tried alcohol and real cigarettes when I turned eighteen and was sick for three days. No way would I ever put that poison into my body or try a something that would mess with my brain. Why do such a thing when life fully lived is the best thing going?

One of the guys has a guitar and we sit listening to folk music and singing. Sharp sparks from the snapping fire shower up into the soft blackness of night, as one of the guys throws on another bunch of sticks. As the fire dies down into glowing embers, we all lie down and fall asleep around the fire.

......

Morning— and a gray mist enfolds the lonely strand of sand. I look around at the slumbering bodies and the gray ashes of the cold fire. I look out at the foggy Pacific and feel the cooling mist condense on my face. The ceaselessly crashing surf thunders in repeated booms that vibrate the air.

I pack our belongings into the microbus, which feels warm and cozy after the chill of the morning, and drive into San Francisco, to Fisherman's Wharf. There, amidst the quaint shops, I buy a sweet roll for me, and a dried fish for Moot, who carries it proudly in her mouth as we walk along.

I huddle in a pay phone. The metallic clink of coins alternates with the voice of the operator. "Kingswood 6 – 6624," I respond in answer to her curt nasal "Number Please."

Ring, ring, ring. I imagine Grampy walking across the piazza to the phone, his dear old body clad in an old cardigan sweater and baggy trousers.

"Grampy! I'm in San Francisco!"

"Where?" His sweet voice sounds shaky.

"San Francisco.... California. I just got here yesterday."

"What are you doing in San Francisco?"

"I just wanted to see the country."

"I was worried about you."

"I'm OK. How are you?"

"When are you coming home?"

"I'm heading home now. I'll be there as soon as I can."

"I miss you."

"I miss you too."

"Be careful, sweetheart."

"I will. I can't wait to see you!"

"I love you," he says.

My voice cracks, "I love you too."

Tears start to run down my face. I hang up.

Moot and I walk back to the van, which is parked on a side street, and get in.

I lie down in the back, which is made up into a bed. Overcome with longing, and grief, I sob and sob as I've never sobbed before, deep visceral sobs. I feel my entire body convulsed with sobs.

I miss my Nana. I want my Nana. I want to be safe and warm, tucked in between Nana and Grampy. I want her to brush the hair out of my eyes and tell me she loves me again. I don't want her to be dead.

My body is wrenched with sobs, the sobs I've kept in all these years of being tough. The sobs I never cried when she died. I want my Nana. I am finally grieving her death.

Moot comes over and puts her paw consolingly on my arm. I feel so utterly vulnerable and lost.

Time passes; night falls.

I pull the curtains on the car windows and stay here in the VW, all night under the street lights, parked on the side of the street near the San Francisco Art Institute.

The next day I feel better, fresher, as if the passing rain shower has clarified the air and relieved me of some long held pent up sorrow. Nana feels close to me now, not only in the vastness of nature but also in the small human things.

Leaving Moot to guard the van, not that it needs guarding, but she likes to have an important job to do while I go into these restrictive, 'human only' places like cafes. I pat her head and put my face up to hers, and say, "When are you going to take off that silly dog suit?"

She knows I feel sad about leaving her and that I will bring a treat for her when I return.

After breakfast, I open the van door and whistle to Moot who jumps out. I give her a hamburger, cooked rare, the way she likes it. I'd felt silly ordering it, "One hamburger to go, nothing on it, rare, hold the bun, please."

"Let's go find a hotel," I say. We saunter up and down the streets admiring the architecture. I think of John and how much he would love to see this.

After some time we enter the lobby of a fine old classic hotel, one of the best in San Francisco. The doorman stops me. "All dogs must be on leash," he commands.

I don't have a leash but I fish out a bit of string from yesterday's fish package and tie it around her neck.

At the desk I register and pay the deposit. The elegant ambiance of this place, the wood paneled interior, the high ceilings feel familiar to me as if I once lived in a palace. Maybe when I was little every house seemed like a palace.

Moot and I gather our belongings from the van and take the elevator up to our room. She carries her food dish.

Here I turn on the classical music station and undress, looking at myself in the mirror for the first time in a month. How strange, seeing myself again, after having no mirrors except in the occasional truck stop ladies room.

Drawing a hot bath, I luxuriate in the suds, sinking deep into the comforting hot water. Suddenly I find myself thinking of that night John and I made love in the lake.

For someone with no money I have exquisitely expensive tastes. It must be the aristocrat in me… or the artist. Every detail of this hotel says quality, wealth and dignity.

After the luxurious bath, I slip on a simple dress and go down to dinner, a sumptuous affair, with candlelight, white linen table clothes and napkins. Chandeliers above.

While I eat I write:

Dear John,

Can you believe it! I'm in San Francisco staying at the fanciest hotel I could find.

How is your summer going?

It has been an amazing journey.

I can't wait to see you again and be at home and tell you all about it.

Love,

Bobby Lou

Strangely I find myself thinking of Paladin, in "Have Gun Will Travel," the TV show I watched as a teenager. This was Paladin's milieu, the fancy hotels of San Francisco, the elegance juxtapose against the tough Wild West in which he imposed a kind of extemporaneous justice for hire.

I put an ad in the paper for someone to share the expense of driving to the East Coast.

"Any messages for me?"

"No sorry."

I hang up.

I stand by the window looking out.

It is morning and I sit at a table with a white linen tablecloth having tea and sweet bread, reading the paper.

The waitress approaches, "Miss Gibb?"

I look up and nod.

"Phone for you," She hands me the phone on an extension cord.

"Yes?... Yes? Really... Oh great. Can you meet me? How about in an hour?... Good." I hand the phone back to the waitress and continue writing and sipping tea.

Three nice looking young men enter. The Maitre de leads them to my table.

"I'm Nick, this is Tony and Pete we're headed back to NYU for fall semester."

"Great. When can you leave?"

"Tomorrow."

"I'll meet you out front at ten o'clock AM."

Chapter 20: The Crash

The next day, the VW, loaded up with duffle bags, three young men, Moot and me, rolls through the streets of San Francisco. I'm driving. Tony sits beside me looking at a map. Moot hangs over the seat looking over my shoulder.

"Tell me if you see a mailbox. I have to mail this letter."

"There's one," Tony points.

I pull over, get out and put my letter to John in the box.

After driving several hours we're over the Bay Bridge and through Sacramento heading east.

"When are we going to stop for lunch?" Nick complains.

"Are you hungry?" I turn off into a truck stop, fuel up and we head for the restaurant. I pick up some sample rocks for my collection. I want to have a cross-section of rocks across the entire continent.

"We can't figure it out," Tony says as we sit munching cheeseburgers and salad. "Are you rich or poor?"

"You're staying in the best hotel in San Francisco," Pete chimes in.

"And then you're driving an old beat up VW across the country," Nick continues... "With a white wolf, who guards you like a mother."

"I've always been the rich little poor little girl," I find myself saying unexpectedly. I never know what is going to come out when I open my mouth.

"And you don't wear lipstick, or curl your hair," Pete adds.

"All the girls we know wear make up and have pierced earrings."

"You don't have any jewelry at all."

"I don't like the feel of makeup, and jewelry could get caught on a bush or something when I'm running in the woods. And I just couldn't do that to my poor soft tender ears, put a sharp piece of metal through them."

"And every time we stop, you pick up rocks."

"Is it to please your teacher?"

"I'm interested in geology, in how the rocks change from place to place. When else am I going to have a chance to pick up samples from across the entire country?"

"You're our Den Mother."

I laugh.

Pete is driving. I am sitting in the passenger's seat, enjoying being able to watch the scenery and not have to think about driving. We're in Nevada.

"So you're headed back to New York?"

"Our family is there. We're all cousins. A lot of our family is still in Greece."

"One of my friends back east, Athena, is from Greece," I offer.

"We're studying business management at NYU."

"Do you like it?"

"It's OK. We want to go into business and make a lot of money."

"Good idea."

"What do you do?"

"Study art n' stuff like that."

"That's what I want to do."

"Maybe you will someday."

"I love Art History. What I really want is to travel and research ancient art," Pete confesses.

"Sounds great."

"Where are we now?"

"We should be near Winnemucca."

I look at the map.

"Yeah. Time to change drivers."

"Hey wake up back there. We're here!"

Nick drowsily, "Where?"

"Winnemucca?"

"Not now."

Tony, elbowing Nick, mutters, "Wise guy. Can't swear in front of our Den Mother."

I laugh.

We pull off into a truck stop and have some coffee.

"Welcome to Utah!" the sign says.

"We've never met a girl like you before. The girls we know paint their fingers, pierce their ears, have sex with the boys and look for husbands."

Tony is still trying to figure me out, to put me in some category, to make me comprehensible to himself. "Nothing wrong with that, but I like other things," I reply.

"Like collecting rocks."

"And studying philosophy and science. And long distance running. And sculpture and painting, and nature and dogs and horses...." I amplify.

"A woman who runs long distance. Who ever heard of such a thing? I didn't know women could run. None of the women I know do. Do you have a boyfriend?"

"Yes."

"Do you love him?"

"Of course. He wouldn't be my boyfriend if I didn't."

"Gunna get married?"

"I'm not sure...maybe."

It's nighttime Tony is driving; Nick is sitting beside him in the front. I'm trying to sleep in the back with Moot and Pete, fighting off a migraine headache.

"You must be tired. You've been driving for hours without a break," Nick says to Tony.

"I don't have the heart to wake up our Den Mother." Tony replies.

"Let me drive again then," Nick offers.

"We're coming up on Cheyenne. Let me take it to there. We need gas anyway."

"She's a funny person isn't she."

"The Den Mother?"

"I've never met anyone like her. You know what I like most about her?"

"What?"

"She just thinks life is the most wonderful thing that ever happened and she's so busy living every minute that she doesn't have time for all the bullshit and vanity that consumes most of us."

Tony looks out the front window. "She's a child-woman in some way... sophisticated yet vulnerable, open like a little kid... But she never let's anyone in too far.... What are those lights up there?"

"I don't know some sort of construction."

"It's a fucking barricade! Shit! Tony turns the wheel abruptly to avoid hitting the barricade and the van careens off the road. I feel the sudden deceleration, jamming us against the front of the car, twisting our bodies with its force.

The entire van circles around as if we are inside a cement mixer.

At the impact I cover my head with my arms. Some instinct tells me to completely relax and let myself roll with the van. I think to myself, "Just relax. Completely relax Go limp." Moot and Pete and I bounce off the side, the ceiling, the other side, the bottom, the side again, the ceiling again and the side again as the van turns over, and we roll down the steep embankment. The guys in front hold on to the dashboard.

I wonder if we are plunging down a thousand foot canyon as the van turns around us. Its like being inside a giant clothes drier rotating around with clothes and blankets dropping off of whatever side is now the ceiling.

"Jesus Christ! What the fuck!" Pete has wakened up beside me to find himself bouncing off the ceiling.

"What the hell is going on?"

The van bounces to a stop.

"Where the fuck's the door?" Pete yells, pounding on the side where the door should be, but finding no door.

"Up there!" I stand up struggling to push the door up like a hatch cover.

"Hey those are my balls you're dancing around on!" Pete yells.

"Get the hell out before it catches on fire," Tony yells.

I open the hatch door out on a perfect still peaceful Wyoming night. The air is cool and clear. The stars twinkle above as though nothing has happened. I crawl out into the sudden still black quiet of a night. The music on the car radio croons on, unaware that its audience is in turmoil.

"Up here!" I yell, holding the door while the other's crawl out.

We stand together looking at the wreck.

"Stand back the engine could catch on fire. The gasoline is leaking," Nick cautions.

"Where is Moot? Mooty?" I call.... "Is Moot still in there?" I run back to the van.

"No!" Tony shouts trying to stop me. "It could catch on fire."

"I know!" I yell, pushing past him and scrambling up the bottom side of the van, onto the side, which is now the top, and looking down at Moot below. Moot is looking up at me. I jump down inside the van and lift Moot up. Tony grabs the dog and I scramble out again, jump down and we all move back away from the van.

We stand there incongruous in the deep silent depths of the universe and its tiny sparkling stars with the music still blaring from the car radio. My van looks like a beached yellow whale, a cow that has fallen on her side and is unable to get up, her side pressed into the dessert sand, her wheels uselessly revolving in air.

"Where is the nearest phone?"

We are contemplating what to do next: Walk to the nearest house, which could be miles away? And it's two A.M.

"Are those sirens?" I ask.

Sure enough in the distance, sirens.

Two police cars pull up.

"Is anyone hurt?" a nice looking, competent police officer asks.

"We're OK," Nick volunteers.

"We were right behind you. We saw you roll and radioed the ambulance and fire trucks," The second police officer says.

We hear ambulance sirens and a fire truck. Another police car drives up.

"Who owns this vehicle?" the first officer asks.

"I do," I say with a lump in my stomach.

"Let me see your registration and driver's license."

"I was driving," Tony blurts out.

After the formalities we are driven to the police station where they offer us coffee and donuts.

"May I make a phone call?" Nick asks.

"Sure."

"I'm looking for a Gus Anastophalos," I overhear Nick saying. I wonder who Gus Anastophalos is, and how he knows anyone here in Cheyenne.

Before long Gus arrives.

"How do you know each other?" I ask.

"I'm a member of the Sons of Greece," Gus says.

"What is that?" I ask, unable to see how that answers my question.

"A fraternal organization," Tony answers.

"Whenever any Greek anywhere is in trouble or needs help, all he has to do is to call the nearest Sons of Greece and help is available," Gus explains

"Oh that's neat," I say.

Gus is a lively old man, thin, stiff and spry. Before long he has found a motel for us and we are on our way, thanking the Cheyenne police for all their help.

We pool our money and take a room for the night; it's all we can afford.

We'll have to share a room.... the four of us and the dog....

We stand looking at the one queen-sized bed in the drab tan-colored room.

Without a word they all settle on the floor with snatches of sleeping bag and blankets pulled over them, and leave the bed for me.

"No," I offer. "I don't mind sleeping on the floor, I'm used to sleeping outside, you guys take the bed."

"The bed's for our den mother," they insist.

"Thanks," I say moved by this unasked for altruistic act of caring.

I snuggle into the bed with my arms around Moot, who presses close to me, a girl and her dog, on a life raft with huge, slumbering men, like logs on the river, floating around us, amidst the flotsam and jetsam of our belongings.

Chapter 21: Gus

The next morning Gus comes into the cafe where we are eating breakfast.

Nick stands up to make room for Gus. It's late; we slept late, past ten o'clock.

"Thanks for coming over," Tony says.

"That's what we Greek brothers do for each other, you'd do the same for me, right?"

"Right," Tony responds.

"My wife and I want to have you over for dinner. We have a spare bedroom for the girl tonight."

"Thanks..."

In Gus's house, his wife, a plump friendly woman in her sixties has prepared a feast. We sit around talking, passing around Greek delicacies, lamb in grape leaves, feta goat cheese.

Gus says to me, "So your father's a chemist?"

"Yeh."

"Does he know anything about coal gas?"

"I'm sure he does."

In his soft Greek accent Gus says, "My friends laughed at me when I bought shares in coal mines. They all became bankers, invested in cattle and real estate and made a fortune. I've been waiting for oil to run out. Do you know why?"

"Why?"

"Because then they'll start making coal slurry into fuel. It doesn't pay unless the price of oil goes way up, but at a certain price it is cheaper to use coal gas. Then my mines will be worth a fortune."

After dinner I help Josephine with dishes. An altar to Virgin Mary is in the hall with a candle burning. I stop to look at Mary intently and think, "The Virgin giving birth to Herself."

Josephine looks and me and says tenderly, "The Mother of God."

We look at each other.

"The Mother of God," I repeat.

"Don't ever forget," she smiles.

"Do you want to use our phone to call home?" Josephine's voice interrupts my thoughts.

I dial the operator, "Long distance please..."

"Bobby Lou! How are you? Where are you?" Gail's voice sounds so familiar to me, as if I'd seen her yesterday.

"Hi! I'm fine...Cheyenne.... Had an accident. No I'm fine so is Moot. And the three guys I'm with.... I'm at Gus's and Josephine's...OK.... In a motel... Yeah It's OK they're great guys. Like my brothers...really.... The car was totaled. The garage gave me a hundred and thirty-five dollars for it. I'm coming home by train.... Probably tomorrow.... I'll be there by Saturday."

"We're here when you get back... But you're parents are back early..."

"My parents!? Oh No".... My poor long suffering parents… "Don't tell them OK?"

"I'll try not to, but it'll be hard.... OK... I know... John's been hanging around...." Gail hangs up and looks out the window. It's Tom, coming up the walk.

"Professor!" shouts Gail cheerily.

Tom comes in the house and they hug, a little too warmly, but a bit stiffly.

"You're probably wondering what the mean old stepmother has done with that daughter of yours."

"It had crossed my mind."

"She'll back home on Saturday."

"Where is she?"

"Drink?"

He nods. She pours out two glasses on the rocks.

"She felt she had to take a trip...."

"Yes?"

"Ah... her best friend, Debby had a baby..."

"Where is she?"

"She just phoned.... She's in Cheyenne. She's fine."

"What is going on?"

"She had a bit of an auto accident but they're all fine, she says."

"They?"

"She's fine. And so are the three guys who are helping her drive the car back... She was too tired to do it all alone, so some very nice guys from New York University... and the dog."

"Dog? What Dog?"

"She has a wonderful puppy..."

"Doesn't she know I'm allergic to dogs?"

"I'm sure she knows but since she's living here now, she didn't think it would matter. We love having her here. And the dog..."

"To hell with the dog. What about the three men? Where are they now?"

"They spent the night at the Cheyenne Motel."

"The Cheyenne hotel. My daughter with three men in a motel... give me that phone..."

"She's not there now."

"Well where the hell is she?"

"Really. She's fine. She's a grown woman now. You have to let go. I guarantee nothing's going on."

"Three men and a woman in a hotel room and nothing is going on...you say... I don't care how old she is. No daughter of mine is going to be in a motel room with three men."

"She's staying with a lovely Greek couple... until the car's fixed."

"Give me that number..."

He grabs the paper. And dials the phone.

In Gus's house after dinner the men are smoking in the living room. The phone rings.

"Want me to get it Gus?" Nick asks.

"Find out who it is."

"Beg your pardon... No there's been no complaint... This is not a motel... This is a private residence..."

To Gus with hand over the mouthpiece, "It's a Professor Gibb looking for his daughter. What a bastard."

"It must be for the Den Mother."

"Ask him about the coal slurries," Gus says excitedly.

Taking the phone...I say, "Hello?" Cheerfully masking a sinking feeling. "Hi Dad! You're back early! Did you have a nice sabbatical?"

"Why do you do this to your mother and me?"

"Do what? I thought you were coming back next week."

"I know about the men in the motel. You're mother's going to be heartbroken."

"They're my friends. Like brothers nothing's going on. Really they're just helping me drive the car back."

"I heard you were in an accident."

"We're OK. I'm taking the train home tomorrow. I'll be there Saturday. No I can get home OK. Really. No please don't pick me up."

As my dad is talking on the Willard's phone, John appears on his motorcycle, parks and saunters up the walk.

Tom slams down the phone and turns around into John who is just coming in the front door.

"Tom, this is John, a friend of Bobby Lou's."

John holding out his hand, says, "Hello, pleased to meet you."

103

Tom, refusing to take John's hand, hisses, "Another one of Bobby Lou's 'friends?'"

He looks disdainfully at John and disapprovingly at Gail, turns on his heel and strides away.

"What's going on?" John asks.

"Bobby Lou's parents got home early. He's really a nice man, he's just upset because he's discovered his daughter is a woman."

"And he can't have her..." John adds.

"Bobby Lou's been in an accident.... She's not hurt. But she was with three guys who were helping her drive back. They had to spend the night in a motel after the car was totaled... I tried to explain to Tom that nothing was going on... And then when he saw you it was the last straw."

"Bobby Lou with three guys?"

"I'm sure nothing is going on. They're just helping her drive the car back."

When I return Gail recounts all this to me.

Many years later John was to confide in me that indeed he had had an affair with another woman that summer. "It was just sex," he had explained. "There was always something missing with her that I only ever found with you."

Chapter 22: Home Again

Looking out of the window of my sleeping compartment, I think of John, as the train rolls serenely along through Nebraska. I am writing.

"Once we see that The Creator is all that really exists, we realize that anything else is just our illusion: our false beliefs. False beliefs cause the world so much suffering and pain. We project our beliefs on the world and mistakenly think that our beliefs are reality."

I'm writing on a scrap of paper, with a wriggly scrawl as the train bounces along, "What it really is we can never know directly.... The Creator is the ultimate existence behind all the diversity of form, behind what we think we see and touch and feel and know. What we're really looking at is the Creator. It is all there really is. And the Creator is pure love; at least that is how I experience it... Do you think I'm completely nuts?"

I look off into the distance and lovingly ruffle Moot's soft white furry ears and think:

Living systems, are self-building, but more than that they are in some sense self-designing, not the way an architect designs a building or a watch maker makes a watch; but over the span of evolutionary time living systems have formed themselves into myriad shapes and sizes to take advantage of the multiple possible niches to which life can adapt and in which it can flourish. This self-formative ability is a type of what I could call intelligence, but it does not necessarily involve a subjective experience.

On the other hand the quality of having a subjective experience does not necessarily explain how a system has the form it does. As I watch the scenery flip by my mind goes blank as I find myself engrossed in the patterns of the landscape. I need more words to designate the difference between the self-formative ability of nature and the ability of some natural systems to have a subjective experience.

I need more words to distinguish these different concepts, but for now I call the one, "Self-formative Intelligence" and the other "Self-experiencing Intelligence" or "Subjective Experience."

Complexification, I have thought for some time, is as fundamental to the cosmos as the tendency to entropic disorder. But what drives this evolution of complexity?

Interaction must be key in understanding nature, whether it is the gravitational interactions of stars and their planetary bodies, which form themselves into solar systems, or whether it is the complex molecular interactions that occur in a living organism, which form themselves into the organism. It is interaction after all that makes formation possible. But how?

And, what really is this subjective experience anyway? How are self-formation and subjective experience related? When I look out the train window I see a scene full of colored objects rushing by. But what is really out there?

The bouncing photons of light fall on my retina and cause some change in the firing of my nerves. These impulses travel up to the brain where I perceive the scene. I have never understood how electric impulses in the brain are seen as subjective experience. It is astounding to me that this material object, the brain, has subjective experience going on inside it and that I, whoever I am, is privy to this subjective experience.

How is this possible? What is really happening?

How is the image of the outside world conveyed to my brain and how do the patterns of neuronal activity become subjective experience?

If there is only one fundamental substance, as I think there is, it must somehow contain the possibility and the actuality of both the material external world and the internal subjective world. It must include both the self formative interactions through which what we call material systems come into being and it must include also the ability to self experience, which at least some complex living systems possess. In nature, there is no mind-body problem. The brain and the mind and the outside world all exist quite happily together.

But what is the mind? Is the mind a thing?

The photons impinge on the retina and trigger a series of events in the complexly organized nervous system that finally result in some change in the activity of my brain, which is perceived by me as this scene before me. All that enters the system anew is the message that some photons impinged on my retina, but because of the highly structured dynamic activity of my brain, which is already in the process of having subjective experiences, these impingings modulate my subjective experience and I am aware of seeing a scene.

The impinging photons don't cause the activity in my brain. My brain is already active. My brain is already highly organized and is intrinsically able to create subjective experiences out of a combination of patterns of activity, through which it presents to itself perceptual images.

But what sort of phenomena is this perceptual image?

Since neither the ability of the brain to have subjective experiences, nor the subjective experience itself is caused by the impinging of information from the sense organs, that means that subjective experience is created somehow in the brain. It is obvious that the brain is already capable of having subjective experiences and is in fact in the midst of having them when the sensory input arrives.

The incoming information merely affects the on going activity and perceptual panorama that is going on in the brain. The sensory receptors are the brain's way of sampling the outside environment and the information conveyed back up the neurons to the brain is incorporated into the brain's ongoing activity. The question is, how does the brain experience all these dynamical patterns of neuronal activity subjectively in the first place?

This ability to experience subjectively that arises in some living systems must be founded on something that is intrinsic to the nature of existence. At some level of complexity, natural systems, in particular living systems, can acquire the ability to have subjective experiences. How? In a completely materialistic universe this would not be possible, at least in the terms that we now understand matter, as purely extended, massive, bits of things that exist out there.

It is clear that the mind is not a thing. The mind is rather is a collection of activities and processes, or rather, billions of interconnected activities and processes perceived subjectively. But how is this possible?

Moot and I spend the days and the nights on the train, cozy in our sleeping compartment, taking walks outside when the train stops. We are both restless.

I leave her in the compartment when I go to eat in the dinning car. Otherwise I spend my time in the compartment reading, looking at the scenery and thinking.

The train rolls across Western Massachusetts. I sit at a window looking out at the lush dark green foliage of late summer. The days are shorter, the light more slanted and golden. It's good to be heading home.

"Back Bay. Back Bay," the conductor mumbles as the train roars into the station.

I struggle down the aisle and out the door with my luggage, books and sleeping roll. Moot follows.

There on the platform looking small and drawn are my parents. My heart sinks.

"Hi Mom. Hi Dad. Really you shouldn't have gone to all the trouble of coming in. Especially with Moot here and all."

We hug awkwardly. Jean is all quivery and acting as if I need to be humored. Dad is stiff and condemning.

"Why do you do this to your mother and me?" Dad starts in.

"Do what? I had a nice trip. I thought I'd be back before you, but you came home early." I feel guilty, small and dirty.

"You're home safely, that's what matters. And now you can get all the help you need."

"I'm fine really."

Jean looks significantly at Dad as if they've discussed something. I get another sinking, out of control feeling.

"I don't think much of a young lady who spends the night with three men in a motel."

"They were just helping me drive the car back. Really. They called me their Den Mother."

Giving me a look of disgust, Dad says, "You're no daughter of mine."

He throws some money at me and says, "Here take the damn dog in a taxi, and get your butt home. You should get the spanking of your life."

......

"I begged and pleaded with your father, but he said 'No!'" Gail commiserates as she pours a cup of tea for each of us. I look out her familiar kitchen window and down at the table with it cups and saucers and jars of jellies, jams and peanut butter.

"If I leave school and get a job, what can I do? I'm not trained for anything. I can't earn enough waiting tables or being a nurses' aid to afford an apartment."

"I told him we'd pay you to stay here and look after the kids."

"Oh Gail, I'd do that for free, just to be here. When I'm here, I'm myself. My mother's convinced I'm insane. My father thinks I'm a whore. How can I live with people who know me so little and see me in such negative terms? It's her sociology courses."

"It's her own neurosis," Gail laughs.

"I sometimes feel that my father's allergic to me, not the dogs. Every time I walk in he starts to wheeze and runs up stairs for his Asthmanefrin... I feel terrible, because I don't want to hurt my parents."

"You're not hurting them. It's their own negative projections that are hurting them."

"Maybe I am crazy. Maybe I am abnormal... a misfit who will never fit in... maybe I should be in a mental hospital somewhere..."

"Don't be ridiculous... You're the sanest person I know... It's the rest of the world that is insane... look at it... violence, wars, drinking, drugs, smoking, abuse, oppression, pornography, poverty, ignorance, ego, money, lying, cheating, stealing, depression, greed, despair, corruption. You don't do any of it. You just like to lead simple life, like Thoreau, sleeping outside under the stars. Breathing the pure, fresh, free air, running free in the woods with the dogs, studying physics and philosophy and painting your murals and doing your sculptures. You're just on your own peaceful journey through the mess... the problem is that's not what your parents, or society, has set out for you as a woman."

"What am I going to do?"

"What about John?"

"I haven't seen him. Has he been by here?"

"Last week he was by. He ran into your father."

"No wonder he's staying away... I know my father loves me and he's trying to protect me. But he's protecting me from the wrong things."

"He still sees you as his little girl with the golden ringlets looking up at him with adoring eyes. It's terribly hard for him to have you leaving and, God forbid, being a mature woman with a man. No man is ever going to be good enough for his baby girl."

"I know... But I just can't be in that house. I love them and I know they love me and are concerned about me, but why can't they give me the love and support I need to become who I really am, instead of trying to force me to be something I'm not?"

"They are doing the best they know how."

"I know. That's what's so heart rending."

Little Lisa shyly slips through the door and on to my lap. "Tell me about the dioxslide and sugar again," she smiles up at me.

"OK." I draw on a piece of paper. "This is the plant here. This green is chlorophyll in the leaves. Here's the air here... and here are the roots, dirt and water. Carbon dioxide is made of one carbon atom here in black and two oxygen atoms here in blue. Water is made of two hydrogen atoms here in yellow and two oxygen atoms in blue..."

"Are these the same oxygen atoms?"

"Yes, the same kind of atom. Atoms are like building blocks, you can put them together in different ways to make different things."

"Well look who's coming," Gail announces.

I turn and, through the curtained window, I see John coming up the walk. Carefully I set Lisa on her feet, leap up and run out the screen door.

"John! John!" My blood is racing!

"I got your letter," John says coolly.

"The one from the train?

"Yeah."

"Did you get the one from San Francisco and Wyoming?"

"Yep I got 'em all."

"I had a great trip. How was your summer?"

"OK...Worked a lot."

"How is Woody?"

"Fine, fine."

Moot comes over and he pats her.

"I'm taking the kids off to do some shopping. Need anything?" Gail shouts over her shoulder.

"Not that I can think of. Thanks."

Gail and the kids leave and John and I sit down on the front porch.

"I didn't know if you'd feel the same when you got back."

"Of course I feel the same. More so in fact. Why is something the matter?"

"No... No."

"You seem like something is bothering you."

"N..no I'm fine. Just a bit of re-entry shock. I'm so used to missing you I can't believe you're really here."

"I'm really here," I laugh. I take his hand and put it on my leg. "See, I'm real."

"Boy are you strong. Boy do you feel good."

He begins to rub his hand over me, then to nuzzle me and butt me with his head, the way he does.

"I wonder if I can still lift you up?"

"Try it and see."

"He lifts me up and carries me into the house.

"Where are we going?"

"To the coal bin."

"My studio... I haven't even seen it yet."

......

John and I are lying on my daybed couch. Light is coming in the back door in dramatic sweeps. John is kissing my hands and lips, face and breasts.

"You got back in the nick of time."

"Why?"

"I was going over the edge."

"I love you so much."

"Oh God. Oh God."

He begins to cry. He sobs and sobs holding on to me. I put my arms around him.

Some time later, the position of the rectangle of sunlight on the floor is longer and more slanted. Several hours have passed. I am lying on the bed-couch. John is lying on top of me asleep with his head on my breast. I am gazing off into the distance out the backdoor and absently twirling a piece of his hair in my fingers. The music has gone off and the only sound is the sound of birds outside and distant dogs barking.

Rousing himself at last he mummers, "Hey how about running to the hemlock grove?"

"Great idea!" I say, getting up and pulling on some rumpled jeans and a shirt. Mooty and the dogs follow us.

We walk out the back door through my garden.

"My garden! Look at it!" All the squash seeds that Lisa and I planted are huge overgrown plants. "And look, Squash!" I exclaim, bending over the thicket of greenery. The backyard is a tangle of tomato plants, squash, beans, cucumber vines covered in a fecund jungle of enthusiastic growth, unkempt, but gloriously prolific. The huge squash leaves fold like green umbrellas. Weeds proliferate as abundantly as the vegetables. The garden is clearly untended.

John is critical. "You went off and neglected your garden and it looks... like the way I feel... uncared for."

As we walk we talk.

"This damn Vietnam war is heating up," John complains. "Steve's draft number is coming up. He's looking into moving to Canada. He'd never survive that war... he can't even kill a bug.... how is he supposed to kill a human being? Worse we'd have to kill women and children? ... That's who they're killing.... with napalm. They're burning them alive... I don't care what they've done... or haven't done... no one deserves to die like that.... or to be maimed, armless, eyeless.... It makes me physically sick."

"Me too," I agree. I can't even watch pretend violence on TV and this is real and it is something America is doing.... what is this "new America"...?

"Not all of America.... Not the American people..." John replies, "You heard about the Gulf of Tonkin Resolution?"

"A little, this summer. I heard about the Buddhists Monks setting themselves on fire and burning themselves to death in protest of the war.... It's a nightmare.... this madness has to stop..." I commiserate.

The whole Tonkin thing was a set-up if you ask me," John says. "Johnson has declared war on the Vietnamese. It's Unconstitutional. Only Congress has the power to declare war. He says it's because they attacked one of our ships, the USS Maddock in international waters. But was it really in international waters? Was it really an attack? What was a U.S. ship doing there in the first place?" John is enraged. "And now he's landed U.S. troops there, not just "advisors" but troops, a quarter million of them and more on the way. They've gone mad. They're defoliating the jungles with toxic chemicals, destroying the crops, wiping out entire villages.

"Who said you can fool some of the people some of the time but you can't fool all of the people all of the time? A lot of well-intended people still think we are fighting to set these people free and if we leave there will be a blood bath as the Vietcong slaughter everyone opposed to them," John sneers.

"There has to be a better way..." I console him and reach out and touch his hand.

We break into a slow run.

The sun is glistening on a perfect September day.

John and I reach the grove and begin to climb one of our hemlock trees. After a few moments, we reach the top. I lie back into the flexible branches that are covered with soft, small, flat needles, dark green on the top, soft pastel green on the underside, which tickle the underside of my arms. The dogs circle below, looking up worriedly and whining. I hold on to the branches, bend back and look up at the sky.

"It's so beautiful!" I exclaim, "You can see the whole Town Forest from here!"

John is just below me climbing up.

"Isn't this great!"

John pulls himself up onto the branch next to me, "This is great!" He gooses me from the rear and I let out a squeal of irritation and delight.

"My parent trees," I say. "This grove is where I'd come to sort things out."

"My parent trees too, remember?"

"Of course I remember! Don't you feel the love in these trees?"

"Yes, I feel it..." John grins at me.

......

"We're very worried about her." My mother and father are seating in a plush office in Cambridge. Dark wood bookcases line the walls and a deep red rug covers the floor. "She was in a car accident this summer," my mother complains. "She's taken to running with the dogs in the woods again and sleeping outside in the backyard."

Dr. Southgate, a comfortably plump middle-aged psychiatrist, leans back in his leather upholstered chair and peers over his solid mahogany desk at my parents who look small and out of place.

My father, who thinks psychiatry is a lot of expensive nonsense, shifts uneasily in his chair.

"Let's set up and appointment for her and I'll see what I can do," the doctor smiles reassuringly.

......

"Can you describe for me these 'feelings of oneness?'" Dr. Southgate croons in a persuasive manner as if talking with a troublesome child. I'm sitting in a leather chair at the side of the doctor's desk.

"It's no big thing... It's just a feeling of happiness realizing that you're connected with everything else," I stammer feeling awkward, and resentful that I'm even here. He scribbles in his note pad.

"Can you tell me what possessed you to take the family car and travel across the entire country?"

"I wanted to see the country and visit my friend who just had a baby."

With a sigh, the good doctor pushes back his chair. "Your parents are very concerned about you. They say you were in an accident with three men, that you sleep outside in the back yard and that you run for miles in the woods with the dogs. They insist that you start sleeping inside and that you stop this running nonsense. Do you like to inflict pain on yourself? Is that why you run?"

"Pain? It's not pain. It feels great to run, so relaxing and energizing. I feel great when I run!"

"It's not normal, especially for a young lady."

......

It is positively weird to be having dinner with my parents again around the family dinner table. The same placemats, the same lamp hanging over the round table, the same chairs... even the same conversation.

"We're glad you gave up physics," my mother says. "That's no subject for a young woman. When I was your age, I was married."

"The only person I'd ever marry is my best friend," I say.

"That's ridiculous. Men and women can't be friends," my dad spouts. "Higamous, hogamous women are monogamous. Hogamous, higamous men are polygamous."

"How do you ever expect to find a husband if you are sleeping outside and running in the woods with the dogs?"

"I'm not looking for a husband."

"Well how are you going to support yourself?"

"You're out of touch with reality."

"This has got to stop. No more running. No more sleeping outside."

"I can't live like this!" I explode. "It's like death." I shove my chair back, get up from the table and slam out of the house.

"What she needs is a strict husband to keep her in line," my dad growls. "We've been too lenient. She's been too free. It's time to break her spirit and make her conform once and for all."

"She's always been a handful," my mother grimaces. "She's never learned to obey."

My mother slowly clears the dining table and my dad goes into the living room, sits down at the piano and plays Beethoven's Appassionata Sonata.

Chapter 23: The Wrath of God

Tonight I am sleeping in my familiar old bedroom, the room I've had since I was nine years old. I've pulled the bed over to the window and have my sleeping bag set up so my head is on the sill so I can look out at my maple tree and hear the sounds of the wind in its branches. This is as close to sleeping outside as I can get. Moot is on the back porch with her head on her paws looking sad. My mind wanders off into the starry night.

Ping, ping... the sound of pebbles on my window wakes me out of my reverie. I look out.

It's John. I pull on my clothes and tiptoe down to the back door. Moot is wagging her tail and looking happy. John wants to come in. I know it is a mistake. I try to explain that this isn't the Willard's.

"Shhhhh, Be quiet. If my dad wakes up he'll kill you and me too," I try to reason with him.

"Let's make a big fire." John pushes his way inside.

"Shhhh. Don't wake up my parents."

John is stacking wood into the fireplace, crinkling paper, lighting a match. Soon the ruddy glow fills the room with heat.

"So was the trip worth it?" John asks gruffly. "Do you think you've found all the answers now?"

"Look... I'm not saying I have the answers. Everyone has to find their own answer. We're all talking about the same thing... the source of our own being, the wonder and mystery of existence. This happens to have come to me. We're all talking about our own models of reality anyway... even this one."

"What do you mean? I can see what reality is. I just look and there it is."

"The universe we think we see, the universe we conceive is not what is really there," I begin shakily.

"What is there then, my little mystic?"

"We can never know what is really here directly. We know only our models of it. ... When you say 'universe' you are talking about the universe you think you see, or the material universe with its mechanical causality, the universe that physics models as real, the big bang, or whatever image of the universe you have at any given period in history. I'm not talking about that. I'm talking about what really exists, the ultimate existence, which we can never know directly but which stands under every other existence and makes it possible. We can't even know if it does exist or what it means to exist in this way."

"That make no sense at all...zero... zip...nada...none. Are you telling me, that this floor isn't real," he says banging his palm on the floor.

"Shhh. You'll wake up my father..."

"I'm not saying it is real or is not real. I'm saying we can't know what it is directly. We only know our perceptions and conceptions of our interactions with it... That it exists, and how it exists, and why we experience it as we experience it we don't know."

"Well if nothing exists, then there is no need of a Deity to explain why it exists," John concludes.

"I'm not saying nothing exists. We assume that things exist, we make that leap of faith, but we can never know for sure if anything really exists, or what it means to really exist, or how things really exist. All we know is our perceptions and conceptions of our interactions with whatever it is," I repeat.

"So where does this leave God?" John asks.

"It depends on what you mean by God," I reply. "What do you mean by God?"

"You know ... a supreme being, a deity with supernatural powers who created, and rules, the world."

"But what is a deity?" I ask.

"You know.... a supernatural superhuman who has supernatural powers."

"I'm talking about the source of our being, the Creator of all existence," I explain.

"You mean a supernatural deity, then!" John exclaims.

"I'm not talking about a deity I'm talking about the Divine Existence. It's much bigger than a deity. It's all that really exists and it's everywhere all the time."

"So is that God?"

"OK," I respond, "I'm not talking about a Being in the world. It's not like you have the world and then you have a Being who walks around in the world and that is the Divine. It may be that that is what a God is, a being with superhuman powers who exists in the world, but that's not what I'm talking about."

"You're talking about a Being who exists outside the world and creates it."

"No I'm not talking about a Being at all... I'm talking about Being itself, what really exists behind what we think we see."

"So you're a transcendentalist?"

"No. I'm not talking about a transcendent world or existence behind reality. I'm not talking about a transcendent existence behind existence. The veil I'm taking about isn't between existence and some transcendent world, just the opposite. It is the veil of our own perceptions and conceptions, covering the reality of what really exists, which we can never know except through our models of it. ..."

"This is ridiculous."

"This real existence is transcendent to our conceptions and perceptions, but it isn't transcendent to existence. It *is* Existence. It is what really exists, behind what we think we know. It's not supernatural, it is what Nature, in its largest sense, is. It is that in which we find ourselves imbedded... what is really here... this huge incomprehensible existence, which is everywhere at all times, the cosmos itself, the universe, all universes, the tiniest subatomic vibration, the quanta, ... everything. It is what is real, behind our conceptions and perceptions and models of it."

"How do we know it exists if we can never know it directly?" John scowls.

"We can't know it in some absolute way. We get along fine acting as if our models are real and projecting them back onto the world, most of the time... unless our models are wrong,"

"If we can't know it what's the good of talking about it?"

"Why is it here? How is it here?" I press on ignoring John's question in an effort to clarify my thoughts. "What is the true origin and nature of its existence? These are all our models of it. I'm talking about what it is itself, beyond our models... And, you know how it got here?"

"No idea."

"It creates Itself… It is in the continuous process of creating Itself into being everywhere at all times."

"Now this is truly insane."

"No. You know why? Because… How did the Creator get here? If something else created it, then that would be the real ultimate creator. Do you see?"

"No," John growls.

I ignore his objections, "And if it exists without being created, then there would be something that exists that is not created by the Creator, and the Creator by definition is that which creates *all* existence, so that would be a contradiction."

"If it creates everything… then how come there is so much evil in the world? How did it create this damn war?"

"What we think we see, what we think exists is not really what exists. We know only our own perceptions and conceptions and models of what is really there. If there is evil in the world it is because we humans create it by hurting each other and by hurting ourselves, not because it has some sort of ultimate reality."

"But this isn't beyond all models. This is just another model." John objects.

I laugh. "Yes, you are right. This is just another model... because that is all we fallible humans can make… What it is in itself is an utter mystery. Why it exists… why anything exists is an unfathomable mystery. And to feel that mystery is a sublime experience that should keep us all humble."

"What about Jesus?"

"Jesus is great. I love Jesus. If believing in Jesus helps people lead better more loving meaningful lives, then great. Perhaps this is what Christ meant when he said, 'God is at hand.' Perhaps he meant: 'God', meaning the loving divine creator and mystery, is already here on all sides, right here all around and within us and that seeing that and feeling and knowing that fills us with love and joy... and leads us naturally to do what is right, that is, to empathize with others and to treat others as we ourselves would want to be treated, which is the fundamental basis of all morality, I think."

"But what you're talking about isn't a supernatural deity at all."

"Right. It has nothing to do with religion. It is perfectly natural, but it's not the nature we think we see and know and measure. In fact it is all that really exists. It's much bigger than the old idea of an anthropomorphic supernatural deity, don't you see. It is the very ground of our Being and it is creating Itself into existence everywhere all the time and its nature is pure love."

John looks skeptical.

"Look," I shrug. "I didn't ask this stuff to come to me. It just came when I opened myself up and asked the questions. It came through me. I never expected this either... If it helps people to feel this sense of love and mystery and evokes a feeling of reverence and gratitude in others as it does in me, then perhaps what came to me on the mountain can do a lot of good."

"I think it's nuts and a poor excuse for leaving me all summer," he mumbles nuzzling my breast.

"Hey, this isn't the Willard's. My parents...." I push him away. John is tugging my clothes off. I'm losing track of where I am, as we passionately kiss and fondle each other. John unzips his jeans and puts my hand on his....

Crash!

I hear the sound of the latch.

The living room doors fling open.

"What the hell is going on!" my dad's voice booms. He is standing there in his pajamas, his dark blue bathrobe, which I gave him for Christmas last year, pulled around him, his voice blasting. His right hand is hanging by his side holding, I see, his heavy black revolver.

"Get the hell out of my living room!" he yells in a rage.

John jolts backwards and reaches for his fly, pulling up his pants as he stands up. He half runs and staggers across the living room away from my father, and lurches through the kitchen door, dragging his one construction boot, and catapults out the back door into the safety of the cool night air.

Moot jumps up wagging her tail but John brushes by like a tornado. I am close behind him.

My dad is furious. I hide on the back porch squeezed in between Moot's doghouse and the outside wall of the kitchen. It is cold but I don't dare move. I huddle in fetal position there in the dark, my head drawn in, like a turtle into her shell, my arms up, like those photos of Vietnamese women hiding from US bombs... like Eve hiding from the fury of God, after the fall, before the expulsion.

I hear my dad stomping back up the stairs, the way he used to when I was a child, when he would give us kids piggy back rides up the stairs, singing the Grandfather theme from Prokofiev's Peter and the Wolf, read us a chapter of Pooh Bear and tuck us in for the night.

I put my arms around my white wolf's neck, like Romulus, and, pressing my face into her warm fur, whisper, "What are we going to do, Mooty?" The cold night closes in around us, my wild wolf and me huddling on the back porch waiting for the fall.

······

"Reverend Richardson? I don't think we've met...Yes. I'm aware of that.... Last night, your son was in my home as an uninvited guest..." The next day, my dad, unknown to me, is on the telephone to John's father.

······

John's sleeping porch is behind his parents' garage. Carrying his boot, I arrive around the far corner of the garage and jump up onto the porch followed by Moot. His half packed suitcase is on the bed. Stacks of beer cans are piled up in towers and architectural designs. Turrets of wine bottles look like castles made of glass, all precariously balanced around the outer perimeter of the floor.

"John?"

No answer. I sit down on the edge of the bed to wait.

I hear something. What is it? Muffled yells. There's a loud argument going on in the house. I can't make out what they are saying, but many years later, John tells me.

"You are forbidden from seeing her again. Her father called this morning and has said if he ever sees you on the premises again he will report you to the police."

"I want to marry her," John yells.

"Marry? How are you going to support her? Do you want to ruin your life? Ruin your career? You'll be forced to drop out of Yale to go to work. I certainly am not going to support the both of you."

"We'll figure out a way."

"If you marry her, I'll pull your tuition."

"What?"

"You heard me. I'll stop paying your tuition."

"You bastard," John mutters as he turns to leave.

 "Get out of this house and don't come back." It is not clear to me if the Reverend hits John or not.

John jumps up on to the sleeping porch and the beer cans fall over noisily.

"Bobby Lou!"

"Hey! I brought your boot back," I say, unaware of what has passed in the house.

John looks down. "There's something I have to tell you."

"What?"

"I can't see you any more."

"What?"

"I can't see you."

"Why? What are you talking about?" A horrible sinking hopeless fear grips me, my heart closes down and shrinks inside.

"I'm all screwed up. I need time to think."

"What's the matter?"

"I'm just fucked up. I can't handle it."

"I don't believe you." I am angry at him, suddenly furious, for destroying this beautiful thing between us, for killing our creation.

"I gotta go. I'm headed back to Yale."

I reach out to stop him. He turns away abruptly, ripping out of my grip.

"Don't call," he yells as he jumps down off the porch with his suitcase, straps it to his motorcycle and takes off.

I watch him in disbelief, my world crumbling like the wine bottles in chaos onto the dirt.

Chapter 24: Run Away

"He'll be back. Don't worry. He just needs time to sort things out." Gail is trying to sooth me as we sit in her kitchen. She pours me some more tea.

"Why doesn't he talk with me about it? We always talk about everything."

"Some things he has to sort out for himself."

"Oh Gail what am I going to do? Living with my parents again, with no John, with no you and the kids..."

"We're here. You can come up anytime."

"But it's not the same. My parents want me to do what they want me to do. They are trying to get me to conform. They say it's for my own good, but it isn't. It's killing me. I don't know what to do. I love them and I know they love me but it's killing me.... I don't even know what it is... And I'm in school again.... Museum School, Art School full time, but I'm not sure this is what I really want either."

......

Finally the moment comes the, moment I've been dreading, the moment I've been avoiding, the moment I have to go back and face my poor distraught parents. I feel so angry, so guilty, so awful.

I slink in the back door after patting Moot who has curled up in the doghouse I've made for her with the cushion inside. I change and put my clothes into the bag marked, 'Dog'.

My mom looks up from the sink as I slither by and glares at me her look full of anxiety, fear, hurt, confusion; I can't tell if its hate or love making her lip quiver.

My dad looks up from his breakfast and glares his most condemning Jehovah-like glare at me as if I am the condemned tribe of Israel, given to licentious fornication, before the flood. He glares his scorched earth glare, his destroying all life on earth glare, from his elevated position on the clouds, gazing at his creation, which he has made, which he possesses, but which has sinned and now must be punished.

His wrath rains down on me. "As long as you are living in my house, young lady, you'll do as I say!" he shouts.

"But I don't want to be living here. I want to live at the Willard's," I yell back.

What's this? Mutinous rebellion on his ship? This is intolerable!

He slams his palm down on the counter making the dishes rattle.

"We don't think you're well enough to live on your own," my mother's quavering voice inserts itself, her white face grimacing in that strange contorted smile.

A red curtain of rage rises up within me, a violence that shocks even me. I scream at the top of my lungs, "You're the ones who are sick. You're the ones who are crazy. I gotta get out of this place." Dimly I realize that this is not having the desired effect of making them reconsider the validity of their position.

Suddenly I feel like a raving manic. I do feel crazy. My dad doesn't dare to try to spank me. My mother, I sense, is afraid of me too, but grimly perseveres in her righteous position that I am crazy and she is sane, and that this too is a burden she must bear, the tragic insanity of her own daughter. It's all, I realize, a drama about her, starring her, by her, about her, for her, and I am playing a part in that drama, not the part I want to play, but the part I'm playing in spite of myself. She is OK and I am not. I feel a fury rising up inside of me like a trapped wild animal, sensing a threat to my being, to my sanity, to my sense of self. I feel the passion of self-justification flooding me, rushing to my own self-defense. The more she drinks the crazier I get.

I want to get out of here. I have to get out of here. It's like being in quicksand, the more I struggle, the more I am sucked down into it. I run back out the door, still clutching the bag of my clothes marked, 'dog.' Grabbing my sleeping bag and ground cloth, I open the back porch gate and, followed by Moot, I flee into the deep woods, where I stuff my sleeping gear under a fallen tree, change back into my running clothes and run and run and run, deeper and deeper into the primeval forest. It's like high school again, that strange disoriented raw, ragged, chaotic feeling of being homeless, of having no one, and nowhere to be.

My thoughts are tumbling in a jumble of feelings. The patterns of trees reel by; late September leaves hang like thin, green, leather hands on the trees. Splashes of riotous color clash with my angry mood. On and on I run. I am strong now, like a wild animal. I can run for miles tirelessly. I have run across an entire continent, sleeping out at night, lost in the stars. Moot is with me, and a couple of the neighborhood dogs. It takes longer to tire me out now. I run until it is late afternoon, in loops through the Fells, which once seemed immense to my small self, but now seems small and confining after the spaciousness of the unending plains.

At sunset I fall into a hollow where a stream runs through a pine woods, near the reservoir. At last I feel peaceful again. I lie here on my back looking up through the woody spokes of pine trees filled with years of accumulated twigs, the shimmering deep green needles, my roof. I smell the tang of pungent pine needles, my rug. I touch the rough reddish bark of the walls of my forest palace. I never want to go home.

I just want to live here where Nana's love still shimmers through the sunlit trees, slanting late into the afternoon and the sun effulges wreathes of photons, which move at the fastest speed possible, blowing as solar winds through the solar system, interacting with the magnetic fields of whirling iron-cored planets, in feathery arrays of radiation, seen by us as light, forever.

Chapter 25: Alas

"Bobby Lou didn't come home last night.... and it turns out she was up in the woods sleeping with the dogs! .... I don't know what we're going to do with her," my mother's shaky voice complains. She reaches into her purse, unscrews the lid on a small bottle, pops a small pill into her mouth and washes it down with a drink provided by Gail.

Outside Gail's living room window, fine drops of rain drift down.

"She's a big girl now... You have to stop trying to control everything she does," Gail observes.

"But she's sick... She's not well..." my mother whines.

"Really? Because she likes to sleep outside? Is she doing anyone any harm? She seems perfectly well to me..."

"I've failed as a mother... I've tried so hard," my mother's voice is wavering.

"Failed?... You have a gifted and unique daughter, who's trying to find her way in a complex often confusing world...."

"When she was a baby, she rolled over on her tummy arched her back and looked around. She was only two days old. The nurse said she'd never seen a child so alert and so bright... and if I raised her right she'd do great things... and I've tried so hard to..to..." my mother moans.

".....To break her spirit and make her conform to what you think she should be...." Gail counters. "Why don't you just try accepting her as she is."

"She can't keep sleeping outside.... and running in the woods with the dogs. How will she ever find a husband and fit into society's expectations?"

"Why should she? Why not let her march to the beat of a different drummer.... Maybe she's happy that way ... happy in a way that the rest of us can't even imagine."

My mother sighs.... "Well she seems to like you and to trust you... So I just came to see... if..."

"We think she's great... a bit eccentric maybe... but great. She's great with the kids... Someday she'll be a wonderful mother... But there are other things she wants to do too.... The world isn't set up for gifted kids.... it's hard to be very sensitive.... it's a handicap to be gifted.... You don't fit in... You feel lonely."

"I grew up in a big huge cold mausoleum mansion in Cleveland Heights. The servants, Luther and Stella raised me.... I was sent away to girl's finishing school.... I never knew what it was like to have a real home...." My mother is breaking down.

"I'm sorry," Gail begins.

"Maybe that's why Bobby Lou likes it here," my mother sniffles ".... It's a real home for her... the home.... I could never give her."

122

"She loves you and Tom," Gail continues, feeling sorry for my mother... "She wants to please you, but she also has to be true to herself...."

"Sleeping out in the woods is being true to herself?"

"She finds something there... some sort of peace... Why don't you just try easing up on her a bit and see how it works...." Gail comforts my mother.

"You seem to be the only person she really trusts..."

"Come up here any time you want to talk," Gail invites.

"I've been staying away.... I guess I felt a little jealous."

Gail looks at my mom feeling compassionate but somehow irritated. "It's OK," she says.

My mother smiles faintly, shyly.... sighs, and gets up to leave... "Thanks," she musters as she walks out the door.

......

"Your mother was here," Gail greets me. Moot and several neighborhood dogs and I burst in the Willards' front door shaking rain off on to the braided rug.

"I figured as much," I say, kicking my boots off onto the pile of Willard boots in the corner. "She had the sheepish guilty look about her she gets when she snoops in my stuff."

"Tea or hot chocolate?"

I glance at the headlines on the crumpled morning paper, "Johnson wins by a landslide."

"Chocolate, thanks."

"It's hard for you to trust anyone isn't it?"

"Yeah," I nod... "Hot chocolate. Thanks."

"So how are you feeling?"

"Better... I miss John...darn it."

"I know.... You've been going through a lot of grieving recently, haven't you?"

I feel a rush of tears behind my eyes, at being so understood and not judged.

I nod... "My Nana...." I begin... but am unable to go on.

Gail looks at me with her clear direct gaze... "John was helping you heal from that... And now he's gone too."

"And Will is gone.... And Lenny is dead... This is not the way it was supposed to have been... I was supposed to marry Prince Charming and live happily ever after in a big castle...."

"Life isn't much of a fairy tale... I'm afraid," Gail commiserates.

"Well what is it then? I really think it's a big beautiful world and we are supposed to be happy... We are meant to be happy in some fundamental way... and all this misery people inflict on themselves and each other is entirely unnecessary.... a big mistake," I find myself spouting.

"You're probably right," Gail agrees, "But no one knows how to do it."

"Well, I feel happy just walking down the road, for no reason at all. Everything seems beautiful to me... And when I don't, I know something is wrong and out of balance and I do what I can to rebalance it," I say... "Go for a run, get some sleep, talk with a friend, eat something, lie on the ground, watch the clouds go by. Whatever it takes."

"I wish it were so simple," Gail sighs, sipping her hot chocolate.

"It is that simple, I'm convinced," I conclude.

"I'm glad you're better," Gail smiles.

"So what did you tell my mother?"

"I told her to ease up."

"That's good. I hope she does for her sake and for everyone else's sake too... Thanks." I smile, feeling that I'm not so alone anymore.

Chapter 26: Lo How a Rose E'er Blooming

Drawing board and newsprint, wedged under my arm, I disembark from the clanging Huntington subway and trudge diagonally across the leaf-strewn front lawn of the Boston Museum of Fine Arts, towards the low brick building that houses the Museum School. It seems strange to see it in the morning light, after years of seeing it in the dark.

Here is my favorite sculpture of an Indian on horse back looking up into the face of the Great Spirit, only instead of looking up into the stars the way I've usually seen him, he's looking up in to the flat, gray, overcast morning sky. I had gone in search of that Great Spirit and found it and felt it. But, now it is crumbling to dust in the face of the renewed onslaught of a different reality, a reality that leaves me feeling empty and raw, like a hurt place.

The hurricane-laden air of late September, with its heavy, green oak leaves blowing in warm gusts of tropical air, has passed into the crispness of October's brilliant clean, blue sky, with brilliant red, yellow and orange leaves letting go and floating down to form carpets of color around the base of each tree becoming bare. And now it is November, four and a half more months of training to the Marathon.

By late November, the hollow, whining moan of winter's wind will tear the ravaged, naked trees. The sharp, stinging hiss of snow and ice, the ache of ears and hands, the sharp edge of biting air in lungs and nose will erase all memory of summer's gentle warmth.

My days begin early. I get up before my parents, gulp a glass of orange juice, take a vitamin pill, give Moot a hug and run to the Museum School. I run along the Mystic Lakes and cut up over the hill by Tufts University dropping down into the Charles River valley. I follow the Charles along to the Fenway, where I turn up and come into the Museum school from the back, having run about eight miles, all the way from Winchester. Eight miles seems like nothing after my summer's running, miles at a stretch.

Each student has a locker where he or she keeps his or her paints, drawing boards, charcoal and smocks. I am taking life-drawing class, anatomy, design and painting. My girl friends, Riddie, Laurie, Sue, Ann, and Emily, and I eat together and draw together. We are like a small herd going everywhere doing everything together. I stay in the middle of the group, seeking its comfort and protection.

Riddie is a quiet, sensible, round-faced girl with glasses. Laurie has bright blue eyes, and an indomitable Nordic spirit. She's served with the Peace Corps in Ecuador and speaks fluent Spanish. Her straight, platinum-blonde hair falls with self-assured abandoned, across her shoulders and part way down her straight back.

Ann is short and blonde and interested in sex. Birth control pills have recently become available. She's taking the new pills she confides to me one day. I'm not very experienced sexually and still fundamentally believe that sex and marriage should go together. But mores are changing and I'm caught in the confusion of the times.

One day at lunch Riddle approaches me followed by a tall, dignified looking young man who turns out to be a Harvard student. "Bobby Lou," Riddle smiles, "I'd like you to meet Branden." I look up into a smiling face with a blunt nose and pair of eager brown eyes.

"Pleased to meet you," he says holding out his hand.

His handshake is warm and firm and I like him immediately, although the pain from John is still too close for me to think about dating yet.

Our afternoon lecture is on humans as creators. "In some sense it is not Homo sapiens that has made us what we are today... But Homo Fabricare, humans the creators," The visiting lecturer proclaims.

After school, I trudge through the crowded rainy streets. Traffic lights blink on and off turning red, yellow and green. This too is the Divine. City lights reflect on wet, hard asphalt. I miss John. I like Art School, but I'm not sure if this is what I'm meant to be doing. I miss science and philosophy. I miss sleeping outside, with Mooty by my side, immersed in the unfathomable mystery of space and time. I'm living at my parents' house. At night I sleep with my head on the windowsill looking out at the silver maple growing up between cement sidewalk and asphalt street. I crane my neck and look up into the infinite universe of stars and dark places between the stars.

The only clear, stable and real part of my life is my running, my training, my goal of running Boston. This, at least, is my true path, but I can't even tell anyone.

......

By Christmas the family rift has healed. It's funny how quickly I forget all the bad things and remember the good things. Having a poor memory is good for some things, I guess.

Next thing I know Dad and I are singing "Lo How a Rose E'er Blooming," and "Lullay Thou Little Tiny Child," and I feel I am safe in the bosom of my loving little family.

Athena and George and their two sons stop by our open house. I've never seen her before out in the world with her family. I've only known her in the intense brief philosophical discussions we have occasionally when she stops me after a run or the couple of times I've stopped in and listened spell-bound to her piano playing. She composes exquisite music. She plays on and on for hours making it up as she goes and no one ever hears it.

"That would be like prostitution!" she snorted angrily the one time I suggested that she play publicly as a professional musician. "My music is for love, not money."

126

"Would you show me your mural?" I'm jarred from my recollections by Athena in person. I look at her dark brown, intense eyes and her tall regal face, like an ancient Persian princess.

"Sure," I say covering my startled sense of being invaded and my shyness at having anyone see my artwork.

I lead her down the dark, creaking cellar stairs to the mural I've painted here as a companion to the mural I painted at the Willard's house.

"Oh this is wonderful!" she exclaims seeing my little art studio den.

After my brother joined the Coast Guard we folded up the ping-pong table and I put a daybed down here, my lantern and a desk, and I made workspace for myself. A philodendron grows in the corner by the cellar window-hole light. Woven madras fabrics cover the bed and the easy chair where I read.

"Is this your mural?" Athena says as I turn on the light and illuminate the rock and cement walls of the basement, which glow rich with the colors and forms of trees, vines and imaginary biological shapes.

"This is incredible. It's so alive!" She stands transfixed, lost in my painting for a long time. Finally, turning, she continues, "It's funny the way nothing ever goes beyond the edges of your mural."

I feel nervous. "What do you mean?"

"I mean all the tree branches are contained within the mural, none of them go off the edge. They all stop at the edge, as if the border of the mural is a real thing, which the trees can sense, if you know what I mean."

"So?" I say a bit hurt.

"So it's interesting... That's all. What does it mean? It's as if you're trying to paint the whole world and there's nothing outside it."

"Well I have always wondered what this world is all about. What is existence, anyway? Why does anything exist? What is existence and how does it get here?" I reply, not knowing what else to say.

"Maybe you just like to create your own world and not see the world that is," she says.

"But maybe the world that people think exists is not really what exists," I persist. "Maybe people mistake their view of reality for what is real."

"Maybe so," she agrees. "Maybe you do too."

We traipse back upstairs where the caroling is just beginning.

"Ah there you are," my dad says, spotting me, "Come sing Good King Wenslaus with us."

My parents are being so nice to me suddenly. I wonder what happened. Maybe something Gail said to my mother helped after all.

I haven't exploded or stamped or yelled at some outrage in a week!

Chapter 27: Blizzard

The temperature drops. Tiny flakes of snow rise with the drafts of cold air up and then down, never seeming to land. The chickadees and blue jays are hunched, hidden in the shrubs. The world is silent and waiting.

Tugging on my boots, wrapping two scarves around my face, pulling on my warm fuzzy, blue mittens, and over them, nylon-covered, puff mittens, I clump to the door, open it and step out into the cold. The flakes are falling faster now and the wind is picking up. Moot looks up at me wagging her tail and grinning. This is her kind of weather.

I rumple her fur, "Moooty Babe....... I hug her. "Hey, its malamute stew for me and you," I sing and laugh. "You're a sheep in wolf's clothing, When are you going to take off that silly dog suit?" She talks to me in a long woo, woo, woo, with intonations and ups and downs. She doesn't bark but only emotes sounds and howls, long whining wolf howls. I remember how Carol and I use to howl to each other, like wolves, when we played as kids in Rockport. How the neighbors must have loved that! "Woo, woo, woo," I answer Moot and she dances around me. "Come on girl, come on. Let's go for a run in the snow!" We leap down the back steps and run along Sargent Road headed for the Fells.

The thought, the possibility, of not running the Boston Marathon never enters my consciousness. Despite Dr. Southgate, my parents, social pressure and the loss of John, this is not something on which I vacillate. This decision has already been made inside of me by something deeper than my conscious mind. This decision has something to do with the way I perceive reality and my relationship to it. It has something to do with who I am and why I came here.

Moot and I run out across the frigid stark white tundra. The wind sweeps loose snow in snaking undulating strands of ghostlike crystals of water, which has become solid like sand. Frozen pinpricks of ice beat against my face and into my eyes, fusing my eyes shut, coating my eyelashes. Flat hexagons tick coldly against the nylon shell of my parka. Impenetrable, gray, white, vibrant pixels of ice, driven by the wind in long eerie swirls, crystallize out of the thin, cold air. We are running across the surface of some other planet, not a warm living earth, but a strange wild planet, Neptune, blue with frozen nitrogen, or Pluto's desolate powdered rock.

Demi-life, wraith-like, swirling, unfolding, tumbling, contortions of gray frozen snow-mist stream like smoke, in white horse tails. Moot and I slide across the primal arctic landscape that has replaced the fecund jungle growth of summer. We've traveled half way around the sun now, and summer is millions of miles away in some distant half-remembered land.

The awe-inspiring Presence is here; it is the same creative force of the elements manifesting itself here as the substrate of our existence, here on this frozen planet. The Divine Creator is here creating Himself into all this wonder.

Moot, matted with ice, trots head down, braced like an ox against the ripping wind. My thighs ache with the unaccustomed lift as I break through the drifts of accumulating snow.

Suddenly as I run I find myself thinking about the mind-body problem again. I haven't felt peaceful enough to think since John left.

I recall my thoughts on the train on the way home from Wyoming. It feels like lifetimes ago, but it was only four and a half months ago. I'd seen that there are two separate but related issues: First, the ability of nature to self-form itself, which comes from the abilities of the parts to interact, and, second, the ability of a system to experience subjectively, that is, to have a subjective experience.

How is it that a material object that is made of atoms and molecules, namely the brain, can have a subjective experience?

If there is no invisible mind substance, if, as I think there are not two explicands, not two separate substances-- mind substance and body substance-- but one substance, then how does the brain produce subjective experience?

Is there some part of the brain like the little man watching the TV screen that is capable of experiencing subjectively, while the rest of the brain is just a mechanical, extended system of neurons, made up of atoms and molecules?

If so, what is so special about the part of the brain that experiences subjectively?

How can the blips of electrical potential firing in patterns of neuronal activity, which the brain generates, be converted, by that part of the brain that experiences subjectively, into subjective experience?

When I look at the body and its brain I see billions of interconnected neurons engaged in dynamic patterns of activities and processes, many of which involve long chains of biochemical reactions and changing electric potentials. I see cells interaction with each other, and inside the cells I see atoms, molecules, electrons and protons all engaged in tremendous self-generated activity, requiring the continual pouring of energy through the system in highly organized ways.

A certain subset of those activities are view by me, whoever I am, inwardly as subjective experience, that is, as sensations, perceptions, thoughts, ideas, memories, feelings, dreams, in short, those numinous inner experiences of which I am directly aware.

What is this 'I' who views? I don't see any separate I in there. All I see are activities and processes in this highly organized dynamic system.

I don't understand how the firings of neurons are experienced by my brain subjectively. Where and how does this conversion from dynamic patterns of neuronal activity to subjective experience occur?

If there is no invisible, insubstantial mind-substance, then the activity of the human brain, or some subset there of, must somehow be subjectively experienced. But how is this subset of activity of the brain subjectively perceived by me?

The brain processes are fluctuations of membrane voltage in cells. The perceptions, conceptions, thoughts are numinous, massless, weightless, subjectively experienced phenomena, like the smell of roses or the blueness of the sky, which seem like entirely different types of thing than patterns of electrical potentials in neurons.

What actually is a subjective experience in my brain? And who am I who perceives it?

The next day thaws and then freezes again. This is a three-day nor'easter. The wind is howling. I get up again, pull on my cold, still damp clothes, which, I tell myself, will warm up once I get moving.

"Why am I running the marathon?"

Take twenty-five billion tons of snow add twenty trillion gallons of freezing, pelting, beating, driving rain, a pinch of salt, and mix, and what do you get? Cold feet.

Sleet blasts my face stinging and freezing my eyelashes together. Melting snow drips off my coat down my neck. Sticks of dark dormant trees poke out of gray snow. Invisible gray skies release torrents of snow and ice mixed with water. My boots slosh and slip on hard ice. There's an exhilaration being out on such a day. I have the world to myself. There's a Presence on these days too, that keeps me company... a wild creative force.

These are the days, in winter that test my determination to run. Never once does it occur to me that I don't have to run the Boston Marathon. Never does it occur to me that I won't run it, possibly even win it, if I can train enough.

Why?

I never stop to ask why. Certainly no one is expecting me to run. At this point I don't even know I am going to make a social statement. What keeps me at it?

Some inner decision has been made inside of me that I will run. There isn't even any money in it, only hours and hours and hours of lonely, arduous training, forging into the unknown... not knowing if I can do it... wondering if my heart will stop beating.

I am in love with the Boston Marathon.

Day in, day out, rain, snow, sleet, I am out here running, working steadily towards my goal, simply because I know that this is what I am meant to do. But I don't know why. There are no extrinsic rewards and there are almost insurmountable obstacles, but doggedly I keep at it.

And doggedly I keep at this mind body problem.

Suppose the mind is some subset of the activities and processes of the brain and not some separate invisible substance that inhabits the brain. How then do the activities of the brain cause subjective experience?

I fall into deep thought as I slog through the slush and snow.

If I imagine that I'm very small and I can walk around inside the brain and look at the ever-changing, dynamic patterns of neuronal activity, nowhere do I see subjective experience, nowhere do I see a scene of a frigid tundra and white snow snaking across the frozen ground, nowhere do I feel the sensation of cold. All I see is neuronal activity. If there is no insubstantial mind substance to look at all this, no little man looking at the T.V. screen, how does all this neuronal activity get converted to subjective experience?

Suddenly it occurs to me that if all there is is neuronal activity then subjective experience would also have to be neuronal activity.

Could it be that the patterns of neuronal activity do not 'cause' subjective experience, but that the patterns of neuronal activity 'are' in fact subjective experience? Could it be that the patterns of neuronal activity are not 'converted' to subjective experience somewhere in the brain, but that the patterns of neuronal activity in the brain, or at least some of them, actually 'are' subjective experience?

This must be true. The solution to the conversion problem must be that there is no conversion from patterns of neuronal activity to subjective experience in the brain, at all, but rather that the patterns, or at least some of the patterns, of neuronal activity are in fact already subjective experience to the brain or at least to the part of the brain that 'has' subjective experience.

But, is a pattern of neuronal activity really a subjective experience?

Not if I am viewing it from the outside. A pattern of activity in my brain is not a subjective experience to someone viewing my brain from the outside.

So it is not enough to say that a subjective experience is an activity or process of the brain. The activity, process and dynamic pattern of neuronal firing is only a subjective experience when viewed or experienced from the inside of the brain whose activity it is.... but here I am back to the same problem... Viewed by what?

If mind is some set of activities of the brain viewed from the inside subjectively.... then what exactly views and what is viewed?

I see now that the exact same event, namely the dynamic patterns of neuronal activity, is seen as the firing of neurons as viewed from the outside and at the same time, that same event is a subjective experience as viewed from the inside of the brain.

But what is this 'viewed from the inside'? What is inside? What views and what is viewed? If all there are are dynamical patterns of highly organized neuronal processes that fire in patterns of activity, then that must be what I, the viewer, am as well. I must be some set of highly organized neuronal activity, which identifies itself as me.

In order for the activities and processes that identify themselves as me to experience subjectively they would have to be viewing their own activities and processes subjectively from the inside.

What is this 'from the inside'? How do patterns of neuronal activity have, from the inside, the subjective quality they do, so that the taste of strawberries is the way it is and the sensation of blue is the way it is? Or to be more exact, how 'are' these patterns of neuronal activity subjective experience? How is it that a pattern of neuronal activity is a subjective experience when viewed from the inside? Viewed by what?

Chapter 28: Yesterday

February grinds on with piles of snow and gravel, from the snowplows, stacked along the streets. I'm eating lots of cheese and protein, liver and eggs to make myself strong, knowing nothing of carbohydrate loading.

The phone rings.

"Hello," my mother says startled at the deep sound of a man's voice. "Just a minute."

My ears strain to hear, a momentary pang of excitement and fear clutches my stomach.

"Bobby Lou," my mother calls anxiously.

"It's some man," she says loud enough so he can hear.

"Shh," I feel irritated at her intrusion.

"Hello," I pick up the receiver, my heart racing, hoping it is John.

"Hello, this is Branden," the voice says. "Remember me?"

"Of course I remember you!" I exclaim. The image of Branden's blunt face and eager brown eyes pops onto the inner movie screen of my mind.

"A bunch of us are having a house party and I was wondering if you would like to come? ... I hope you don't mind... I got your number from Riddie."

"Of course I don't mind… Thank you... I'd love to…"

Well, actually the idea terrifies me. A house party at Harvard.

Branden dressed in a tweed jacket, jeans and a tie arrives to pick me up. My insides are fluttering wildly. This man has incredible presence. He's tall, towering over my Dad, and dignified... And, you can feel the power of his mind.

"Hello, I'm Branden." He extends his hand to my dad, who is at the door, and then to my mother who is behind my dad.

"This is more like it," I can hear my dad thinking, a Harvard man, who has enough grace to come to the door and meet the parents before seducing his daughter, unlike that other one he had driven off, that minister's son... what was his name?

They act as if... the business of marriage and finding the appropriate mate.... the art of seduction and selection...is some kind of...paternalistic business deal.

Branden is definitely way up there on the scale of appropriate mates, but of course I don't have wit enough to realize that this is what this is all about. I am looking for my spiritual other, my transcendent partner. But this is about as close to Prince Charming as you can get in this imperfect world, a charming intelligent, gentleman in Harvard, destined for Harvard Medical School.... and I like him.

We drive through the starry night to the parking lot behind his dorm, a huge brick edifice near the River behind Harvard Square. My nearsighted eyes can't quite read the name. He takes my arm in his arm and escorts me through the door.

Inside I hear the din of Beatles music and a couple dozen male and female voices talking and laughing. The thick wooden door opens and we walk into the suite. A fire crackles in the large fireplace and elegant thick rugs cover the hardwood floors. The ceilings are high, and carved wainscoting reaches up waist high around the elegant room.

Like my Grandmom-Christina's house this suite has that same sense of grandeur and connection with the past, past successes in business enterprises and in life, hard work, intelligent risks and good decisions, that entitle one to well earned comforts and rewards of stability, status and peace of mind that well-earned wealth brings, or at least I hope it was well-earned.

Being shy I find the energetic intensity of all these people overwhelming and I'm glad the lights are low. Branden introduces me around the room to this collection of sophisticated young people destined for success. I shake hands and smile and make polite conversation even though my insides are cringing and I feel more inadequate with each passing moment.

Oh how I wish I were curled up with a good book, Descartes perhaps, at the Willard's. Or sleeping with Moot and the dogs in the woods tonight instead of being here where I feel so entirely awkward and out of place.

"Wine?"

"Oh no thanks," I say and the man looks hurt.

"Well, OK then," I say not wanting to hurt his feelings.

I pretend to take a sip and set it down on a coaster on a mahogany end table near the couch where gorgeous young women are flirting with self assured Harvard men. I suddenly wish I knew how to flirt...

"She loves me... Yeah, yeah, yeah... She gives all her love to me.... and tenderly.... Yeah, yeah, yeah, She loves me," the music croons. Branden swoops me up and we dance around the room, my forgetful feet stepping on his shoes, trying to remember Mr. Curry's high school Dance class.

Other men cut in, though I don't understand why. I am in a disconnected daze.

Finally it gets too much for my overwhelmed senses and I escape to the bathroom, where I pour half my wine down the sink so people won't know that I'm not drinking. I stand looking at my drawn ugly face in the mirror feeling entirely lost and unworthy. What am I, a poor blundering, tongue-tied fool, doing in the midst of all these intelligent successful people? I feel terrible. I don't want to go out into the room. I just want to curl up and disappear.

Bang. Bang. Bang.

Oh darn someone else wants to use the John.

I open the door and smile at the young man who beams at me.

Branden, who has been looking for me, picks up my hand and we start dancing again, this time to "I Want to Hold Your Hand," Branden dances like a crane in flight, his coat flying, his arms outstretched, his long legs tangling and untangling. I smile as I gyrate, not knowing what I'm doing.

Another man cuts in and then another. When Branden finally catches me again for "A Hard Day's Night," he whispers, "Boy you sure are popular."

"Me?" I exclaim incredulously. "You're kidding."

"No," he says, I can barely get to dance with you."

Now I'm totally confused. Branden must be teasing me. I feel completely out of it, ashamed of being so ugly and stupid, in the midst of all these handsome and brilliant people.

Chapter 29: A Hard Day's Night

Aware that the Marathon is only two and a half months away, I'm pushing my training harder. I'm going out every single day, rain, wind, sleet, snow, ice and pushing to my limits. This, and keeping up the work at the Museum School, drawing class, anatomy, design and painting is wearing me out,

After one particularly hard run, I'm in the back hall changing when Ring! Ring! Ring! The phone rings.

I pull a towel around me and dash to pick it up, wildly hoping it might be John.

"Hello?"

"Hey," Branden says, "A bunch of us are going to see, 'A Hard Day's Night,' can you come?"

"Really?.... Sure... I'd like that."

Black and white, the Beetle's film reminds me of the old-time comedies, like Laurel and Hardy, police chases on foot, the mischievous clean old man, Paul McCartney's grandfather, the rollicking good humor, liveliness, energy, and over all, the playfulness of a new generation born out of the calamity of WWII, which, though only twenty years ago, is all but forgotten,

This new generation, my generation, barely remembers D-day, the push of Allied troops towards Germany, the thousands, the millions of deaths, that made our freedom possible, and here we are like new spring grass growing as happily as if nothing had ever happened, healing all the wounds with laughter and song.

A Hard Day's Night, She Loves Me; I love Her... If I give my heart to you... The sliding minor major transitions, the close harmonies, the tight rhythm brings a new twist to the rock scene with the charm of British accents, clear boyish faces, and a beguiling openness that makes me smile inside.

Branden slips his hand over mine.

Girls scream, the Beetles sing: "I give her all my love, that's all I do. If you saw my love, you'd love her too. She gives me everything and tenderly, and I love her; A love like this could never die, I know this love of mine will never die; ...If I give my heart to you, I must be sure from the start that you would love me more than her."

And.... "I should have known better with a girl like you, that I would love everything you do; I'm so happy when you dance with me; She loves me ya ya ya, she loves me...."

I like Branden. He's aloof, an aristocrat, yet amiable and considerate. He loves words and speaks well.

After the film we walk back to his dorm, where we find Stewart, Kirk, Gardner, a couple of other guys and some coeds playing a word game in the living room, with the fire crackling in the fire place. The object of the game is to stump the person next to you on a word. Esoteric words fly through the air. At the end of each round Stewart looks up the word in the unabridged dictionary and gives its meaning derivation and spelling. They are all speaking with various accents, which change, with each new round, German, Cockney, King's English, Spanish, and Chinese.

I like words too. I had forgotten. Playfulness characterizes these people, and I like that. I am delighted to find how playful I am too. I prefer being with the men, laughing, talking, and beginning to flirt. I like learning too. I want to know things. I feel that I have let myself down, that there is a whole different self that I could be... if I let myself. I'm too awkward to relax enough to try an accent, but I smile shyly. Branden likes to do the talking. I feel too self conscious and inadequate to try to do much talking myself.

Later that night Branden drives me home. The snow swirls down hard in white sheets, which shimmer in the headlights. We drive slowly through the deserted, half plowed streets, which are illuminated periodically by glowing, conical pools of streetlamp light. My parents have gone to bed already but they have left the front porch light on for me. Branden opens the car door for me and helps me out of the car. He puts his arm around me as we slip and slide on the icy walk.

At the door we pause as I fumble for the key. The wind is gusting, blowing up under my skirt and I am cold. I feel his arm tugging at me and I turn around. He leans toward me and kisses me long and tenderly on the mouth. I feel my heart contracting and running away and at the same time fluttering and flying up to meet him. I'm still in love with John, and am confused to find myself responding to Branden.

He hugs me warmly and says, "Good night. Thank you."

"Thank you too. It was a lovely evening," I stammer.

He turns and walks away and I open the front door and step inside pausing to turn and watch Branden make his way through the blasting snow, get into the car and start the engine. His windshield wipers start jerkily and he reaches a hand out the door to scrape the snow away. He slams the door again. Just then I hear a rustle in the bushes and turn to look into the dark.

"Probably one of the dogs," I think and open the door a little wider, calling, "Rinty? Briggy?" But no answer. I hear Mooty whining on the back porch and run to see her.

Opening the back porch door, I kneel down and take her head and shoulders into my arms and press my face into her soft fur, "Oh Mooty, Mooty, I miss the old days, when it was just you and me and we were sleeping outside under the stars."

Many years later John tells me what happened that night.

John meanwhile who has been crouched in the front bushes moans to himself and walks away, dejected. He walks aimlessly through the night, not even knowing where he is going. His walk turns to a run and he realizes that he is headed for the Hemlock grove.

Whining wind moans through the trees, bending and swaying the bare branches in a crazy dance. Hard, frozen snow mixed with sleet hits against his parka making nervous ticking sounds and his feet squeak as his boots crunch through the frigid white powder. Icy air cuts against his face. Rain has turned to sleet has turned to snow.

He runs on through the night lost in the mysterious strange otherworldly forest, until he finds the Hemlock grove and enters under its snow-covered branches. He feels the huge, strong wooden trunks around him like pillars in a church. He smells their damp cold bark. Snow sifts delicately down through the needles, and inside the grove he feels its peace.

"I see why Bobby Lou comes here," he thinks to himself remembering how it was to be here together. "Damn, What am I doing? Why don't I do something?"

Anguish rises in his soul.

"Damn!" he shouts... "Damn, damn, damn."

Filled with despair, he has the urgent urge to merge himself with the storm with the cold the wind, to escape the constraints that bind him, to sever the shackles that eat deep into his soul and keep him from ever really embracing life.

"How does she do it? How does she feel so at one with life?" He remembers the first time he saw me swimming across Seaward Cove, lolling on the seaweed, "She's so much a part of everything around her!"

In desperation he rips off his clothes, throws his parka his pants and his underwear into the snow, and, naked in the raging storm, he grabs a hemlock branch and pulls himself up. He feels the sting of snow and the frigid slashing of wind against his naked body.

"At least, at last, I feel... something!"

He climbs higher and higher into the swaying branches, the cold numbing and slowing his muscles.

He climbs up to where the wind howls through the branches and needles make sifting, singing, whining, moaning sounds. He sings with the wind. He sings his agony into the night.

From the deepest core of his being issues a beast-like roar. He feels the power of the sound of himself vibrating within his body. "Roar, Roar, Roar," he repeats each time louder and more primal that the last. He throws his head back and roars again and again into the storm feeling the anguish and despair of not being able to feel, trying to feel the anguish of his despair.

At last frigid with cold, he unlocks his blue fingers from their clutch on the branch and slowly, carefully, barely able to move, he descends barefoot, bare bottomed, bare bodied, from branch to branch until he is at last standing on the snowy ground again. He tips back his head and roars again, but it sounds, he thinks, hollow, fake, unreal, contrived. He pulls on his clothes using the palms of his hands and his teeth and wrists. His fingers no longer move, nor his lips when he tries to speak. He trudges home to his parent's house and falls defeated into bed.

Chapter 30: Trick or Treat

Only one more month to the Marathon!

I have to really concentrate on my training now. I'm running eight miles a day every day into the museum school, and sometimes eight miles back at night. In March it's still cold and snowy, but I run along the edges of the streets and on the sidewalk when and if it is plowed. Snow melts and freezes into slippery ice making running treacherous and difficult. I keep a pair of shoes and dry socks in my locker and run in rubber boots with buckles up the front, over layers of socks. I wear layers of long underwear, which I peel off in the ladies room at school and change into a skirt or pants, depending what classes I have, and a smock.

Diligently I learn anatomy. I learn to draw all the bones and all the muscles, of the human body. I know how they look from every different angle. Our quizzes consist of our having to draw the skeleton from various angles in various poses and then to put the muscles on the bones from memory.

From Biology last year, with Dr. Payne I remember a skeleton in the closet in Barnum Hall, the old stone biology building at Tufts on the hill, where Jumbo, the great stuffed elephant, which is the symbol of Tufts, stands. The massive mastodon was given to the University by Barnum of Barnum and Bailey's Circus. I open the closet and sit for hours sketching the form of the human skeleton.

Isn't it funny that we each have a skeleton inside us and all of our skeletons are so similar to one another. We, our larger Self, knows how to make our skeletons but the smaller self, who we think we are, doesn't even know how it looks and has to learn.

Clams and scallops, lobsters and crabs have their skeletons on the outside and their soft muscles and nerves safe inside. We, on the other hand, have our soft muscles and nerves vulnerably, but flexibly, on the outside.

I'm getting nervous and pushing the training, never missing a day. Yellowish brown sodden grass begins to show in frozen pools of water melting. On the weekends I take long runs in the woods. The paths in the woods are knee deep in mud, which freezes and thaws. The snow turns to rain.

Then, just as March turns to April, the woodland bogs are filled with the primal pulsing songs of frogs. Today I run in the Town Forest and visit my hemlock grove, to luxuriate in its peaceful grandeur and to feel its love, as I delight in every small detail of its being.

On my way back I have to cross the busy Main Street. As I reach the other side with my herd of dogs I realize that Brigadoon is behind us, and has stopped in the middle of the road in front of an on coming car. I run back, grab his ruff and pull him.

In my disoriented rush, I fail to see the curbstone under the slush. I fall into the street, and, still clutching Brigadoon by the scruff of the neck, I roll into the slippery gutter. Moot jumps on top of me, licking my face and trying to protect me from whatever it is. I try to stand up but can't. Shrieking pain lacerates my ankles.

My clothes are soaked through. I crawl on my hands and knees to the sidewalk. What to do? I start crawling on my hands and knees, towards the Willard's. The cold is soaking through my skin to my bones. I can imagine people driving by, and staring at me out of the window of their car, through their bifocals, and thinking that I've gone entirely mad, crawling along on my hands and knees with the dogs. Despite the pain in my ankles, I chuckle to myself that the neighbors will just think its one more eccentric trick of that strange Gibb girl. Now she thinks she really is a dog... or some such thing.

Moot is trying to mother me, licking my face. All the dogs are excited by this new fun game and they wag their tails in delight.

Knock! Knock! Knock! I've crawled up the front stairs onto the porch and reach up to bang on the storm door. The dogs press around me, keeping me warm, their wet fur smelling like old, mouldering cushions that have been left in a flooded basement all winter. The solicitous wet licks from their pink tongues are supposed to heal me.

"Yes?" Gail opens the inner door, pulling it backwards, towards her and looks out the storm door seeing a blank window.

"Trick or treat!" I say from below.

She looks down not knowing whether to laugh...

"What the...?"

"I can't stand up," I explain. "I hurt my ankles."

She opens the door and I crawl in.

"What happened?"

"I was running and didn't see the curb."

She gets me seated in a hard-backed wooden chair. When you slow down you start to freeze up out there. If I had fallen in the woods, in the winter, I would not have made it home before I froze. Funny, I never thought of that.

Moot comes and rests her white head on my lap. I love these times with Moot, like the old days, us running together being at the Willard's together.

"God, I hope my ankles heal in time for the Marathon," I lament.

"The what?" Gail exclaims.

"Oh, darn. I forgot. I wanted to tell you... I've been training to run the Boston Marathon for almost a year now. Please don't tell my parents. If they found out they'd try to stop me. They'd have me locked up for sure."

"Of course I won't tell them if you don't want me to."

Gail looks up at me with a strange pitying, indulgent affectionate look, the look a parent might give to a cute but misguided child.

"I doubt if you'll be running any marathon with these."

My poor ankles have ballooned up, swollen like two ecru and blue gourds... Nature's way of making a cast, of keeping the joint immobile while it brings healing nutrients to the joint.

"I have to run the marathon... I.... I've trained for an entire year.... I can't not run it... don't you see?"

Gail ferrets out a dusty dishpan from under the sink. Knocking a few dead flies out of it, she fills the basin with hot water and shakes in some epsom salts.

"Here, soak your ankles in this," She says spilling water on the floor as she sets down the tub.

Ah, the hot water feels good on my frozen feet.

She takes my ankles and moves them back and forth. "At least you didn't break them... just be happy about that."

She puts on water for tea and we sit sipping tea into the late afternoon as dusk falls outside and rain drums wildly on the window glass, running down in transparent rivulets of tears.

After several hours she gets up and gets a towel. She takes my feet and wipes them careful. She wraps both ankles in some old ace bandages she's scuffled out of a medicine closet somewhere in the upper regions, up the carpeted stairs where I seldom go. In another moment she's found some crutches.

"These are left over from the time Lorrie broke her leg. They're adjustable.... see!" She says pulling the crutches out to full length.

Memories of Nana flood over me bringing me almost to the point of tears, just to feel the kindness of this friend, to not have to be fighting against something all the time, not to have to be protecting myself from assault and criticism, but to be able to relax and to be cared for. I've almost forgotten how.

"Is it too tight?" she asks. A shadow passes over her face.

"It's fine. Thanks," I smile.

"Well, that'll do you for now," She murmurs standing up.

"I wish I didn't have to go home. I wish I could just stay here and be the way we were before," I lament.

"Me too," She says putting her hand comfortingly on my arm.

"Thanks a lot," I say.

"It's OK," She says.

"Well I'm not giving up yet," I say as I hobble down the stairs and stagger off on the borrowed crutches. She watches from the door with a look of affection and something I can't quite place, sadness? Amusement? I wish I knew her thought at that moment.

Chapter 31: Ginn Field

The next day I am up and out, practicing running on crutches. I pick up a cantering sort of gait, swinging on my crutches, up over the hill down to Ginn Field where I run loops on the flat melted area. Around and around and around I canter, swinging the crutches forward, touching my feet lightly to the earth, still aiming to run the Boston Marathon on April 19, 1965. I am unwilling to admit defeat. The dogs nose about in the slushy, gray Aberjona River, which flows along side the playing field.

A moment of calm descends upon me. The moist air is cool on my face. The round silvery disc of the sun cloaked behind bare white clouds looks like the moon. Peepers sing in the marshy places along the banks of the swollen river, silencing each time the dogs approach too closely. Frogs are good watchdogs. They let you know if anything is coming, even at night.

Having nothing to do but to run laps around and around on the only piece of flat semi-cleared ground I can find, I have time to think again—To continue my inquiry into the nature of subjective experience.

As a child I'd wondered, "Do other people see the same thing I do when I see green? How would I ever know?" Freddie, my first love, and I had discussed this at length at age seven or eight.

Does sound and the seeing exist out there in the world just as I see it and hear it? Do we all just tune into it? If so how? Is there some sort of mind out there? How does the tree out there get into my head as a sort of picture of a tree? What really is an idea?

My dad had asked us the riddle about if a tree falls in the woods and there is no one to hear it, is there any sound? I'd puzzled over this at length unable to come up with an answer. "Doesn't it depend on whether sound is in the airwaves or whether sound is in your ear?" I'd asked. I'd begun to think about what really is sound?

I see the muddy yellow brown field and the dogs nosing about the river, but these are images my eye-brain has constructed from its interactions with photons of light bouncing off the surfaces in my environment.

I pick up the thoughts that have been gestating in my mind ever since my run in the February blizzard.

I had realized that, the activities of neurons, or at least some subset of neurons, are not "converted" to subjective experience, but must, themselves, be subjective experience.

I had seen that both what is viewed as subjective experience and what views the subjective experience must be the highly organized processes and activities of the brain and nervous system because that is all there is in the brain… at least all I can detect from the outside.

How can the activities of clusters of neurons that are made of atoms, molecules and electrons actually be subjective experience from the inside?

What is the inside? Is the subjective experience inside the neurons? Or is the subjective experience outside the neurons, but inside the clusters of interacting, synchronized groups of neurons, organized in complex arrays of patterned of activity?

All I can say for certain is that the subjective experience is inside the brain somehow. And I'm not even sure of that. Perhaps there is some sort of global consciousness out there and our brains just tune into it.

What actually experiences the activities of the brain subjectively? How can the processes and activities of the system be experienced by the system whose processes and activities they are? How can the processes and activities of the system both be, and be experienced by, the processes and activities of the system?

What do I mean by inside view?

What is viewing the neuronal activity of the nervous system? If there is no insubstantial other substance inside the brain viewing its activities, no little man watching the TV, I am led to a circularity of neurons viewing other neurons, and nowhere does this explain how to get an inside view of the system.

Suddenly it occurs to me that this is the same sort of paradoxical self-activity that I'd seen in living systems, where what is done is what is doing. In the brain, what is viewed is what is viewing.

This insideness of view is a paradoxical, recursive activity.

It's not as if I am outside the house viewing it and then I go inside the house and view it from the inside. It's more paradoxical and subtle than that. When I'm inside the house physically, I'm still viewing the outside of the inside of the house. I am still something other than the house viewing it. There is still a subject, me, which is different from the object, house. The subject does the viewing of the house, which is the object.

What I'm talking about is a reflexive self-viewing from the inside such that the system is viewing itself. It would be as if the house were capable of viewing itself from the inside, not as something else viewing it from the inside, but as itself self-viewing itself from the inside.

My crutches swing rhythmically, punctuating the half frozen ground and puddles, with their rubber tips. I feel the pressure in my armpits, and forearms as I canter over the rough terrain. Now, like the dogs, I am once again a four-legged creature.

This insideness of view is a paradoxical self-reflexivity where there is no subject-object split. This would be an identity-reflexivity where that which is seen as subjective experience is in fact the subjective experience that it sees. The activity that views the subjective experience is the activity that is the subjective experience. This is as impossible to think as the Divine Self Creating Paradox, in which what is created is that which is creating. How can it act to create itself until it exists? But how can it exist until it creates itself? The Ultimate Paradox.

The subjective experience is that activity, which both is, and is that which views the subjective experience... The subjective experience would be nothing in addition to the activities and processes of the neurons... The subjective experience would be the activities and processes of the interconnected neurons working in synchrony viewed from the inside by the very activities and processes of the neurons that are compiled in the systems, whose activities and processes they are.

This would be the inside of the house viewing itself in contrast to something inside the house viewing the inside of the house.

As soon as there is a subject/object split I have one thing or one activity viewing another thing or another activity and as soon as I have one thing or activity viewing another, that thing or activity must view the outside of the other thing or activity. So to be more rigorous in explaining subjective experience, I am looking for something that truly views itself, not just recoursively, but identically-self-reflexively, where the subject and object are identically that which views and that which is viewed.

This is almost impossible to think.

I am getting dizzy so I reverse direction and canter on my crutches the other way. I run through the line of thought again from a different angle.

For a moment let's consider what happens when I say that there is one part of the brain that can view subjectively and the other parts do not. That one part of the brain, whose activities and processes are subjectively experienced by it, would view the activities and processes of the other parts of the brain objectively. For as soon as it views something other than itself it is looking at the outside of that other thing.

Only when that part of the brain, which is capable of viewing subjectively, is viewing its own activities within itself, is it viewing subjectively and self-reflexively. So the activities and processes of the other parts of the brain would have to act to make some kind of changes in the activities of the part-that-is-viewing-subjectively and it would be those activities, which the part-that-views-subjectively would actually be able to view subjectively.

But how does the system actually act to view its own activities and processes? Those activities and processes must <u>be</u> subjective experience to the system. Those neuronal patterns of activities, in those various subsets of neuronal networks, in that-part-of-the-brain-that-views-subjectively, must actually <u>be</u> the blueness of the sky and the sweetness of sugar to that-part-of the-brain-that-views-subjectively.

So the only reason the system can experience its own processes and activities subjectively is that those processes and activities are, in fact, subjective experience to the processes and activities, which comprise the system that is reflexively self-viewing. That is, the self-activities that self-experience themselves as subjective experience, are in fact what the system is.

At least some of the activities and processes of the system, then, are in fact subjective experience to the system whose activities and processes they are.

This insideness of view, this self-identically, subjective self-viewing is not something anticipated by physics or even biology. It is not consistent with the proposition that these systems are entirely materialistic since matter is defined as what is extended out there in the physical world and this subjective, self-identically self-viewing is not out there in the material physical extended world. And yet, my thesis is consistent with the concept of a paradoxical self-creation, and self-formation, which I have discovered characterizes natural existence.

So what does the existence of paradoxical, self-reflexive, self-identically, subjectively experiencing activities and processes within the nervous system imply about the nature of the so-called physical or material world?

After an hour and a half of cantering circles, I call the dogs, who come joyously bounding, wagging their muddy tails. I pick up a stick and throw it. We play fetch the stick and tug of war and end up in a wet, smelly, muddy heap.

Chapter 32: Marathon '65

The day of the Boston Marathon comes. Gail, the kids and I pile into the station wagon and drive to see the marathon. Moot is with us wagging at everyone. I stand by the side of the road, on crutches, watching, heartsick. My dream of running the Boston Marathon is crushed, after an entire year of training. The very core of my life is being eaten away by losses.

"I can't see..." Lisa whines.

"Com'ere" I say grabbing her and swinging her up onto my shoulders. She squeals and holds onto my head, blocking my eyes with her little fingers.

Gail turns and smiles at me with a look of indulgent affection.

I watch these runners and feel the dignity, the quiet strength, the elegance, the endurance, the integrity it takes to run like this. This digs deep into the human spirit, this primal gait, as ancient as the first steps made by the first humans who walked upright across the African plains, millions of years ago. This upright gait— the rhythm of it, and the balance of it—is uniquely human. I am meant to run this race. I'm meant to be part of this celebration of life, part of this deep reuniting with the soul of our physical bodies that is rooted back in time, even before we had words to convey meaning.

The conviction is even more firmly rooted in my soul, to run, to be part of this race. I don't know why, all I know is that I am supposed to run this, to be part of this. This is my vision of the roots of human existence, born anew here in the modern world. Something fundamental to the human spirit has been all but lost in modern civilization, but, running has brought me back to myself and given me a freedom and autonomy, a strength I never knew I had, and has joined me now with these runners and with all humanity.

"Ok," I say to Gail, "Next year.... for sure."

Gail gives me another of her quizzical, indulgent looks, filled with that deep affection, which I've come to trust. Perhaps she loves my father in me... that eccentric, passionate, creative person he never let himself be. But there is the ethereal otherworldliness of my mother in me too. What a strange combination.

I remember a year ago when Dad and I had watched this race together. I feel a wash of remorse and guilt for crashing his VW camper microbus... my dear sweet dad... my poor lost mom... and my little brother... I miss them more than I'd realized... I miss our old family, the way we used to be... sailing on the East Wind living in our dear little white Cape Cod house in Marblehead. We were so much more innocent and younger then.

......

Suddenly it is hot— seventy degrees. Every seed is bursting, every leaf straining to break out of its confining, shiny brown, encasing bud-coat and to burst into green fragile leaves that unfold like tiny wings and hang like newly washed laundry to dry in the sultry, simmering sun. Bugs hatch and buzz uncomfortably around my neck and face taking small nips, which hurt and itch.

My ankles are healing fast and I am running again in the woods.

Moot and the other dogs look motley, with tuffs of last winter's fur hanging from their sides as they shed. I pull off enough hunks of wool in my fists to knit two or three sweaters. They roll on the ground and rub up against rough branches and wriggle and smile and look up at me lovingly.

With the pack of dogs pressing around me, I make my way over a ledge and down the slippery pine needle-covered bank to my secret stream, which is filled with rushy melted snow, overflowing its banks, gurgling in joyful disarray, bubbling, frothing, leaping, feeling young, vigorous and full of life as it plunges down from ledge to ledge splashing. How I've missed my woodland bowers and thickets.

The dogs lie in the swishing, swirling water. I sit down and hang my feet and ankles into the cool healing waters and watch how the currents of water pile up into sustainable forms, through their interactions with each other and with solid objects. I see this as key in the wonder of self-formation, this dynamic interaction of flow in which the material is constantly changing even while the shape of the heap of water remains, and where interaction defines form.

I lie back and look up into the brilliant blue sky feeling the soft cool earth beneath me. I am returning to myself again. Each tiny flower seems to speak to me again in a language without words. Each seems to be aware of itself in some way, saying with its very being, "I am alive! Here I am! I am reborn, as I had perfect faith, I would be."

The Divine is present in all this so strongly, bursting forth on all sides from behind the veil of my conceptions and perceptions. Just here. I reach out my hand and touch the air. Moot noses my hand. "Yes, you too are the Divine becoming Itself as you," I laugh. "The Divine as Moot nosing about the Divine as hand, waving in the Divine as air, in the Divine as forest, on the Divine as planet, in the Divine as solar system, in the Divine as Universe in the Divine as Cosmos."

The Divine Self-Creator is both what touches and what is touched, what sees and is seen, what thinks and is thought. It's like subjective experience in being characterized by a identity-reflexivity where there is no subject/object split. The Self-Creating Miracle, which is paradoxically creating itself into existence, is both what creates and what is created. The Self-Creator embodies a unity where there is no subject/object split – a paradoxical self-reflexivity that is impossible to think.

In my theory, Divine Self-Creating Existence is continuously creating itself into all that really exists and this precedes and is prior to any mind body split, which split is just a human misconception.

A purely material world does not contemplate inner subjective experience in material objects, and yet my brain is a material object, in that it is made up of atoms and molecules, yet, it thinks.

I'd come to realize that the exact same activities, which from the outside look like patterned blips of electrical energy passing through a highly organized nervous system are, from the inside of the nervous system, subjective experience — the smell of the earth, the sound of the rushing brook, the blueness of the sky, a mathematical equation, the memory of my Nana. It seems impossible, and yet that is exactly what happens. There is nothing inside the system viewing it; it is viewing itself in this strangely recoursive, self-reflexive way where what is viewed is what is viewing.

But how would this explain the actual subjectivity of the experience, the greenness of green, the sweetness of sugar, the saltiness of salt, the sadness of sad. Why would that type of neuronal pattern in that particular area of the brain have that particular type of subjective experience associated with it. Why would I not perceive the sky as tasting like salt and perceive salt to be the color blue?

Clearly it has to do with which area of the brain is stimulated in what way. The sense organs input to specific parts of the brain, which represent that stimulation with that type of subjective experience. What would happen if I rewired the brain so that the olfactory input went to the visual cortex, would I have the subjective experience of red when I smelled a rose?

Probably if this were possible, I would, but that still doesn't explain how, even if patterns of neuronal activity are identically self-experienced in the context of the whole dynamic brain and its functioning, as subjective experience, how the self-experiencing patterns of neuronal activity would be, to themselves, and to the system whose processes and activities they are, the sensations they are, or, indeed, sensations at all.

Why would green be green and not just a pattern of dots on a screen? Or even if perceived as a pattern of dots, why and how does this or any perception arise and exist at all? How about bees who see in the ultraviolet? Bees probably have a type of subjective experience that presents ultraviolet that we humans don't, but still it is a subjective experience. So there are two questions: Why and how are the particular types of subjective experience experienced? And more profoundly: Why and how does the subjectivity of the experience exist at all?

When I think, it's as if I'm in an inner room filled with places to put things. I don't actually see the things I put around this room, somehow I feel them abstractly and I experiment with the relationships among them. I try one configuration then I try another. I experiment with how they might relate. It's like taking pieces of a puzzle and trying them in different places. But the pieces themselves are made of pieces and I can enlarge each piece and look at the pieces that compose it. I can think in words, and in images, but I can also think in relationships.

Even words are abstract. When I say, "The dog jumps over the fence," I know exactly what I mean, I have an image of a dog jumping over a fence but it is an undefined image. If I say, "A black dog jumps over a white picket fence," The abstract image becomes more defined. If I say, "A spotted dog jumps over a rail fence," I have a different yet similar image. So even when I think in words, I'm thinking semi-abstractly, in terms of in relationships.

What is this inner thinking space that I have inside me where I can plan things out, design things, imagine things, create things, and remember things?

I'm not at all subjectively aware that my brain is made up of neurons and astroglia and operates by means of tiny electrical currents and membrane voltage changes. I've learned about the mechanics of my brain from the outside and now I'm struggling to associate that outside materialistic perspective with the inside subjective perspective, all the while knowing that all I'm really doing is making models.

I lie on my side and open and close one eye and then the other watching how the scene jumps back and forth from one perspective to another. When I shut one eye the subjective experience of depth disappears and when I open it the subjective experience of depth reappears. There is an actual feelable sensation of 'depth' associated with having the input of both eyes combined somewhere in the brain.

Even granted that the patterns of neuronal activity are experiencing themselves, and that the same activities, which are viewed, are also viewing, how can the brain come up with this particular way of representing depth to itself as this particular sensation of depth? How can the material processes and activities of the brain actually be subjective experience to the brain whose activities and processes they are? What does this say about the nature of mind? What does this say about the nature of matter?

I roll over onto my back and look up through the spokes of the hemlock trees to the blue sky beyond and realize again how little of this world I really understand.

Chapter 33: Vietnam

"So what's going wrong in Vietnam?" I ask Branden the next time we are together.

"It's about resources," he says. "All wars are about resources and territory; it's a competition. If the Soviets win, they get the territory and the resources and if we win we do. The same with South America or the Mid East, anywhere... China."

"Really? What about democracy? Don't we want to set up democracies where people are free and have good lives. Aren't we trying to free people?"

"Sure, we want to do business with other free nations."

"Well isn't that good?"

"It's better than doing business with corrupt dictatorships as we are in Vietnam and in half the other places we do business," Branden replies.

"Then why do we do business with corrupt dictatorships?"

"Because that's who's in power and that's who'll do business with us... unfortunately our Government, including Kennedy, put Diem in power in South Vietnam, not realizing that he too was corrupt..."

"Well both Kennedy and Diem are dead now, both assassinated... Weird and terrible," I muse.

"Yeah weird," Branden looks distracted for a moment, and then continues, "When the communists take over they confiscate private property and then no one can own any property any more. All property belongs to the government and if that government will no longer do business with us then we are cut off from those resources and we lose the businesses we had there."

"But do U.S. corporations help people or hurt them?"

"Some of each, I suspect," Branden says... "but on the whole, I'd say they help people, giving them jobs, raising the standard of living... bringing in modern medicine. Many of the third world countries that have natural resources, are still living a Paleolithic lifestyle, small subsistence farms, chickens, goats, primitive housing, no plumbing, no electricity. We didn't make them live like this. This is the way they were living when we arrived, caught up in the power struggles of petty chieftains and warlords of the region. This is the way they've been living for thousands of years. We had to do business with whom ever was in power."

Branden is a Catholic and he explains about the Catholic Church, something of which I know little.

"The Vatican is the ninth largest economy in the world and it owns billions of dollars worth of real estate, banks, and industry here and in Europe, South America, Asia—everywhere," he explains. "They are invested in armaments, drugs, manufacturing, mining, chemicals, oil... You name it.

"The Catholic Hierarchy strongly supports the war in Vietnam. Cardinal Spellman is an articulate advocate of that war."

"Why?" I ask.

"Because Vietnam under the French was a Catholic country. Those Vietnamese that fled the communists were Catholic."

"So how did we get involved?" I query.

"Vietnam is a mess," Branden sighs. "After WW II, Ho Chi Minh was the leader of a united Vietnam briefly. He supported the allied forces."

"Then what went wrong?"

"According to the peace accords in 1945, after Germany was defeated, all the colonies that Germany had captured from the French and Belgians, during the war, ended up belonging to the victorious British and Americans. The British and Americans gave the colonies back to whatever European country had owned them before the war. What had been the French Colonies were given back to the French. The Chinese Nationalists, still under Chiang Kai-shek, had to give the Northern part of Indochina back to the French also."

"Maybe that was the mistake, giving the colonies back to France, as colonies, instead of doing what we did in Europe, and helping the countries of South East Asia become independent and democratic nations," I comment.

"Ho Chi Minh wanted a united Vietnam under a democratic constitution patterned on the American Constitution," Branden agreed. "That was what the Atlantic Charter had set out."

"Then why didn't it happen?" I ask.

"The resources of South East Asia were vital to American and British security, oil, tin, rubber."

"Well why couldn't the Vietnamese develop these resources and trade with us?"

"They lacked the capital, the know-how, the technology. It was United States who had developed these technologies and the British and Northern Europeans, including Germany and France and the Netherlands. And in fact it was private research and development and private enterprise, which developed the technologies that make the modern world possible.... Well in all fairness a great deal of it was from U.S. government supported programs and research as well, especially in agriculture, science, medicine and war technology."

"So maybe our corporations could have cooperated with the Vietnamese and brought prosperity and education there, in a way that was fair and not exploitive," I venture — "A Southeast Asian Marshall Plan."

"The problem was that as soon as WWII ended, the powers realigned. The Soviet Union and China, after the communist revolution under Mao Tse, became the new enemy. What was on Eisenhower's mind was now the containment of communism. John Dulles, the Secretary of State, and John's brother, Alan Dulles, the head of the CIA concurred, and, in fact, took the lead in the new cold war against communism."

"Then how did we get involved with Vietnam again?" I query.

"The Vietnamese under Ho Chi Minh refused to submit to being made a colony of France again and fought the French."

"And what happened?"

"In 1954 the French realized that even with the millions of dollars of United States aid which Eisenhower was sending, they couldn't win a war against the Vietnamese and they submitted the conflict resolution to Geneva, where it was agreed that the French would withdrew temporarily to the Southern part of Vietnam and in two years nationwide elections would be held."

"So what went wrong?"

"Those elections were never held."

"Why?"

"Because by then the communists under Mao Tse Tsung had taken over China and the United States feared that the Chinese communists were controlling Ho Chi Minh and North Vietnam and that, were elections held, and were Ho Chi Minh to win, as he most certainly would, that Vietnam and from there all of South East Asia would fall to the communists."

"So we would be cut off from all those resources," I conclude.

"Precisely."

"So, we inherited the mess the French left there and we find ourselves in the midst of a civil war which the North, under Ho Chi Minh, already won once.

"And there is another factor," Branden concludes.

"What?"

"Drugs... A very lucrative drug trade from the region of South East Asia called the Golden Triangle, where opium poppies grow in profusion. Someone wants to control that trade."

"I wish I knew the best way to make a world where people... all people.... are healthy, happy, secure, educated, doing what they love and free.... no one exploited, no one profiting unfairly, everyone able to be and to become the best they can be," I lament.

"Well, it ain't what we're doing in Vietnam," Branden comments ruefully.

"What would happen if we just packed up and went home?"

"A blood bath, a civil war in which the communists would massacre the non-communists and then build a united Vietnam, under Ho Chi Minh if he lives long enough, which if they have their way will be independent. But no doubt neighboring Cambodia and

Laos would join the fray, and the Khmer Rouge extend their bloody grip on South East Asia," Branden states unequivocally.

I'm amazed at this man. His mind is like a steel trap. I wish I could be that sure of things...

Chapter 34: Manhattan Morning

The elm trees along Commonwealth Avenue flower into tiny white blossoms, which ripen into minute green seeds encased in a small membranous flat, oval, winged fruit that fall and blow along sideways, randomly finding crevasses in which to burrow, and, nourished by evening thunderstorms, burst into the roots and shoots of next year's trees.

I finish up my finals at the Museum School. In my anatomy exam we have to draw from memory a skeleton sitting in a chair and then draw the same figure, in perspective, with all the muscles correctly placed.

I'm still running from Winchester to Boston every day. I run along the esplanade, an expanse of green that graces the Charles River as it bends, with Boston on one side and Cambridge on the other. These grassy islands, where ducks gather and people stroll, make a wonderful place to run, though I am the only one running.

Startled people look up as I whisk by at a full gallop, wondering if their eyes are deceiving them, or whether a young woman with long reddish blonde hair and piercing blue eyes, really did just roar by, running like the wind. No one else runs. I wish they did. I wish everyone would find in running the same joy that I do.

One young man, probably a college student, turns, looks after me and yells, "Goddess! Goddess! You are a Goddess!" Perhaps he's been drinking too much.

The frenzy of May's new growth turns into the euphoria of June's ecstatic discovery that it is really true, the long winter is over. The bright, clean green of new leaves, the lacey pink of unfolding blossoms fragrant with sweet promise, the soft winds and warm sun fill the world with hope.

In June, another Harvard class graduates. The dowdy brown, dismal gray and dirty white of rotting snow, which had enshrouded the Quad for months, is gone and in its place springs forth brand new vibrant green fuzz. In succession, the lavender and white crocuses, the brilliant yellow daffodils, the multi colored tulips, the deep purple, heavily fragrant lilacs, the pink azaleas and the magenta rhododendrons dazzle the senses with color. And, under foot, no longer is the slippery ice, granular dirty snow and wet mud of winter, but glorious green grass, mowed to perfect flatness by invisible gardeners. The cut grass fills the air with a sugary scent that reminds me of the horse pastures in the broad rolling hills of Vermont.

Branden has invited me to sit with his family at graduation and then to come to his parents' home in New York City. Our whole gang is here: Kirk, Gardner, Jeff, Stewart, and their families and girl friends.

Mr. Beujoi is a powerfully set man with close-cropped hair, a New York Investment banker, who sits with his willowy, tall, blonde, artistic wife and Branden's dark-haired younger sister, Mia.

We watch the solemn procession, the black robes, the flat, square hats with tassels, and we listen to the sonorous speeches that are filled with visions of a new world, new lives to be led, and new discoveries to be made.

A few days later Stewart and Shirley are married in the Harvard chapel, a colonial brick structure, with white painted wooden trim and Greek style white pillars, set bucolically on the old Harvard campus. Conservative, blond, blue-eyed Stewart, and flamboyant, tempestuous, dark-haired, olive skinned, Shirley, the Italian dancer, are committing themselves to each other for life. How does anyone make that enormous decision?

Stewart's parents look stiff, as if they are perpetually holding their breaths in fear of inhaling some foreign odor or germ. Shirley's fat short smiling parents talk rapidly in Italian to half a dozen cousins. The camp is clearly divided into tall blonds and short dark folk who have little in common except these Romeo and Juliet offspring. The notion that family prejudice is anything to consider and genetic continuity matters is something that clearly and wonderfully escapes my generation.

Branden and I go with our friends to New York for the graduation party. Branden's parents live on the Upper East Side in a palatial suite overlooking Central Park. They don't seem at all to notice that Branden and I occupy the same bedroom. I wonder if this is because they are Catholic, part of the Catholic aristocracy, and are free of the Puritanical constraints, which govern so much of our family's New England and Midwestern heritage.

Branden drives me around Manhattan in his father's Porsche and we are much enamored. We drive out to Oyster Bay on Long Island, to Riddie's parents' estate, for yet another party then back to the city again.

One of Branden's cousins is marrying a Count from Europe. We attend the wedding in Saint Patrick's Cathedral, which reminds me of the redwood grove I'd discovered near Muir beach. It has similar majesty and silent, meditative spaciousness. The rows of burning candles, the serenity, and the music reminds me of somewhere I've known before. Our protestant churches are clean, light airy and empty when unoccupied by the congregation. This church seems like an ancient forest—fertile, like the inside of a womb, warm, dim, carpeted, inhabited.

After the ceremony, we attend the wedding party where Branden introduces me to his grandfather, who had been an ambassador to some South American country. His handshake feels weak, cold and damp, like kleenex, and his painted face looks like a mask to me. Afterwards Branden takes me dining and dancing at the wedding party. I am dazed by the splendor. And yet as I gaze into the drawn puffy faces, witness the artificial smiles, and smell the interior erosion of alcohol, cigarettes and rich food on their breath, I sense that these people are neither happy nor free. Wealth and power have never really interested me. The pursuit of vast sums of money has always seemed so empty, so sad, so misguided, and so tragic to me.

The deep part of me longs to return to the woods and to Moot. I love a simple life, living close to the earth. I love to create and to think. I miss the sound of wind in the trees and the stars that stretch out into infinite space and time. At night after the nightclub party, as Branden opens the door of his father's Porsche, I instinctively look up at the stars as if to get my bearings and to feel connected again to the greater Being, the Divine Self-Creating Miracle, the source of all being.

......

It's early Sunday morning in New York City. I've arisen before the household is stirring. I've pulled on my nurses' shoes, taken the elevator down to ground level, and walked to Central Park. The city gradually wakes up. Yellow cabs race each other along the clean broad straight streets. Traffic lights flash green, yellow and red. I cross the street and enter the park. This park is immense compared to the Boston Common.

A few people are sitting on benches. Others walk dogs on leashes, stopping at trees and trashcans. There are no other runners here. I am the sole runner in Central Park and I feel weird and out of place. People stare at me as if I were some aborigine or a wild animal, or perhaps Lady Godiva, naked on her horse. I long for the safety and privacy of my woodland retreat, and yet find comfort in the luxuriously foliaged, well-watered trees that line the small lake, and canopy the park. In the distance I can hear the city sounds, honking cars, the increasing roar of traffic, a siren wailing, and I can smell the sultry, heavy, toxic exhaust fumes that hang on the warming air.

I feel my body heating up as I begin to push my pace. I'm lulled by the cadence and rhythm of my own breathing in and out, and by the diagonal back and forth of my arms and legs. "In, two three four, out, two three four. In, two three, out, two three," the words drift through my brain in time with my breathing and in time with my stride. I miss the dogs.

I watch the trees revolve by and delight in the dappling morning sun shimmering through the heavy green leaves of summer. I look in admiration at the cement and steel skyscrapers that grow like gigantic rectangular towers in orderly array. Here in the quiet Sunday park I continue the thought that have been turning themselves over in my mind since my run in Ginn Field and my meditations in the woods, in the glen by the babbling brook.

I see that in order to understand subjective experience and how it arises in a material brain I need to understand what is the nature of matter. Since subjective experience can and does arise, the

159

world cannot be as presently conceived, as purely extended matter, made of atoms and molecules that exclusively exist objectively in the outside physical world.

What would the nature of the physical world have to be like in order for subjective experience to be able to arise in the human brain, or for that matter in any nervous system? Was Dr. Payne right that the workings of biological systems can be reduced to physical movements of matter? What about living systems that have nervous systems and are capable of subjective experience? Physical movements of matter cannot explain the existence of subjective experience, at least not as we now understand matter. What is matter?

I remember how much I loved my physics course at Tufts with Professor Tessman. I remember how I'd stewed over the concept of mass and struggled to understand gravity. We had learned Newton's Law of Gravity—that massive bodies attract each other with a force that is directly proportional to the product of the masses of the two bodies and indirectly proportional to the square of the distance between their centers of gravity. For days I had thrown snowballs up into the air and, with childlike delight, watched the perfect parabola of their trajectories unfold. But... something was missing. There was something that bothered me, something I couldn't understand. While the rest of the class forged ahead doing their homework assignments grasping the concepts, I was bogged down in the first and most fundamental chapter, feeling more and more stupid each day. Maybe it was true that girls couldn't understand physics after all...

Finally I knocked on Professor Tessman's office door.

"Come in..." He peered at me over his glasses.

"I don't understand something.." I had begun hesitantly.

He nodded and listened.

"I understand why when you throw a projectile up it gradually looses speed because the gravitational pull of the earth is dampening the force used to propel it."

He nodded.

"But I don't understand why when it gets to the top of its trajectory it doesn't fall straight down very quickly; rather, it gains speed gradually. If gravity were the only force acting on it, it would fall abruptly down. It's acting as if another force is pulling it outward and keeping it from speeding up..."

He looked startled. "Did you figure this out on your own?" he queried.

"What? I can't figure it out. That's the problem." I felt very dumb.

"There is another force. It's called 'inertia.' It acts to keep a massive object from changing velocity. For some reason that no one understands the gravitational mass is always equal to the inertial mass. You're the second student in my entire career who has noticed that. If you were a man, I'd urge you to go into physics."

I hadn't known what to say but it seemed to me that mass wasn't just some property of the object, but rather that it had to do with the interaction of the object with the entire universe. I recalled Foucault's pendulum. It had seemed to me that the entire universe was a huge mass and that each massive object in it contributed to that mass and interacted with the whole of it. Moreover, intuitively, it seemed to me that the small masses of stars would not be enough to keep the whole universe together but that rather the stars must be imbedded in some kind of huge invisible mass. I had thought that this was what mass was— the interaction of the individual massive object with the whole—and so as Professor Tessman spoke, I immediately thought that the inertial mass would be equivalent to the gravitational mass, because it was just a different way of measuring same thing, namely, the interaction of the individual mass with all the masses arrayed around it.

Professor Tessman rummaged in his desk. "Here, take this," he said handing me a small book. I looked down at the title, "Relativity Theory," by Albert Einstein.

That night I had devoured the small book, not understanding much of it. For months, I kept reading it over and over, taking days on just one page. I kept thinking about relativity and matter, time and energy and marveling about what I was learning in that amazing physics class.

What is matter? What is mass? What is energy? Why does light travel at constant speed in vacuo, and why does that speed always appear to be the same to all uniformly moving observers, no matter how fast they are traveling? Nowhere in all this did I see an explanation of subjective experience. And yet to understand how the same terms can be created to describe and to explain both matter and mind, I need to understand what matter is.

Refreshed and restored even by this brief contact with nature, and relaxed by my run, I return and slip into the shower, hoping that no one will notice my strange and eccentric, secret affair with running, unheard of in these days, especially for a woman,… and by herself, too.

Now, Branden and I sprawl comfortably reading the New York Times and yesterday's Barrons. Finance interests me, though I know nothing about it. The economic system is a scary mystery to me. I have no idea how I am going to make a living when I grow up. The idea that I'm supposed to find some man to support me hasn't quite dawned on me, and when it does, it's not something that really appeals to me.

Financial support was not mentioned in Snow White or Cinderella. It was love I was supposed to be finding. I was supposed to be above bodily functions or needs, and certainly I should have no need of something as gross and base as money. Somehow I was supposed to be a goddess on a pedestal, and goddesses just live, they have secret source of all good things and never need money. I am supposed to be like that.

Money was never discussed in our family... except that we had to save money and so the water heater was turned low all the time, meaning all our showers and baths were lukewarm. When I had moved to the Willards' and had hot showers I had thought it the height of extravagance. At Branden's house the showers are steaming hot.

"It's positively Malthusian!" Mr. Beujoi is exclaiming when I sit down at breakfast with the family.

"Malthusian?" Branden replies.

"Listen to this, 'Population has a constant tendency to increase beyond the means of subsistence.' He believed that if wages rise above the level of subsistence that the laboring class will just have more children producing a surplus of unemployed laborers and so if war and disease don't reduce population, starvation will," Mr. Beujoi continues.

"Who is this?" Asks Mrs. Beujoi.

"Thomas Malthus, a British economist who wrote, 'Essay upon the Principle of Population,' in 1798."

"You don't believe that do you?" she asked.

"Dad is saying that it's part of Laissez-faire," Branden replies... and I'm saying that was Adam Smith."

"Adam Smith?"

"The Scottish economist who wrote, 'Inquiry into the Nature and Causes of the Wealth of Nations,' in 1776," Mr. Beujoi replies impatiently...

"The same year as the Revolutionary War," she observes."

"Ludwig van Beethoven was six," Mia, chimes in.

"Thirteen years before the storming of the Bastille," Branden replies, not to be out done by his little sister.

"Seventeen years before the execution of Louis the Sixteenth, Twenty-four years before the rise of Napoleon Bonaparte to power in France and thirty-nine year before his Waterloo," pronouns Mr. Beujoi with an air of amused authority and irony.

"So what's the point?" Branden asks.

"That this war between conservatives and liberals has been going on for centuries," Mrs. Beujoi interjects with a sidelong glance at her husband.

"Napoleon claimed to have been creating peace in Europe," Mr. Beujoi replies. "He saw himself as forging a great empire in which his law, the Napoleonic Code, would bring equity and justice, abolish primogeniture, abolish the Catholic Inquisition in Spain, promote religious tolerance, obliterate borders, end wars, build transcontinental highways, create a common coinage, and forge a peaceful European Empire..."

"Ruled by him...of course."

"Of course... He saw himself as a visionary and a humanitarian, freeing the European populace from the tyranny of their respective monarchies, as the French revolution had freed France of its monarchy."

"Never mind that it plunged the country into bloodshed and chaos," Mrs. Beujoi argues, "and then brought carnage and war, instead of peace, to Europe."

"And then came the Congress of Vienna, which was an assemblage of statesmen and rulers whose individual hegemons had been threatened by Napoleon's war. These were the conservatives... and they banded together to protect their common interest in defeating any attempt of Europeans to create democracies.

"They saw themselves as the saviors of civilization fighting for the right and the good, the bringers of peace and prosperity, annihilating the tyrannical threat of Napoleon and the French Empire. The last thing they wanted was for people to have power. This they could agree on. Democracy was a disaster as you could see from the French Revolution, which had instituted, in the end, not democracy but empire, under a totalitarian dictatorship... And so the Congress, which was made up of the English, Russian, Prussian, and Austrian aristocracy cooperated to fight against their common enemy, the ignorant, violent masses."

"Their common enemy... the proletariat... the liberals, the middle class bourgeoisie, those who wanted to be free, those who wanted some kind of representative government," Branden argues.

"But who instead, brought chaos and disorder and bloodshed," Mr. Beujoi asserts, "through their own ineptitude, squabbling, ambition, and unrealistic idealism, and corruption."

"Metternich," Mrs. Beujoi dredges up the name from her college history class, "was the Austrian who wanted to restore the Hapsburg Empire... and ...Who was it? That peculiar name... yes, Tallyrand, the representative of the restored monarch Louis the Eighteenth of France... represented their respective emperors and kings at the Congress of Vienna, the full circle in just twenty-five years," Mrs. Beujoi observes wryly.

"And all this time great music being written by Mozart from 1756 to 1791, J.C. Bach, J.S. Bach's son, from 1735 to 1782, Haydn from 1732 to 1809 and Beethoven 1770 to 1827," Mia adds. "How did they manage to write such exquisite music through all this chaos and disruption and war?"

"It was strange," Branden comments, "speaking of population. In the seventeen hundreds, European populations increased rapidly. Britain went from six to nine million; France went from nineteen to twenty-six million. And general affluence increased with increased market for goods and services."

"Why?" I asked.

"Why what?"

"Why was the population rising rapidly?"

"Well what's the usual way that populations increase!" Mr. Beujoi laughs.

Mrs. Beujoi giggles... "Early to bed, late to rise..."

"The rising, no pun intended," Branden grins, "middle class of shop keepers and merchants who had become established after the French Revolution were flourishing, and new technologies were coming on line to meet the increasing demand for cotton and linen fabrics—the cotton gin in 1793 invented by Eli Whitney and the improved the mechanical looms developed by Richard Arkwright in Britain, in 1769. In 1807, Robert Fulton's steamboat was built in America. Starting in 1820, railroads were constructed like mad in America and Europe. Strangely, the birth rate declined in France after 1815, after the end of Napoleon."

"Why?" I ask.

"Some say it was because of the end of primogeniture. A father could no longer leave his estate intact to the oldest son."

"Why would that matter?" I wonder.

"The eldest son could continue the family business and support his family. But if the estate had to be divided among all the children, there was no longer enough for everyone. So they solved the problem by having fewer children."

"Some say it was because of Malthus," Branden comments.

"How so?"

"Because the rising middle class saw that the only way they and their children could stay in the middle class and not get pulled down into the impoverished proletariat, was to have fewer children. Thanks to Malthus they saw that it was this habit of having huge numbers of children that they couldn't support, which gave the wealthy class a pool of desperate starving workers to exploit. So they figured if they cut down the numbers of children, the wages would have to go up for the workers who were left." Branden explains.

"Yes, it sounds so good, but how about the workers who *were* exploited? In some places in Britain, Germany, and America... don't forget this was before the civil war and the emancipation proclamation... and child labor, in the northern mills, was as bad as slavery. It was a disgrace..." Mrs. Beujoi interjects again.

"What is happening now is that masses of third world and Mid Eastern populations are beginning to swarm into Europe to take up the menial and low paid jobs that the dwindling numbers of aging Europeans don't want, and these foreign populations are beginning to multiply rapidly, which I predict will become a major problem for Europeans. The same thing happened with the Roman Empire. Slaves and people from the conquered lands swarmed into Rome looking for money, and they simply out bred the Romans and over populated the Roman Empire. And of course the Roman Christian Church proselytized and drew its support from the poor and disenfranchised, encouraged them to breed to the max, and used them to gain power," Branden sighs.

"But," responds Mr. Beujoi, "don't forget Robert Owen and New Lanark."

"What was that?"

"Owen was a factory owner and philanthropist who built an entire industrial community, with nice houses, schools, and restrictions on child labor and limits on the hours workers were forced to work... and he made sure that the workers owned shares in the ownership and shares of the factory and a say in how it was run."

"So why doesn't Grampa do that with his mine workers?" Mia chimes in.

"That's enough, Mia!" Mr. Branden chastises her gruffly. "Any more of that noxious brew you call coffee, Dear?" He holds out his cup as if begging for alms.

Chapter 35: The Ent Forest

This summer I'm taking a summer school course at Tufts in philosophy — Nietzsche, Kierkegaard, Husserl, Heidegger — The Existentialists. I've been missing science and philosophy and math and the challenge of thinking about things. Well I think about things anyway. I'm always thinking about things.... But art is mushier... Well I take that back. It's terribly hard to see what you are looking at. This requires a huge amount of concentration. But it's a different kind of concentration... It's almost like having to be empty, so that no thoughts interfere with what you are seeing. What you are seeing has no words. There is no word for the way the cheek bends into the flare of the nostril or for the space between the edge of the eye the side of the forehead. I can feel myself using a different part of my mind, a part that has no words.

Branden, Kirk, Gardner and Jeff have rented a big old brown house on Delle Ave, in Roxbury, not far from the Harvard Medical School and the Museum of Fine Arts. Riddie, Emily and Ann, who have rented a big gray house on Fort Hill, not far away, have asked if I would like to join them. And, so now I am living on Fort Hill in Roxbury. Yet, I find living in the city away from my forests, confining. Moot, though uncomplaining and cheerful as always, misses our woodland rambles... but at least she can be with me now in my room.

When I ask if they would like me to paint a mural in their stairwell, Kirk, Branden, Gardner and Jeff reply in the affirmative and so begins my mural painting at Delle Ave. Moot accompanies me, following me back and forth as I work. The comfortable, motherly women behind the counter at the donut and coffee shop next door let her come in and sprawl on the cool floor, while I take a break from painting and sit and eat and read some esoteric tome.

I grab the newspaper and read the headlines, "Voting Rights Act Passed!" The National Voting Rights Act of 1965, which outlaws discriminatory voting qualifications that have been used to disenfranchise African American people in the South, had passed the Senate on May 26. Now, on July 9, 1965, the House version has passed!

…...

By mid July Boston is hot and some dozen of us, Stewart, Shirley, Branden, me, Kirk, Gardner, Riddie, Jeff, and several other art and med school cronies take off in a cavalcade of cars laden with backpacks, hiking boots, water jugs and sleeping bags to the White Mountains, for a weekend of hiking. We hike south on the Appalachian Trail over Mounts Madison, Adams and Jefferson.

We are all reading Tolkien's "Lord of the Ring" trilogy, which is now experiencing a renaissance among college kids. Branden has memorized great stretches of it, which he recites to us as we walk through the primeval forests that drip with melting ice from the last ice age. We breathe in the scent of damp mists from the jungle vegetation, which I imagine is left over from the Mesozoic era when huge dinosaurs luxuriated for one hundred and sixty-three million years.

Warming up, I feel restless and soon I'm jumping from boulder to boulder, up and up, running on ahead of the group, way up the mountain, turning around and running back again. I run in laps up to the top, back down again, up to the top again back down again, as they walk sedately up the mountain. My body remembers Nevada and the mountains there. My soul remembers my great discovery, which is mouldering in the closet of respectability and convention. My mind remembers the wildness. I remember camp and my youth, Audrey and the campfires, the comforting munching of horses chewing hay and rain on the barn roof.

We reach our cabin in the late afternoon and set about gathering firewood and making a fire. We have brought steaks and eggs, vegetables, dessert. But before we begin the job of cooking we pause and look out over the valley, which is filling with mist as it cools at the end of a day. Fog lies like a heavy cloud in its valley bed. We each wander off on our own for a while reading, resting, looking at flora.

I find a little spring and sit down. I've been pondering the question, "What is matter?" since my run in Central Park. I pick up my line of thought and continue.

What kind of universe would it have to be in order for systems that have the ability to experience subjectively to arise?

I watch the clear liquid bubble up from some underground source and listen to the tintabulation of its tiny voice as it gurgles forth in shy insistence. It is the transparent messenger from the underworld, a dark cool place where invisible monarchs hold sway over populations of unimaginable creatures.

If there is to be a monistic substance, or single explanation, it will have to explain, in the same terms, both this internal subjectivity of experience, and the external world, which is experienced and modeled by the mind.

Perhaps the problem is in the way mind and matter have been defined. If mind is defined as the some incorporeal, insubstantial, weightless substance, which inheres in the body and is intimately connected with it during life but which has a life of its own that continues after death, as Descartes thought, and if body is defined as the material physical existence characterized by being extended, having mass, location, durability, then the two substances, are mutually exclusive by definition from the outset and so there is little hope of reconciling them.

If there is to be one unitary substance or explanation of existence, then it cannot be either matter or mind, but has to embrace and explain the characteristics of both in some way.

I'd seen that mind, at least human mind, is not a thing, but is an activity. Mind is an activity that has a curious, paradoxical ability to self-view itself. In humans, mind is a combination of activities and processes in the brain as viewed by the brain in that recursive, self-reflexive way. So if

I redefine mind to be the inner subjective experience of my brain's activities, or some subset of my brain's activities, and processes am I closer to an understanding that would embrace both mind and matter?

Clearly other animals have subjective experiences; dogs, cats, horses, fish even insects no doubt have some sort of inner experience. And yet these are living systems, made of matter.

What is matter?

Ever since my high school chemistry class with Miss Travis, I'd marveled at the periodic table of the elements and noticed how the elements themselves had seemed to have evolved, in very hot cores of stars, from the simple and most abundant hydrogen into more the complex elements like oxygen, carbon, iron and sulfur and the even more complex elements like uranium. It was at this time that I first thought that complexification was as fundamental to the universe as entropy. But why and how?

In my college physics book there was a chapter entitled, "The Structure of Matter." Matter was taken to be the atoms and molecules out of which the physical world is made. Atoms and molecules join together in various ways to form the objects we detect out there in the physical world. In my philosophy courses matter is most often thought of as the hard, heavy, solid, locatable, bits of things that are taken to exist out there in the physical external world.

But what is the physical world?

Is it the total cosmos? Is the Cosmos really made of matter as everyone thinks? It seems to be made of atoms and molecules, or whatever out there corresponds to what we detect as atoms and molecules with our measuring devices. But ever since Rutherford's experiments, it has been known that most of the inside of an atom is the space between the nucleus and the electrons and it isn't solid at all. Now with quantum physics, these particles of matter are seen to be not as locatable as previously believed. So what is matter?

Newton had thought that the objects of the physical world were the thoughts in the mind of God. Plato had thought that the Ideal Forms or Ideas exist as templates of material objects in a transcendent realm. Is the Cosmos like a huge vast mind?

If everything is mind, then what are atoms and molecules? Are atoms conscious? Is everything conscious? Is consciousness everywhere, even between, as well as within, objects? Are objects actually thoughts, as the idealists say? What could that possibly mean? What is consciousness? What is matter? How do the two things coexist in the universe? Does consciousness spring into existence anew at high levels of complexity in sensate living creatures or is there some sort of consciousness in everything? Is consciousness a product of highly developed nervous systems? Is nervous system the product of a highly developed consciousness of some sort?

It depends in part on how I define consciousness.

If by consciousness I mean some sort of innerness of experience, some sort of numinous inner subjectivity then the term, 'consciousness', can be quite broad. If I mean by consciousness, human waking awareness, then it is quite specific. Although it still leaves the question of whether the human mind is tuning into some greater Mind or whether the human mind is solely the processes and activities of the human brain experiencing its own activity subjectively... and even if it is, is this the product of some greater Mind?

In order to grapple with this coexistence of mind and matter, I need to explore the question of what is matter?

What is matter? Matter is not generally considered to have any inner subjectivity of experience. Indeed matter is explicitly defined as being extended, being external, not having an inside view, not having an innerness of experience.

Molecules are organizations of atoms. Atoms are organizations of subatomic particles. If matter is defined as what is made of atoms, then matter is not the fundamental substance because atoms are built up from more basic subatomic particles. Are subatomic particles then the fundamental substance? Do subatomic particles have some sort of innerness, or innerness of experience?

In my first year at the Tufts School of Special Studies in 1961 to 1962, I'd read in my physics books about the baffling array of elementary particles that had emerged when physicists bombard atoms and nuclei with high-energy particles. And I'd wondered why there were so many elementary particles. Could these elementary particles really be the fundamental building blocks of matter?

Something about the search for the smallest particle had struck me as strange. Finding the smallest particle would be like finding the smallest brick out of which a house is made by bombarding the house and looking at the rubble. Finding the smallest brick would never explain how the house was organized and built.

What is a particle after all? A particle is thought of as a very small, massive, extended bit of matter, but what it really is is a system of interacting parts. Each part is in turn made of smaller systems of smaller parts. Each of these nested systems is comprised of dynamically interacting parts. So looking for a smallest particle would be like looking for a system with no parts, because if the system were made of parts, then those parts would be yet smaller. But this is a contradiction.

If matter is defined as atoms and molecules then that out of which atoms and molecules are composed is not matter. Why? Because atoms and molecules are not composed of atoms and molecules, they are composed of something smaller. Cleverly, some philosophical materialists had redefined matter as being 'that out of which everything is made.' But this is a tautology since whatever it turns out is the fundamental substance out of which everything is made, these philosophers have already named it 'matter.' I needed to find another word for, and a new understanding of, that out of which everything is made.

What could that be?

It seemed to me that what was happening was that each time physicists bombarded a small entity, the internal system of dynamic interactions of that entity broke apart and reconfigured to include the new energy provided by the bombardment. This resulted in new configurations. Thus, each time physicists interacted with the system, by bombarding it, that interaction changed the net systemic activity so that the system reconfigured. This means that for each type of interaction a different type of dynamic configuration results. The same types of interactions will lead to the same types of dynamic reconfigurations and different types of interactions will lead to different types of dynamic reconfiguration.

I had called these resultant configurations, "interactons", not fundamental 'particles', but 'interactons'. The interactons were not particles in the sense of bricks. They were not material particles. Rather they were dynamic configurations of activity. The interactons I hypothesized were dynamical systems. But were these interactons made of still smaller systems?

When I look at smaller and smaller subatomic systems finally I get to the point where there has to be a smallest system and this means a system not made up of smaller systems. A system not made up of parts.

This system not made up of parts would have to be the smallest system, but what could it be? A system not made of parts is a paradox, since a system is defined as an organized interaction of parts.

It was becoming clear to me that matter defined as atoms and molecules could not possibly be the fundamental substance of existence. Mind, on the other hand was too ambiguous a term to be useful. And the concept "consciousness" was multifaceted, myriad with no clear referent and even more ambiguous that the term 'matter.'

If there is a single explanation for what we now term mind and matter, what could it be? Could my insight of a Divine Self-Creating Existence help?

"So this is where you are?" My thoughts are interrupted by Branden. I smile and my thoughts evaporate like mist. He sits next to me, puts his long arm around me and pulls me close.

"Come on you guys. Let's sing!" Stewart interrupts us.

"OK!" we scramble up eager to play. I love these people and their incessant invention of ever-new ways of having fun.

"What'll we sing?"

"Let's sing the mountains and the clouds! See, you take the top line of mountains; you take the next range of mountains. You take the upper line of trees and Branden takes the lower line of trees!" Stewart exclaims pointing out over the misty valley filled with thick forests trees.

"And I'll take the clouds!" I exclaim.

Stewart moves his arm and hand slowly from left to right along the scene and we stand together, arms locked around each others shoulders, looking out over the folding valleys and graceful ranges of mountains to the west and singing the mountains, trees and clouds making wonderful druid like disharmonies and harmonies in an enchanting song of nature.

Pleased with our work, we set to making supper, opening knapsacks, pulling out plastic containers dripping with melting ice that contain steaks, vegetables, and rustling folding metal pans that clink together with a ringing sound. We all work, spontaneously doing what needs to be done, with no one telling anyone else what to do or how to do it.

We pause now and then to sing a different section of mountains and trees. Branden reads Tolkien to us and it seems the forest Ents are right here around us.

At sunset Branden announces that he is looking for the green flash.

"The what?" Stewart responds.

"The green flash... I saw it in California last year. When the sun sets into the Pacific on a clear night like this one, just at the final moment there is a bright green flash. No one can figure out what it is," Branden explains.

We all line up watching as our meal cooks. The deep orange sun sinks behind the black mountains and no green flash.

After supper we each take a character from Lord of the Rings and read together by the orange, glittering light of our campfire that burns in the soft dark universe, which whispers with its own sleepy thoughts.

It is chilly in the evenings in the late August mountains. Branden has brought his binoculars and we look up into the night sky at my old friends the stars.

"There's the Big Dipper!"

" There's ... Where's Orion?" Stewart exclaims.

"Orion we can no longer see in the evening," I elucidate to Stewart.

"Why?" he asks.

"He is on the other side of the sun from us now," I remember my high school observations. "But in late summer, if you get up very early in morning while it's still dark, you'll see the winter sky, including Orion, coming back into view as we move around the sun, through the universe."

"Olber's paradox is a good riddle, since you like riddles so much," Kirk says to Branden.

"What is it?"

"Do you know how we know that there are not an infinite number of stars in an infinite space?"

I strain to hear the answer.

"If there were an infinite amount of stars in an infinite space the night sky would be completely filled with the light from stars, it would appear as a continuous sheet of light."

Would it? I wonder. I make a note to think about this and to think about the green flash too.

"What's this?" Kirk asks sliding a small book out of my pocket.

I've brought a little blue book, De Toqueville, *Democracy in America,* written in 1832 by a Frenchman visiting this country.

"How was it that in America the Constitutional Congress, despite its ponderous blundering, managed to write and to enact one of the most brilliant evolutions in social and political thought that has ever existed?" I muse.

"Well it is being sorely tested in these times," Gardner quips.

Chapter 36: The Heisenberg Uncertainty Principle

By the time we arrive back to Cambridge I'm thinking about the Heisenburg Uncertainty Principle. Cramped after the long ride, I take a long run with Moot out along the Charles River to clear my head and have time to think. The question "What is matter?" is still rattling around in my head.

It is clear to me that what we take to be matter, that is, extended, massive particles, the atoms and molecules, cannot be the fundamental substance.

Atoms are built up of smaller entities. Indeed the search for the smallest particle goes on.

But the smallest entity cannot be a particle, in my opinion, at least in the sense of an extended bit of something, like a particle of dust or a very minute brick. I wondered if my idea of interactons could provide more insight into the nature of the fundamental entity.

The Uncertainty Principle says that when I try to measure both the position and the velocity or momentum of a small particle, the more accurately I define the position the less I know about the velocity or momentum, and the more accurately I define the velocity or momentum the less I know about the position. I can see that each time I measure the velocity, or the momentum, or the position of a particle I have to interact with it, and that interaction changes the velocity or momentum and position of that which I am measuring, so that when I'm measuring very small quantities, the very act of measuring changes what I'm measuring.

The mechanisms that I devise to measure velocity or momentum are such that the more accurately I can describe the velocity or momentum of a particle, the less I know about its position. Likewise the mechanisms that I devise to measure the position of a particle are such that the more accurately I can describe the position the less I know about its momentum and velocity.

But more than that, in quantum theory, the Heisenburg Uncertainty Principle says that the observer can only know one half of the parameters of that which he or she is measuring. Why could this be? What does this say about what must be the fundamental substance of nature?

Physicists debate about how quantum physics, which treats the natural world as discontinuous quanta, and relativity theory, which treats the natural world as a space-time-gravitational continuum, can be reconciled. Can the idea of "field" help reconcile these two theories? The idea of 'field' is very important in physics. A force field, for example, is the force that a unit test object would experience at each point in space if the unit test object were actually there. The idea of field started out as a shorthand way to account for the forces of interaction among objects, but it acquired a kind of conceptual reality that was solidified by Relativity Theory into a physically extant thing – the space-time field or the Riemann gravitational continuum, which, in the Theory of General Relativity, is what really exists out there in the extended world. So Relativity conceives of a continuous field while quantum dynamics conceives of a matrix of discontinuities, which have both wave-like and particle-

like properties. The concept of field then doesn't seem to resolve the conflict. In no case did this have anything at all to do with subjective experience.

And yet it seems to me that one thing quantum physics and relativity have in common is the centrality of the observer.

In quantum physics the observer can know only one half of the parameters in any given interaction, and in relativity theory, the measurements of distance, duration and even mass and energy depend on the relative states of motion of the observers.

Who or what is this observer?

Can my ideas about interaction help?

When two entities interact they form a dynamic boundary of interaction. Each participant 'experiences' the interaction from its own perspective. Whether this is simply an interaction in the sense of physical action-between or whether this involves some kind of subjective experience of the interaction I'm not sure yet. But thinking in terms of interaction I can suddenly see why only one half of the parameters can be known by the observer.

In an interaction each participant is the observer from its point of view. The whole interaction is comprised of the two halves, each from its own perspective. So that each participant in the interaction is the observer from its point of view and the other is the observed. Thus, each observer can 'know' only one half of the total parameters of the interaction. There is the same sort of reciprocity of observation as I saw in relativity theory.

In relativity theory an observer riding along on a uniformly moving coordinate system looks over at another observer riding along on a different uniformly moving coordinate system and each measures the other's clocks to be running slower and measuring rods to be contracted in the direction of the relative motion. There is no objective way to tell which measuring rods are actually contracting and which clocks are objectively running slower. In fact the rods do not actually contract; they only appear to be contracted and the clocks don't objectively slow down; they only appear to be running slower. So there is no one over-all-observer. In relativity theory each observer is associated with a particular coordinate system and so, in some way, mixed in with the observation.

And here in quantum physics I am seeing the same thing. The observer is mixed in with the observation in this curious way, in which the only way the observer can measure or even detect something is to interact with it either directly or indirectly and that interaction changes both participants.

It had seemed to me, even three years ago when I first started studying physics, that the concept of interaction was fundamental.

What is interaction?

Interaction means action between. Indeed I'd seen that the self-formative power of nature is comprised of exactly this type of interaction of systems of systems of systems each composed of patterns of dynamic interactions. The entire cosmos is a system of interacting parts. Gravitation itself can be seen as an interaction, that is, an action between, in which the velocities of the interacting parts are mutually changed. In this case the interaction is defined by the presence of a gravitational continuum that defines a four dimensional spacetime tensor, which is like a field in that it assumes different values at different points, but whether it has some kind of objective physical reality, as Einstein assumed, depends on how we define external reality.

It strikes me again as I run along the river that whatever I take as my fundamental remains undefined and undefinable within the context of the hypothesis that is presented. This I find extremely frustrating. Force is an undefined quantity in classical physics. When you ask: "What is force?" you have to find other terms in which to explain the given. What is a force? It is a presumed invisible causal agent. All I see and measure is a change of velocity or momentum. To explain this the concept of force was invented. There must be a force, physicists reasoned, to cause the change in velocity. But what the real nature of this invisible force is remains undefinable in the theory.

So now I'm doing the same thing with "interaction." Is not an interaction simply a force? Or vice versa? What is the advantage of calling it an "interaction?" The advantage is that I'm not hypothesizing some metaphysical invisible agent that causes the change in velocity. I'm simply saying that the observed velocities of material bodies change when they interact and that an interaction is just that, an action between, which acts to change each of the participants in the interaction in someway. It is only through interaction that anything can be detected. If I can't interact with it I can't detect it. If it produces no change in anything it is not only invisible, it is undetectable. So does this mean that it is unable to cause or to be caused in terms of physical manifestation? On the surface it appears to be so.

So where does this leave quantum physics, relativity theory and subjective experience?

Newton said that an object remains in a state of uniform motion unless acted on by a force. I could as well say that an object remains in a state of uniform motion unless it participates in a type interaction through which its state of motion is changed. And yet in my view, every part of the cosmos is already in a state of continuous dynamic communion with every other part. I'd seen this in Foucault's pendulum and in my considerations of Gravity.

I'd hypothesized that inertial mass was just this: The continuing interaction of the individual part with the entire cosmos, which is arrayed, from its point of view, around it. And yet a force is something that tends to cause the motion of something to change. How could I reconcile this ongoing communion of each part with the whole of the cosmos in an immediate way with the action of a force?

As I'd gazed up into the night sky all those nights of sleeping outside it had not seemed to me that the universe could be held together by the force of attraction between those tiny specks of stars. It seemed rather to me that the entire universe was all one whole huge vast matrix of something that had incredible massiveness. But what is mass?

Relativity theory says that the mass of a material object is equal to its internal energy, that is, its rest mass, plus its kinetic energy, that is, its energy of motion, all multiplied times the velocity of light squared. This had fallen out of the Lorentz equations, which the great Dutch physicist had *invented to explain how it was that the speed of light is measured to be a constant no matter what the uniform rectangular speed of the observer who measures it.*

At the turn of the century it had been a shock to physicists to learn that there was no ether, no invisible medium that served as a medium in which light could travel; to learn that there was no absolute space and time; and, to learn that the speed of light was measured to be the same no matter what the uniform speed of the observer. The experiments of Michelson and Morley had demonstrated that the velocity of light was not affected either by the supposed motion of the hypothetical ether or by the motion of the earth. No matter how fast one travels towards an oncoming light beam or how fast one travels away from it, the light beam always appears to be approaching at the same speed.

When I first read this in my magical physics book in 1962 I was astounded and I still am amazed at this. What is so special about light? Why is its speed an absolute? What does this say about the nature of the universe?

Lorentz had invented a series of transformation equations to let us transform among uniformly moving coordinate systems that have differing velocities with respect to one another, in such a way that the speed of electromagnetic radiation will always be constant. It had been Einstein, who, with his brilliant first wife, a Serbian, Mileva Maric, had reinterpreted the Lorentz equations based on the work of Mach and Poincare.

Whereas Lorentz had thought that the lengths of objects actually shrank in the direction of motion, and the local time of events, a concept invented by Lorentz, was simply an epiphenomenon, and that somewhere there was an absolute time, the Einsteins had realized that lengths only appear to shorten and local time only appears to expand, and that these appearances have to do with the relative motions of the observers to one another and to the events and objects that are being measured. I continued to wonder if this insight had been Mileva's.

This fascinated me. What kind of universe is this where the lengths of material, extended objects only "appear" to lengthen and shorten and the time between events only "appears" to expand or contract depending on the relative motions of observers? Where does that leave external, extended, material reality? What does this say about matter?

What is matter in this new theoretical context? If I take matter to be that which is built up of atoms, then matter, as I had seen, cannot be fundamental because atoms are built up of even smaller systems. But now I see that when the Lorentz equations are applied both to Newton's laws of interactions of material bodies and to Maxwell's equations that describe the propagation of electromagnetic radiation, one comes up with the famous equation that the energy of a material body is equal to the mass of the body times the velocity of light squared. What could this mean? Does it mean that energy and mass are the same? No. It means that the measure of something called 'energy' is proportional to the measure of something call 'mass' and the proportionality constant is the velocity of light squared.

What is energy? Energy is defined as the capacity of a system to do work. What does that mean? Work is defined as a force applied multiplied by a distance moved. Thus the work of a bulldozer pushing against a solid wall and remaining in place is zero, where as the work of a goat pulling a cart is equal to the force exerted by the goat on the cart times the distance the cart moves. Mass on the other hand is a measure of the ratio of the force applied to a material object divided by the acceleration produced by that force, in Newtonian terms.

Is mass then the same as matter? No. If matter is that which is made out of atoms, then matter has mass, but matter is not its mass. Matter is that which is composed of systems of interacting atoms. Is it fair to say that all matter has mass? Yes, I think it is. Is it then fair to say that that which has mass is matter?

I fall into deep thought. Not everything that has mass may be composed of systems of interacting atoms. Many elementary particles have mass; a traveling beam of light has mass. That is to say that these tiny particles can and do interact with gravitational fields and it takes force to change their velocities.

What if I redefine matter to mean 'that which has mass'? Does this help or does this make things more confusing? What else would I call things that have mass but are not composed of atoms? These are the subatomic particles that I called interactons because I saw that they are not solid bits of things like particles or tiny bricks at all, but they are dynamical configurations of something... Of what? Of energy?

Is energy the fundamental substance? Energy is the capacity to do work. How can that be a fundamental substance? Energy and mass are different measures of the same thing. What? When I say the rest mass of a material object is its internal energy, what do I mean? When I say that the kinetic energy of a moving object adds to its mass, what do I mean? Especially since, whether, and how fast, something is moving depends on from what coordinate system I measure its velocity.

I pause for a moment to notice the quiet flow of the river and to remember how my father had taken me kayaking as a small child in our bright yellow canvas kayak, when we lived in Watertown. I resume my thoughts as my feet find their way over the dirt path that follows along on the grassy bank of the river.

The internal energy of a material object is a measure of all the energies of interaction among its internal parts. In a chemical reaction, when the atoms of molecules dissociate from one another, the chemical energy or bonding energy, is released. This happens when paper burns.

The nucleus of an atom is held together by tremendous forces of interaction. When the nucleus of an atom is broken apart, the internal energy that was locked in the interactions inside that nucleus is released as kinetic energy. The rest mass of the object is the sum total of the energy of all the internal interactions that are going on inside that object. The total energy of the system is the rest mass plus the kinetic mass or energy that the system has because of its motion relative to its surroundings.

When a material object is moving very fast relative to the observer who is measuring its mass, the mass of that object appears to increase. But, I muse, since no object can travel faster than the speed of light, there is an upper bound on how fast and object can travel and hence on how massive the object can get, that is, on how heavy it can appear to get.

Can mass be the fundamental substance? No. Mass is the measure of a property of a system of interacting parts. Can energy be the fundamental substance? No. Energy is a measure of a property of a system of interacting parts. If there were no systems of interacting parts there could be neither energy nor mass. Matter is comprised of systems of interacting parts. A material body is simply a system of interacting parts.

And when I look for the smallest part what do I find? In order to be the smallest part, it must be a part made up of no smaller parts. The smallest part must be a system composed of no parts, which is a contradiction, because a system is defined as an organized interactions of parts.

Max Planck, the great German scientist discovered that light is emitted in very small discrete bits, called photons. Could this be the smallest particle? The photon has no rest mass, and hence no internal mass or energy. What does this mean?

Suddenly I look up startled to see the white shingled Cambridge Boat Club building and docks. I follow the path around it, past a red boat barn and through a dank tunnel, which is a pedestrian underpass under a highway. I follow a dirt path along the bank of the Charles River next to a marshy area where cattails grow. I bet Native Americans used this same path hundreds of years ago.

What is a photon of electromagnetic radiation?

I have been enthralled with light ever since I first learned about what it is. It is a very strange thing. No material object can travel faster than light. Light, the electromagnetic entity, travels at a constant speed in vacuo, and that speed appears to be always the same and always constant, to any uniformly moving observer who measures it. Moreover, a moving beam of light interacts with gravitational as well as magnetic and electrical fields. Astoundingly, when a photon is released it is born already traveling at the speed of light, that is, it takes no time to go from zero to the fastest speed possible. All this is taken for granted in modern physics, but to me it is a miraculous paradox of immense proportions.

Somehow light must be absolutely fundamental to the universe. But how?

How does all this long review of my fundamental physic course bring me any closer to understanding how subjective experience and human consciousness can arise?

I finish my run and meet Branden for a quick supper at Pasims, a basement coffeehouse that opened a few years ago, on the little alleyway near the Harvard Coop. I change in the ladies room. Branden doesn't participate in my life the way John had. He is busy with Medical School and work, but its fun to meet him like this. Tonight live guitar music accompanies our dinner.

Chapter 37: Woodstock Vermont Hundred Mile

It is August 1965. Our cities are scenes of major social unrest as African American communities erupt in violence. In Watts, Los Angeles, on August 11th, the arrest of an African American for driving under the influence, by a white patrolman escalates into a five-day rampage in which thirty-four people die, over a thousand people are injured and three thousand, nine-hundred and fifty-two people are arrested. The rioters set fires, break into stores, and generally create havoc. Thirteen-thousand-nine-hundred National Guardsmen have been called in to help the police and fire fighters already on the scene. I watch the tragedy unfold on TV.

As August draws to an end, I decide to go up to Woodstock Vermont and run all or part of the Woodstock Hundred Mile equestrian event. For years I've been thinking of running the event on foot... ever since camp, ever since I'd run along with Jan and her horse, Nikki, as they trained.

Yes, I will do it! It will be a good test to see if I'm ready to run Boston. At least I'll try to run twenty-six miles of it and see how I do.

After a summer of hiking with Branden, Gardner and Kirk in the White Mountains, and after long runs in the Fells, which seems now so confining after last summer's endless prairies and mountain ranges, running Woodstock will be just the thing. If I can run Woodstock, at least twenty-six miles of it, then I will know I am ready for Boston.... and it's beautiful in Vermont this time of year, early fall, with it heavy thick green leaves and splashes of yellow foliage.

My parents are away cruising in their rented yawl with the Kriebles and I'm living in the house alone, sleeping out in the back yard again, with Moot. Being out under the stars is restoring my soul and reconnecting me with the earth I love. I feel a sense of peace that has escaped me—a simplicity and rightness that is me. Moot will stay with Gail and the kids for the weekend. Both she and I are at the Willard's most of the time anyway.

In early September, the day before the Woodstock equestrian event, I board a bus in Boston and five hours later step off into the charming bucolic splendor of downtown Woodstock, Vermont. The Inn is too expensive and so I wander down toward South Woodstock on foot looking for a place to camp out, perhaps a little patch of woods.

Feeling conspicuous with my pack and sleeping bag, although hikers are a common sight, I look uneasily for some place to camp, which is not someone's backyard or someone's pasture. I find an old mill along side a small river and enter into the shop, which now inhabits the building. I like the feel of this spacious, brown-boarded place and the friendliness of the people.

The young woman behind the counter smiles and asks if she can help.

"I'm looking for a place to camp," I explain. "I've come up to see the Hundred Mile and...."

She smiles again and I feel compelled to tell her the truth.... "Well, actually, I'm going to try to run it."

"Run the hundred mile? On foot?"

I nod.

She looks at me blankly, her face registering astonishment.

I smile and shift uneasily.

"Well I don't have any place to camp... but I have a loft you can stay in if you like cats," she smiles.

"Cats? I love cats," I say, thinking of Molly and how Nana used to let her sleep on my bed when I was little.

"There's a mother cat and kittens who will probably sleep with you," she says leading me up a set of wooden stairs.

"Oh how cute!" I gush when I see the mother pick up her head and turn her ears towards our noisy clumping sounds, as the tiny kittens nurse along her belly.

After a quick supper at the local café, I spread out in a confused array of puffs, quilts and blankets on a huge feather bed. The cat purrs rhythmically beside me, the heavy autumn leaves softly rustle in the afternoon breeze and the stream, which runs right along the foundation of the building, gurgles, tinkles, babbles and splashes.

When I awake it is absolutely dark and silent except for the sound of the brook. I've never heard a silence so deep and heavy and dark as this one. The utter blackness makes me feel helplessly pinned to the bed. I cannot see even to find my pack and my flashlight. The thick, dark silence is not empty but is filled with something. Whether that something is a nocturnal predator or scurrying mice and rats I do not have time to access before the heavy veils of sleep engulf me again and I sink into peaceful oblivion convinced that whatever fills the silent darkness is benevolent.

Next I know, sparrows are twittering and rays of welcome sunlight are streaming through a high window into the dusty loft. I wake up refreshed, hungry and eager to be on my way to the start of the race.

The air is cold on my skin and my breath condenses in clouds of vapor as I pull on my bathing suit, my bermuda shorts, shirt and nurses' shoes.

"Brrrrrr!" I say to the cats. "You're lucky you have fur coats."

Not wanting to load my stomach down with a lot of food, I nibble on an apple and jog along the road towards the start of the race. The horses and riders have been up since before dawn and the judges are already assembling.

As the first horse goes out, I head off down the road looking for the trail markers — red, white and blue, one color for each of the three days.

Today, Friday, I am running forty miles, tomorrow, Saturday, forty miles and on Sunday twenty miles.... or whatever part of it I can... Warming up, I jog slowly down the edge of the road looking at the quaint houses and the huge lumbering trees.

Before long, the horses start to pass me, trotting energetically along, clip clop clip clop, their strong legs beating out a syncopated rhythm on the tarred road. The riders post crisply up and down, up and down. How I remember those years of riding instruction in the hot dusty ring with Audrey yelling, "Up down up down, keep those knees in. Watch where you're going. Keep to the rail," And then the years after that when I yelled the same thing to my students in the same hot dusty ring.

The sound of horses' feet on pavement has excited me since I can remember, since I first started to ride, as a four year old; since the days when as eight year olds Carol and I would run from my grandmother's porch to the edge of the road to watch Smitty's horses go by, listening to that same ancient beat, clip clop clip clop, and how each precious Saturday I would ride a horse for one hour, from Smitty's old barn out along the road to the old riding ring across from Lane's Farm...clip clop clip clop.

How I love these mythic animals, the graceful curve of their smooth bellies, the broad haunches, the long, swishing filaments of tail, the mane and forelock, the strong arching crest of the neck that rises and falls with each powerful stride, the sturdy square legs, the strong bunches of muscle between the forelegs, the big rounded barrel rib cage, the hind legs put on backwards with the knees facing to the rear, not knees but really the heel of an elongated foot, the curve of the rump, the delicate fetlocks and tiny U-shaped feet.

What power these animals have and yet such gentleness... the long face, the velvety soft nose, the blunt flat teeth, the adorable fuzzy ears that twitch in all directions following you as you currycomb and brush their big warm bodies, the gentle bulging brown eyes, which can see forward down and back, and the long curved eyelashes. Now to be running with horses, feeling that same energy that courses through these huge ancient beasts coursing through me, feeling my body strong, my legs firm, keeping my own rhythm, a softer lighter version of clip clop clip clop. I feel that same old excitement rising within me.

The markers lead us abruptly to the right from the paved road onto a dirt road that winds up a steep hill. After a time, the markers lead us off the dirt road, up an even steeper slope, across a field and onto an old muddy logging road. I'm climbing slowly, steadily, keeping my pace, lifting my knees to clear the mud and negotiate the hill. Covered with mud to my shins, I pause for a moment to glance out over the morning valley, which steams with rising mist. The triumphant sun rises steadily, banishing darkness, warming the chilled earth and reviving me.

A magnificent, dark-green, lush forest encloses us, punctuated by swaths of fields, vibrant green with the recent rain and new growth of grass just before winter. Here, on the top of the hill, frost has touched the tallest trees and turned their crests to golden yellow. Spaciousness, the feeling of flying, the sense of the height of the hill that we are climbing and the openness of the valley below fill me with a kind of airy intoxication.

Five miles. Only thirty-five more to go. We are descending now, which takes less energy but which is much harder on the leg muscles. I dash from side to side as if skiing to ease the strain, skipping the way Gardner and I did, fast down the mountainsides. Without a pack I can go so much faster. Here nestled on the mountainside is a cozy white farmhouse surrounded by a white fence. I wonder who lives here. I wonder what it would be like to live here. What would you do? Who would you talk with? I can't imaging being away from a university where I can go listen to lectures and take classes, or an art school where I can learn how to be an artist... and yet someday it would be neat to live on a farm and have animals and children and a family of my own.... It's something I've always wanted.

At ten miles I'm surprised to see a cluster of horses standing, riders dismounting and an assembly of cars bringing food. It looks like some kind of brunch. I recognize many of the riders who had posted past me so fast without a word this morning. Now they are stopped and I am passing them doggedly, the tortoise.

"Hey... Still running?" one of them calls out.

I smile and wave. The others look up and watch me go by.

After a while the horses and riders pass me again, horses snorting, riders chattering away to each other.

"Are you running the race on foot?" one of them asks.

"Yes," I smile. "As much of it as I can."

Word travels fast, and as the day progresses, more and more riders call out to me as they pass by asking me how I'm doing. I smile and laugh and say, "Fine... Slow but sure... What a beautiful horse...."

I wonder how far I will be able to run.

......

At lunchtime the horses and riders stop again and again I run by, and this time people wave and smile, and I wave and smile back. "How's it going?" They ask.

"Great!" I say or "So far so good."

"Are you going the whole way?"

"I hope so." And, I trot by.

I'm grateful for the watering troughs along the way where water gushes freely from springs. I stop and scoop the precious fluid into my mouth and let it dribble down my throat. The day is turning hot.

I glory in the scenic beauty of the place— stone walls made of glacial rocks laboriously pulled from the fields by ancestors who farmed the unyielding ground, pastured herds of cows grazing, red barns and metal silos and well-kept farm houses. The open sky arches over all in a great blue dome filled with gently blowing air. I marvel at the immense, wooden trees silently growing here in the moist deciduous forests, the gray-barked oaks, the soft-bodied red pines, the smooth sinews of the sweet maples, with their familiar hand-shaped flat green leaves, and the birches, which slash the green foliage with streaks of white and stunning black stripes, their fine ragged, heart-shaped leaves already turning light yellow.

I draw in a deep breath and smell the moist wetness of woods, the fungi growing under damp logs, the sweet greenness of growing grass, the pungent scent of cows, the cinnamon spice scent of fallen leaves, the sneezy scent of late ragweed and goldenrod, and the far scent of the air that encircles the earth, bringing with it the smells of far away places, the cold glacial fields to the north, the hot prairies to the west, the luxurious, vegetal swamps to the south and the tang of salt oceans to the east.

I think of the earth, how it must look from space, how the colors change in succession, moving down from the north. Here is the advancing edge of yellow and red. Further to the north, the already leafless trees stand knee deep in their own crumbled brown foliage and further north still, the white snow blows in arctic blizzards across the barren tundra as the procession of seasons moves southward.

Already great numbers of geese are gathering and winging south in long quivering v-shapes, honking through the night and day, muscles warm under feathers, delicate bits of life, newly hatched goslings already grown and flying with the flock, their first migration south. They follow the ancient sky-paths of their ancestors, paths these birds were flying for eighty million years before the first primate stood up on the plains of central Africa.

We, who think we own things and have dominion, better look again. Nature never lies. Nature is absolutely and totally honest. Nature takes everything into account, nothing is ever lost.... or gained, but something else is gained or lost. Infinitely providing, infinitely creating, infinitely patient, infinitely loving, Nature goes on giving and giving and giving, giving us air to breath, giving us the sun for warmth, giving us the earth to till, giving us food to eat, trees for lumber, ore from mines, giving us the atoms and molecules of our existence, giving us ourselves, our brains, our ability to invent, our ability to love and to procreate.

All this is given and we are absolutely dependent on this pouring forth of being, despite all our posturing and egotism, we are dust, holy dust and to holy dust we return.... all of us, but what is that holy dust? It is the divine Herself, giving Herself to us as every form we are

183

and every form we will be. In the end we are Her becoming Herself as us, as anything she pleases, we are Her and She is us because She is all that exists and each form She takes is a dance in time, a laugh on the breeze, a playful sporting of Her infinite creating mind. Being becomes Itself over and over again in so many infinitely evolving forms, each one sacred, each one divine, each one Her holy Oneness, each one Her creativity at play.

I think again of the insight that had come to me on the mountain in Nevada. It seems so long ago, as if I'm losing something.

The miracle of this Divine Self creativity fills me again with that same honey golden peace and love. I see that everything is gloriously beautiful, filled with a celestial beauty and perfection that can only come from a love beyond our comprehension.

The sound of horses' hooves beating up the trail behind me stirs me from my reverie. Lunch is over and the food-carrying cars have loaded up the trash and have headed back to Woodstock. I feel the earth pass under the noon meridian into the afternoon. The tenor of the light changes, the sounds of birds change, even the leaves on the trees feel it, drooping into an afternoon nap. The rising hot air currents of the morning cease, the wind shifts direction and the day begins to ebb.

After six hours of steady running my legs and arms are feeling tight. I need food. My head swims and my stomach contracts. Woodstock is ahead of us, nestled like a tiny toy village down in the valley, a quiet valley, which lies open like a tide pool in the noonday sun. Eons ago, the earth heaved up the flat sea floor into ripples of rounded rising ridges, mounting up into the sky and eroding again. Then millions of years of rain and snow took it, particle by particle, down the rushing slopes into rivers to the sea again, where, even now, layers of sediments are building up on the sea floor, which in millions of years, after these hills are worn away, will be pushed up into a new sky, by the old earth to form the mountains of tomorrow.

Will there still be humans millions of years from now? Modern humans first appeared one hundred thousand years ago, a tiny millisecond compared with the age of the earth, four billion years, and the age of the universe. Will humans evolve? They will have to evolve. Perhaps we are already evolving, because if we do not, we will blow ourselves out of existence with our fancy war technologies. We will either evolve into a more loving peaceful species or we will destroy ourselves. I take a deep breath and begin the descent into Woodstock.

Seven and a half hours, forty miles. Let's see how many miles per hour is that? Hm you take forty and divide it by seven and a half... and um... I can't think too well.. Well let's see, eight into forty... four times eight is thirty-two and forty minus thirty-two... I feel as if I am in third grade again learning long division... or was it fourth grade ... I can't even remember it seems so long ago...so many lives ago.... and yet it seems like only a few days ago... time is funny that way. What is time anyway? It's not time... it's memory that is time. Suddenly the present moment overwhelms me with its reality.

Oh dear, my legs are hurting as I run down this long hill and now there is hard pavement. I hate running on pavement... it hurts my feet and legs. I love the feel of dirt; of real earth beneath my feet.... this pavement is jamming my legs. I hear the rise and fall of cheers and clapping up ahead, as each horse passes by a small informal throng of spectators.

"Did you run the whole way?" one man calls out.

"Yes!" I yell back. There is a round of applause.

"How do you feel?" a lady yells.

"Hungry," I yell back.

Her companion hands me a carrot.

"Thanks!" I shout, taking the proffered root and nibbling on it as I finish the race. At the finish line, the judges scribble on their note pads noting the gait and condition of each horse. The timer presses the timing clock. I cross the finish line to one side so as not to disturb the horses, noting that no judges pay the slightest attention to my gait or my condition, in fact they do not seem to even see me, probably thinking I am just some spectator hurrying to meet a friend, with no idea that I have just run forty miles.

……

The next day I arise before dawn and set out again, following the dots on trees trotting along with the horses. I feel stiff. I hope I warm up a bit. As the day progresses my knees begin to ache. I run up and down hills and my knees hurt. It's not a sharp pain; it's just uncomfortable, should I push on?

I run on for about twenty-five miles wondering whether I should stop or not.

What if I injure myself, hurt my knees, and I'm not able to run the Boston Marathon? What's the point of doing that? The whole reason I came to Woodstock was to train for Boston, to see if I can run twenty-six miles and I've already run forty miles yesterday... and now today I've run another twenty-five miles...

I better not take a risk on an injury.... I better stop now. O.K. I'll run until the next main road.

Ah... I hear traffic on a road up ahead.

I walk along the side of the road heading back to South Woodstock with my thumb out. A trucker stops and picks me up.

"Thanks," I smile as I open the heavy door and climb up and into the cab.

"Where ya headed?" He asks.

"Back to South Woodstock, the barns..." I reply.

"Oh, are you riding in the hundred mile?" he asks turning to look at me.

"No, not riding... I'm running the Woodstock Hundred Mile, on foot."

185

"On foot?... Is that possible?"

"Sure... but I decided to stop because my knees hurt."

"Too, bad," he commiserates... "Better luck next year."

He lets me off by the barns in South Woodstock. These barns remind me of the imaginary barns Jeanie and I designed when we played Arabian Horse Ranch in Marblehead when I was seven. The barns are long western style double-sided wooden sheds with roomy box stalls and large protective roofs extending out over the walkways, which are held up by natural wood posts.

"Thanks," I call out to the trucker, waving as he drives away.

"Well... that's that," I'm glad to be back. I ran sixty-five miles of the Woodstock Hundred Mile... I guess I'm ready to run Boston!

Relieved of the burden of having to run, I hike into downtown Woodstock and wander around town hungrily searching for a restaurant. Always a sucker for white linen tablecloths, I end up at the lovely Woodstock Inn. I order a huge lunch and as I eat I take out my notebook and write, continuing to explore the question that I have been pursuing for months, and years: What is matter and how is it related with our ability to perceive, conceive and think subjectively?

I look at the bowl of sugar on the table and marvel at how much of what we take as the extended world out there is a product of our own nervous system. When I try to describe the physical properties of sugar objectively I find myself listing such items as: white, sweet, crystalline substance that dissolves in warm water and melts at a certain temperature. It is made up of sucrose molecules, which are in turn made up of rings of carbon atoms with hydrogen atoms attached. Each carbon atom has a molecular weight of 12.011 grams per mole and is made up of a nucleus comprised of six protons and six neutrons, surrounded by six electrons, the whole taking on a tetrahedral shape. Each hydrogen atom is comprised of one proton surrounded by one electron. Sugar is taken as being extended, out there in the world, as we perceive and conceive it to be. It is taken to be a material object, having weight and location out there in the extended world independent of us.

And yet just to describe it as being sweet is to confer onto it a property of my own sensate awareness. My subjective experience of its interaction with my taste receptors is a sensation of sweetness. So I say that the sugar is sweet, but is it? Not really. The sugar molecule triggers the stimulation of certain taste receptors that relay electrical impulses to my brain, which experiences sweetness. That sweetness is in the interaction between that molecule and me. I am describing how that interaction is perceived by my brain, not how that molecule is in and of itself... and, I'd seen that this is all I can know... my own perceptions and conceptions of my interactions with whatever is out there. I had concluded that I can never know directly what is out there.

Does this mean that I should stop making models of reality? Of course not. My ability to function in the world, my ability to navigate in that world, to manipulate the world, to create, to invent technologies, and indeed, to maintain my own existence is dependent on my ability to model the world. The better are my models the more successful I am and the more I can create. And yet this new model of a physics that includes an observer as part of every observation intrigues me. I see in this concept of the participatory observer a possible way of reconciling quantum physics with relativity theory.

I sit eating for hours, scribbling diagrams on scraps of paper and rereading Einstein's little book on relativity. I keep an eye out to make sure other people aren't waiting to use the table. I leave a huge tip to make up for my long stay. And take the bus back to Boston.

Chapter 38: The Mothers

I watch the muddy river, the full, deep-green trees and the white-trimmed, brick Harvard dorms flip by. Branden has to make a quick stop at Lamont Library to pick up a book. We pile out of the car, three men and me. We walk up the stairs and into the library. The attendant at the front desk reaches out to me and says, "Sorry, You're not allowed in the library."

I look around to see if they are talking to me. "Me?"

"No women allowed in the library!" the attendant repeats. The other people at the desk look up.

"Me? Not allowed in a *library* because I'm a woman? .... Not allowed in a library because I'm a *woman*?"

Suddenly, some blinding curtain of outrage lowers over me. The same outrage I used to feel at my mother when she did something degrading or unfair. A deep visceral red scream of anger rises up within me. It's the kind of outrage that every woman, every oppressed person feels, and instead of stifling it the way I'm supposed to, the way good girls are supposed to, the way women have done for generations of repressed anger, I let it come out in all its terror and glory.

I stand in the library and scream. At first there are no words only a scream. I scream at the top of my lungs, from the depths of my being. My soul screams a scream of outrage. The human soul hates injustice and unfairness, wherever, however, whenever it occurs.

Branden, Gardner and Stewart turn and look at me stunned. I scream and scream and scream again and finally the words come. "This is an outrage! I'm not allowed in the library because I'm a woman. Women are not allowed in the library! This is insane. This is an outrage! What do you think a woman is going to do in your precious library... read? Maybe think? Maybe.... contribute something to society, perhaps.... learn something? Discover something? It all a lie! It's all a huge lie! Damn it!"

The half remembered history of half the human race pours over me and I feel the bone-crushing weight of all the stupidity, violence, neglect, unfairness, persecution, torture, deprivation, oppression, envy, and sadism of that insidious disease: misogyny. When will it stop? For centuries women were not allowed to learn to read or to write. Even now women are not allowed into Harvard or MIT or Yale or Princeton. Women are not considered to have minds. I have a mind and I am outraged. I am furious at this humiliation and injustice, this deprivation, this binding of my mind and soul.

I am not allowed to have a mind and here it is again. "If you were a man I'd suggest you go into physics," Dr. Tessman had said. If I were a man I could go to medical school or law school or graduate school. My mind is as good as any man's mind. Don't you see we are losing half our talent and intelligence as a society? I feel trapped. I feel the trap closing in again. If you are a woman there is no place to go.

I scream again and turn and run out the door. I run and run and run. All the anger of the centuries burns within me. I run to the River and follow its moist grassy banks upstream. On and on I run steaming, boiling with outrage. I run past the Harvard Boat Club, for men only, and on out along Soldiers Field Road. A men's only racing shell is following along beside me, like a Viking Ship, the oarsmen bending and straining rhythmically to the coxswain's beat. The ancient ship races on like a Roman or Greek warship. I am angry. I will run this damn warship to the ground. I increase my speed. I run faster and faster, I am keeping pace with it. I am out running it. It falls behind me and I am free.

On and on I run, following the Charles River in its winding course out through Watertown. Finally late in the afternoon I turn and run back to Cambridge. My friends are gone.

Maybe my parents are right. Maybe I am crazy. All these tumultuous emotions. What would Dr. Southgate think of my screaming in the absolute quiet of the inner sanctum of the all male Harvard Library?

Wearily I head home to Winchester and to my parents. Suddenly I see what the repressed rage in my mother is…. It is this… and what I hate is that instead of helping me get free, she incessantly tries to make me bend to this outrage, to accept the injustice, to smile a brave, bitter smile the way she does and to feel my life being taken away from me. I'm supposed to be a good sport about it to pretend that somehow it doesn't matter or that what I get in return makes up for my loss of freedom and for my inability to ever become who I am. As if the safety and routine feeding of a zoo animal, a lioness, or a she-bear, can ever make up for her loss of freedom even with all the dangers and challenges that freedom entails.

My mind is grinding this over and over as I watch my mother's once beautiful body bending over the sink scrubbing tonight's pans with the strange flickering, grimacing smile tensing her face. I feel a wave of compassion for her, but I dare not show it, for fear that she will see it as a weakness in my armor to be used and exploited somehow to my detriment and her advantage. God this is frustrating! And so unnecessary! Arrrrrrrgggggghhhhh! There has to be away to make this right…. to change this!

The insidious thing is it's not only outside; it is inside. It's in me. It's in everyone, put there somehow in a way that is so insidious we can't even see it… this hideous degradation … this … desecration.

I'm forgetting my trip west last summer. I'm feeling shallow, off balance, even as my parents are pleased with my acculturation progress, I feel myself slipping dangerously close to the vacuous emptiness, the sense that women have that they don't really exist.

The way women are forced to live, or force themselves to live, makes them feel that they don't really exist. Their vitality is being robbed, their life force dribbled way in a round of meaningless repetitive tasks. Somehow getting married is still the ticket to a woman's survival and social status, in which she gives up her autonomy, her own life, her own mind, sacrificed for what? And yet living alone, childless is an equally un-alluring and arid prospect. Can't there be something else? An equal partnership in which both men and women fulfill their potentials as complete human beings?

Branden is looking for a wife who will keep the house raise the kids and fulfill the social role. He doesn't want to marry a woman who is also a doctor, because then who would keep the house who would raise the kids, important, but non-paying, non-status jobs? I can have social status, a good income, children, and dabble in art, like his mother, not a bad life.... living as an adjunct to an important man. There is a beguiling security to it a sense of being useful, without the challenge of freedom, without the work of finding my own life. I would have the comfort of fitting into a ready-made life, a life that is known and approved of, a way of avoiding the terror of the unknown, but I would know inside that I am haunted, crushed, by the insidious deadness in not finding my own life, my own unique path, in not using my own God given gifts.

Why does it seem so oppressive to me, like such a cop out? It would certainly be easier than the life I've chosen. The difference between being a prize cow, fed, cared for, safe, pampered, and a wild deer, shot at, eking out a living in frozen tundra, prey to the hazards of life in the wild and yet invigorated by the contest with hardship and danger.

Like my Viking forbearers who thrived taunting the wild North Atlantic, there is a wildness in me that has not been bred out, a soul that thrills to the earth in all her seasons, to its aliveness, to knowing this wildness of nature, untamed in all her intricate, holy, wild beauty.

The one unmoving fulcrum in all this mess remains my running, my training, my goal of running Boston, my dream of being part of that celebration of life, part of my vision of what it means to be human... to be free... to be who I am meant to be.

......

A few days later I'm sitting at the kitchen table of the Delle Ave house, still fuming. Branden enters with three large volumes and thumps them down on the table.

"Here, read these," he proclaims.

I look at the title, "The Mothers" by Robert Briffault and look at Branden blankly, wondering if this is some push to hint that perhaps I should become a mother.

"It will change your entire understanding of history," he says. "There was a time when women were the great leaders of magnificent cultures, mathematicians, inventors, astronomers, architects, religious leader, and the Great Mother was the Creator and Sustainer of the Universe."

"Thanks," I smile looking up into Branden's eager brown eyes, noting the tousled brown curls that tumble onto his forehead.

"You're welcome," he says with a puff. "That ought to keep you out of trouble for a little while."

Eagerly I pick up Volume one and open it. "The Mothers by Robert Briffault, New York, The MacMillan Company 1927."

Outside rain splatters down flatly on the large dark-green maple leaves and drips onto the soft ground below. The delicate fringed blue blossoms of the wild asters that have rooted in the dead leaf mulch, in the cracks and crevasses of the backyard patio, droop and nod, while water gurgles in gutters and splashes onto cement below. I put Mozart's Mass in C Minor on the record player. Moot curls up by my feet under the table.

These late summer, overcast days are great for holing up with a good book. In amazement, I read through the chapter titles: 'In the Beginning Was the Word,' 'Traditional Heredity,' 'The Evolution of Motherhood,' 'The Origin of Love.'... I flip through chapters with beguiling titles like: 'Women as hunters and fishers, Women as warriors, Manufacture of pottery carried out exclusively by women, Women as the builders of primitive homes, Medicine and surgery women as the chief medical practitioners in primitive communities, Primitive trade, Primitive industry, leatherwork, embroidery, weaving and basketry.'

Then onto Marriage... 'group marriage, sexual communism, polyandry'.... so much for higamous hogamous... 'Promiscuity and Individual Marriage. Individual marriage regarded as an economic institution and not originally associated with claims to exclusive sexual possession... freedom as regards sexual relations unrestricted before marriage in most uncultured societies, Polygamy.

'Tabu, The Totem, The Priestess, The Moon, ...The Resurrection and The Life... The Moon God, Primitive Cosmic Religions...The Cosmic Religion of Ancient Egypt... The Magical Origin of Queens, The Great Mothers, The Mother Goddess, The Divine Mother and The Divine Son in Greek Religion, The Mother and Child, The Virgin Mother, Holy Matrimony, Modesty, Purity, Romance, The Christianization of Pagan literature, The Mothers.'

It is a little scary and weird but suddenly a window onto the past and into the human psyche is flung open before me. A whole new concept of women and the importance of women in the invention of culture... agriculture, astronomy, medicine, religion, trade, commerce, written language, weaving, architecture, politics and leadership as well as reproduction… presents itself to me.

I page on through the volumes. " The yam-digging stick is among the Australian aborigines as inseparable and personal a part of the woman as weapons are appurtenances of the man." The invention of agriculture is ascribed to women. Fertility was the province of women both her own and that of the earth. "Fire is everywhere accounted sacred."

Not only were the primitive cultures bound up with the power of women but for tens of thousands of years, throughout the history of the world's greatest civilizations in India, China, Babylonia, Egypt, Asia Minor, Crete, Greece and Rome, the female Goddess, the Queen of Heaven, the Divine Creatrix of heaven and earth, the inventor and bringer of civilization was female.

I am surprised to read that the moon was thought to function as the real husband of all women, and the source of all fertility, and was hence masculine, where as the sun was thought to be his wife. The moon however had a mother, the Mother of God. Often in myth this Mother of God is also the mother of the human race and of the ancestors of the tribe. The Mother Goddess is also the mother of animals and food. The Earth Mother or Great Goddess is the bringer of new life, children, bountiful harvests, but she also controls death.

Women possess the magic that causes seeds to grow. The plant comes out of the earth's womb as the child comes out of the mother's womb.

These connections of divine, human and earth were not confined to primitive tribes but permeated the consciousness and beliefs of the great civilizations where the great Mother, Queen of the Universe was worshipped for millennia.

I read on an on in this strange text of gods and goddesses, myths, religions sometimes weird and bloody, sometimes exalted and numinous, life and death, birth and procreation, sex, war, and behind it all the continuous need to procreate, to bear and to raise children, to eat the food produced from the earth and this tended to by women and the Great Goddess, the Mother of heaven and earth.

As human populations grew, another class of gods evolved who were political gods representing various cities or states especially throughout the Mid-East, "A cosmic god representing a universal force of nature stands in the same relation to all countries and to all men; a nationalistic and local god cannot assume cosmic functions without weakening his nationalism and patriotism," Briffault writes. And, this cosmic god was female.

Numerous variations and permutation on the identities and functions and gender of gods and goddesses evolved, the father god could appear as the son god or the mother or sister or daughter god all being identical.

But the concept of the Great Mother Goddess emerged as monotheistic, not only in primitive cultures but in the most advanced civilizations of Mesopotamia, with its capital at

192

the ancient city of Ur, and then in Babylonia. The Great Goddess, Ishtar, also known as Nana, Innini, was the one supreme and universal God.

Nana? Suddenly I understand who my Nana is in mythic terms. She is the Creatrix of all things and governess of the universe, the mother of men and the mother of the gods. She is said to have made men out of clay and is called the Potter. She presides over childbirth, she is huntress, goddess of battles, and legislator... the Queen of Heaven, the moon cow, just as the moon-god was the moon bull.

This is amazing... Here is a prayer to her written, how many thousand years ago? Five or six or more ... carved in ancient cuneiform script on sacred tablets and recited in temples in the most advanced civilization:

"I beseech thee, Lady of ladies, Goddess of goddesses, Ishtar, Queen of all cities, leader of all men.

Thou art the light of the world, thou art the light of heaven, mighty daughter of Sinn. (The ancient moon god)

Thou leadest the hosts in battle and ordainest the combat;

Thou givest forth all commands and deckest thyself with the crown of kings.

Supreme is thy might, O Lady, exalted art thou above all gods.

Thou renderest judgment and thy decision is righteous;

Unto thee are subject the laws of the earth and the laws of heaven, the laws of the temple and of the shrine, and the laws of the private apartment and of the secret chamber.

Where is the place where thy name is not, and where is the spot where thy commandments are not known?

At thy name the earth and the heavens shake, and the gods they tremble; the spirits of heaven tremble at thy name and the men hold it in awe.

Thou art great, thou art exalted; all the men of Sumer, and all creatures, and all mankind glorify thy name.

With righteousness dost thou judge the deeds of men, even thou;

Thou lookest upon the oppressed and to the down-trodden thou bringest justice every day.

How long, Queen of Heaven and of Earth, how long,

How long, Shepherdess of pale-faced men, wilt thou tarry?

How long, O Queen whose feet are not weary and whose knees make haste?

How long, Lady of Hosts, Lady of battles?

Glorious one whom all the spirits of heaven fear, who subduest all angry gods; mighty above all rulers, who holds the reins of kings.

Opener of the womb of all women, great is thy light.

Shining light of heaven, light of the world, enlightener of all the places where men dwell, who gatherest together the hosts of the nations.

Goddess of men, Divinity of women, thy counsel passeth understanding.

Where thou glancest the dead come to life, and the sick rise and walk; and the mind that is diseased is healed when it looks upon thy face.

How long, O Lady, shall mine enemy triumph over me?

Command, and at thy command the angry god will turn back.

Ishtar is great! Ishtar is Queen! My Lady is exalted, My Lady is There none like unto her."

(Reference L. W. King, 'The Seven Tablets of Creation, R. W. Rogers, "Cuneiform parallels to the Old Testament," F. Delitzsch, "Babel und Bibel.")

"This is amazing!" I call out to Branden.

No response. I arise, followed by Moot, and rummage in the refrigerator hungry for lunch.

Sitting down with a sandwich and a glass of milk, I resume my reading.

In Arabia the Great Mother was the triune or Triple Goddess, Three in One. Throughout the Mid-East, Her consort Tames, known as Adonis to the Greeks, was her son/ lover/ spouse. His name, Tames or Dumas or Dame means 'true son.' His yearly death and resurrection corresponded to the harvest and regrowing of the Earth Mother Goddess. Women assisted in his rebirth with basin vases containing representative seedlings. This dying and resurrection of the divine son traced back at least four thousand years BC.

This is amazing!

The Sumerians had a very advanced culture even five to six thousand years B.C. and the Divine Son of the Divine Mother was associated with the waters of the rivers and of the rains and oceans. This belief appeared in India, Egypt and among the North American Indians. He was also known as the Healer and the Savior or Shepard and may have been originally a moon-god who dies and was resurrected each month.

This ancient Divine Son of the Divine Mother Goddess was also known as the anointed one, translated in Hebrew as the Messiah and in Greek as the Christ.

The myths we inherited from the Hebrews really came from the Babylonian captivity where the Hebrews had been immersed in the Great Mother. After they had taken her myths, powers and rituals, they renamed her: "The Whore of Babylon."

One of the lamentations sung by these ancient Mesopotamian worshipers of the Queen of Heaven was the song of sorrow of the mother for her dead son.

"For him who has been taken away there is wailing,
Ah me, my child has been taken away,
My Damu that has been taken away,
My Christ that has been taken away,
From the sacred cedar where the Mother bore him.
The wailing is for the plants, they grow not;
For the houses and for the flockes; they produce not;
For the perishing wedded couples, for perishing children, the people of Sumer, they
reproduce not.
The wailing is for the great river, it brings the flood no more.
The wailing is for the fish-ponds; the fish spawn not.
The wailing is for the forests; the tamarisks grow not.
The wailing is for the store-house; the honey and wine are not produced.
The wailing is for the palace; life unto old age is not."

And another Sumerian psalm from about five thousand years before Christ,

"Why have they slain him, him of the plains?
The Shepherd, the Man of Wisdom,
The Man of Sorrow why have they slain?
The Lady of the Vine languishes,
The lambs and the calves languish.
The Lord, The Shepherd of the folds lives no more,
The spouse of the Queen of Heaven lives no more,
The lord of the cattle stalls lives no more.
When he slumbers, the sheep and the lambs slumber also."

The Sumerian culture was no primitive tribal religion, but a highly developed
sophisticated theology, science and religion, which lasted for thousands of years. It spawned
and was the foundation of Western civilization.

The Great Mother was worshipped in the most advanced cultures of Egypt, Persia,
Crete, Greece and Rome. It appeared in the literature of Homer and later in the Hellenistic
times, The Great Mother was worshipped throughout the Roman Empire, for centuries, to
500 AD when it was suppressed by the Christian Church, which continued the suppression
began by the Hebrew priests of Jerusalem, through the Dark Ages. But the Great Mother
continues in the form of the Virgin Mary and her Divine Son even to this day.

The Queen of Heaven was worshipped by the advanced agricultural societies. Herding people looked with contempt and some jealousy on agricultural people who greatly outnumbered them and who enjoyed a far superior degree of cultural development. When these herding people conquered or were conquered by an agricultural region they took over the Great Mother religion often changing it to make their tribal deities take on the characteristics of the Goddess.

In Greece, men were excluded from the temple, which represented the birth-chamber of Dionysos at Thebes. Men were excluded from the thesmophoria or seed sowing festival. The women visited the shrine of Eleusis in Attica and brought back lalathos or sacred kernos large mouth earthen pots, inside which compartments called kotyloi contained seeds and seedling of rye, barley peas, lentils, and other grains and vegetables.

When men attended similar rituals they wore women's robes and clothes.

Dionysos, a male moon/planting god and also the god of the grapevine, was able to turn water into wine. And here is another aspect of religion coming in. Soma or Homa was an Aryan god of the ivy vine, which was fermented into an intoxicating drink. According to myth, Ahura Mazda, the god of good, as opposed to Ahramin, the god of evil in the later Persian religion, first planted this ivy vine in the fountains of life and it was thought that whoever drinks of its juice never dies.

In the Old Testament we have the Garden of Eden, the tree of knowledge and the tree of eternal life, which are, but restatements of these earlier myths.

Dionysos was the moon god similar to Osiris, Tammuz, Mithra, and Yahweh, who was once the consort of the Great Goddess until Hebrew priests fashioned him in a new image. His rites and mysteries were attended by the drinking of fermented fruit, grain juices and some say hallucinogenic fungi. Clearly in many places, in both the New and Old World, religious rites came to be associated with induced states of mental and emotional hallucinations brought about by the eating or drinking of certain fungi and plant juices often fermented.

The three-fold Mother Goddess was ubiquitous in Greek, Semitic, Teutonic, Celtic religions. Ishtar the Great Mother Goddess is called the Virgin, the Holy Virgin, the Virgin Mother meaning unwed. She is also the virgin prostitute, the Sacred Prostitute and the sacred prostitutes in her temple were called holy virgins. A virgin was an unwed woman and children born to virgins were called virgin-born. In many cultures women who had given birth to children before marriage were more desirable because they were proven fertile and desired of other men.

The Great Goddess of Chams had ninety-seven lovers and no husband. A virgin woman is unmarried and free. In Egypt Isis, the Great Goddess was married, but she was married to her brother and conceived of him after his death and was at the same time his mother.

The Son God, the Divine Son of the Great Mother is identified with the fruit of the Divine Mother, the bread is his body as it is her body, the juice of the grape his blood as it is her blood. The Divine Son of the Great Mother is born and dies each year and descends to the underworld and is resurrected. He is persecuted, and killed by his enemies, lamented, rites held, leading to his resurrection. This cycle includes and predates the agricultural cycles, in the moon cycles, which represent life and death and rebirth of all creatures.

Initiation into the mysteries of Dionysos was thought to bring eternal life. It is the Great Mother alone who possesses the secret of eternal life and she gives her son to the world so that men may be saved and live. The death of the moon like the death of a scapegoat is thought to absolve evil.

"The Great Mother differed fundamentally from the tribal deities, the political gods and the triumphant Sun-gods. She was not tribal, not national, not the jealous deity of a chosen people. She was the Mother of all, without respect of persons; and the brotherhood of her children was not tribal brotherhood, but the brotherhood of all men."

"'I am Nature, the mother of all things,' Apuleius made her say, 'the ruler of the elements, the original principle of the ages, the supreme divinity, the queen of souls, the first in heaven, the one presentment of all gods and of all goddesses. The luminous spheres of heaven, and the health-giving breath of the sea, and the dark silence of Hades obey my laws. There is no other power but I; I am worshipped under as many aspects, under as many forms, with as many rites as there are people on the earth...'"

In some parts of the world women still make little sweet cakes for the Divine Queen of Heaven, the Mother Goddess and offer them at a sacred place.........

I can't put this book down. I read on and on into the night, fighting sleep, my eyes blurry. This book fills some huge gap, some terrible rift in my soul, some horrible empty loneliness that has come to haunt our materialistic culture. I find here strangely, in the Divine Mother, the same present power and love I find running in the woods and fields, where I feel the sun dapple down through the pine boughs in some secret corner of the forests, where a stream pools, and furry dogs pressed around me.... this primal, glorious sense of life itself, despite all the superstitions and perversions, distortions and erasures which have obliterated it for centuries.

If I can only free this cosmic sense of life from all the human perversions, superstitions, bizarre rituals, mind altering substance abuse and false beliefs that have plagued it, and reunite life with its fundamental truth... the primal paradoxical, Divine Self-Creating Miracle... face to face...brimming with love... as I did on the mountain... to feel its reality and presence all the time everywhere, I could heal the world. This is what I want more than anything to know this divine wonder, to feel it... every moment of every day.

What am I to do with my experience of the Divine Self-Creator, the paradoxical Divine Self-Creating Miracle, DiMa?

I keep my secret to myself.

Chapter 39: My Twenty-Third Birthday

Today is November 2, 1965, my twenty-third birthday. The Vietnam War is raging. Norman Morris, a thirty-two year old pacifist, a father of three children, stands below War Secretary McNamara's Pentagon office, douses himself with kerosene, sets himself on fire, and burns himself to death in protest of the Vietnamese war.

The ghastly horror of this human torch, the agony of this man's last minutes, the charred stiff remains of his inert body hangs over our nation, over both the Hawks and the Doves. The insanity of killing, of war, of murder, like MacBeth's knife dangles in front of us, like all the lifeless carcasses, millions lost to the sickness of war, which like a plague sweeps across a land where human life no longer has value and where oligarchic greed masquerades as National Pride. Where the lie grows larger with each breath and Bob Dylan belts out, "A Hard Rain's Gonna Fall," and Joan Baez sings "We Shall Overcome Someday." And Peter Paul and Mary croon, "Where have all the young men gone? Gone to soldiers every one. Gone to soldiers every one. And where have all the soldier gone? Gone to flowers everyone..."

"The illusion that America is altruistically fighting for freedom and democracy against an oppressive dictatorship is becoming harder and harder to maintain. And gradually before our unwilling eyes a different reality asserts itself, as hideous and disillusioning as the sewer of corruption, which was revealed to us the day Kennedy was murdered," Kirk is spouting. "Most of us Americans are good people who want to help others and to build, and to make the world a better happier healthier place for everyone, and now we are angry that we have been lied to and deceived, and involved in something that is not as it was represented to be."

Gardner agrees, "We have been lied to by a small group of people who remain hidden from view, with purposes of their own, a small group of people who are co-opting our government, of the people, for the people, and by the people, and turning it into a means for themselves to acquire power and wealth at the expense of the rest of us."

My dad still insists that we are defending the Vietnamese from the Chinese communists... "Containing Communism," he says... the old Dulles/Eisenhower policy.

"Wars," Branden asserts, "are not a matter of ideology but of economics."

I sit in a daze unable to sort it all out but feeling sad inside.

My birthday comes and goes unnoticed except by my mother who makes me her special birthday layer cake with sugar butter and cream frosting. I lick the frosting out of the bowl and off the beater, just as my brother and I did as children. Suddenly I am filled with nostalgia for our family, I want to go on like this forever with all of us together, with Mother making cakes and Paul and I licking the frosting. Paul, my little baby brother, is now a full-grown man in the Coast Guard.

"Fascism could never raise its ugly head in America," Branden proclaims.

"Why not?" Kirk queries. "People under stress, people in fear will do crazy things."

"But we're not in fear or want here..." Gardner chimes in.

"But we are under stress and there are irrational elements.... especially in the various religious sects, where the fires of intolerance and fear are being fanned by those who hold out the hope of earthly power, their own, in particular, and eternal salvation," Kirk replies.

"It happened in Germany and in Italy," Gardner concedes....

"Why did it happen?" I ask.

But my question goes unnoticed.

......

"You miss her too, don't you," my mother says to Moot, as she shyly places a bowl of fresh water on the porch floor. I've been staying at my parents' house again, so Mooty and I can run in the woods.

I am at the Museum School all day long. I leave early in the morning and run the eight miles to Boston. I arrive back home late after taking buses and trolleys and subways for hours through rush hour traffic. November rains beat down. Cars honk, traffic piles up. People are brusque and angry on the streets. Subways are crowded with frowning, unhappy people.

I arrive home in Winchester and as always call, "Moot! Mooty?"

No answer.

She always waits for me on the back porch. And greets me with her wolf talk, which is a long soliloquy wooo wooooooo woooooo woooo with intonations, a low howl and whine, telling me about her day. I hug her and we sit together and maybe go for a run or play in the yard with a stick. Often the other dogs are around too. Where is everyone? I think to myself with a sudden sinking sensation of dread in my gut.

"Mom! Mom! Have you seen Moot anywhere?"

"She was here this morning."

"She's not here now."

"Maybe she's at the Willard's."

"Is Moot here?" I poke my head in the Willard's front door. Cold rain is falling.

"She was here this morning," Gail shouts.

"I can't find her," I shout back, and then shut the door and began to run through the neighborhood calling loudly. Maybe she went into someone's house, out of the rain.

I run for several hours through the neighborhood, up into the woods, calling frantically, my heart sinking with each moment that passes.

I call the police. I call Angel Memorial Hospital to see if any injured dogs have been brought it.

That night, after setting out food for her, I lie, heart sick and worried, with my head on the window sill looking out at the bare maple tree, listening to the rain beat down hard, filling up the water table before the winter's freeze. All is not well with my life. Something is going wrong. Mooty is gone.

What am I doing? What am I going to do? I'm running out of time and money and I feel trapped and confused. I feel like a cornered animal. Perhaps this is at the basis of my troubles with my mother, this deep fear of never being who I am, of never getting to find out who I am or what I can do, of living the empty life set out for me, the life she is forced to live, the life she is trying to force me to live, the non-life of women in this culture, the sense that I don't exist. And, this is a primal fear of death, that down feeling, colder and colder as you move away from your divine path and away from your sense of the presence of the divine.

The next day, unable to sleep, I rise early and search through the woods. My brain spins around and around as I run. The joy has gone out of the world, the forests that delighted me, the streams and swamps into which Moot would nose, the paths we followed together all seem empty now. I run on looking blindly for her, my friend. I run until darkness falls and I can run and shout no more. I run up and down the streets through the entire neighborhood, looking for her, asking for her.

Brigadoon is missing too, the Atkinson's tell me.

The next day, I call the police again. It seems a number of dogs are missing. It could be an interstate gang, they say.

"What do they do with the dogs?" I ask.

"They take them across state lines and sell them through pet stores or disreputable kennels."

I think of medical school experiments. Do they sell them to medical schools? I call Harvard medical school.

I sit in the living room feeling dead.

"I'll be back in an hour or so," I call, "I'm going to look for Moot."

In the weeks that follow I call every veterinary, every animal shelter, every police department, the pounds, animal rescue leagues, I run miles and miles, further and further, calling and searching as winter closes in. I put pathetic ads in the paper. One time in Boston I see a gang of boys surrounding a light tan furred dog. My heart leaps up. "Mooty?" I run towards her and see that the gangs of boys, teenage boys, are throwing rocks at the hurt, frightened animal.

"Stop that!" I order. They look as though they will throw rocks at me too.

"It's a dangerous dog!" they shout.

"Nonsense!" I exclaim. "She's just frightened."

I walk towards her and scoop her up in my arms. She bites my arm and then looks ashamed of herself. I carry her to my mother's gray Chevy, which I've borrowed, and gently put her in the back seat. The gang of boys looks at me in awe and disbelief, my wild reddish hair flowing, my arm bleeding, my pale blue eyes glistening, like some Viking warrior of old.

I drive her home and we keep her on the porch. I put an ad in the paper. After a few weeks a woman comes and takes her away.

Still no Moot. My heart is broken. My life is out of balance. It's not me anymore. It's not my life. It's something that someone else wants, not me. Moot is the wild part of me and it is getting lost. I'm feeling dead in a way I never felt dead before, like an automaton, going through the motions, doing what I'm supposed to do; but I am not there.

Everyone is so pleased with my progress, but I am no longer here, not the unique me that I really am. Not the me that rejoices in the full extent of the universe at night and the wonder of angular momentum, the me that is enthralled with Foucault's pendulum, the me that loves to paint murals of the woods, to roll with John and the dogs and the kids in front of the fire at the Willard's, the me that wants to know things, to think about what life is and what the soul is, to write, to read Aristotle, Thoreau and John Muir, to camp on mountain tops and run across continents.

This is not the life my soul wants. But there's a huge economic system out there, an inhuman thing, that I don't understand, which wants me to serve it, not my own soul. Like my parents and Dr. Southgate and society, the economy is not interested in whether I find my own authentic life and create what I am meant to create, at all. Having a soul, following one's soul's path is a luxury that most people cannot afford, or so they think. But if one gives up one's soul's path, what is left? I feel scared and lost. I want to go home but I don't know where home is anymore.

I miss my Nana. I miss John. I miss the Willard's. I miss Moot. I miss myself.

"Oh Mooty, my sweet dog, where are you?"

My mind is in turmoil. I am overcome with grief. My Mooty is gone.

It's been a year since John left and now Mooty's gone too. What is happening to my life?

I need to get back to something solid, something basic. I'm losing track of who I am. A dammed up sorrow wells up inside me and fills my head with prickly sawdust. Lenny is dead. John is gone. Moot is gone. Branden, I think doesn't love me, doesn't even know me. Will has gone.

I need to get back to the woods.

......

The November woods are silent and still. Bare trees stand forlornly, mauve, purple, brown and black. Gone are the shimmering green groves of summer with their rustling leaves and singing birds. The world seems now like an empty closet.

The air is heavy and cold. It feels like snow.

Vapor lifts from the dark liquid surface of the pond, which looks slick and slippery like mercury. Brown, broken stalks of last summer grass, now dead, stand shoulder deep in swamp muck. Two or three dark ducks float near the shore, heads tucked under wings, except for one who watches. Stiff twigs stand stark and still silhouetted darkly against the milk white sky, a sky that has descended to the earth today.

I walk slowly to my hemlock grove. Here I stand leaning against the largest trunk, looking up through its spokes of reddish branches feeling the quiet strength and power of this living tree, remembering my Nana. Thinking of how happy I was with John and Moot playing in this grove in another lifetime, eons ago. The delicate small, flat needles, dark green on the top side and dusty pastel green on the bottom side, give off a subtle sweet tangy fragrance. A lone chickadee hops from branch to branch and stops to tilt his head back and forth eyeing me with his bright round eyes. Chick, chick, chick. He says as if bringing a message from another world, a world I cannot see, just behind the veil.

I feel the peace of Nana's love again. The whole earth is her garden now. With a sigh I slide down the trunk and sit on the carpet of light brown hemlock needles. Home at last!

These trees never change in their love for me. Their loving, calm, indifferent presence soothes my troubled seething mind. Slowly the words stop tumbling around my head and the feelings stop rampaging around my insides. Only the present moment remains in all its relentless reality. What is this present moment? How utterly astounding that it exists at all. That it has existed in the past where we can no longer see it and in the future where we cannot yet see it. How strange that we can only see the present moment and that there are no words here.

My eyes drift over the subtle forms and somber tones of the late November day.

Hearing a rustle in the brush, I turn, the frantic hope rising within me that Moot has followed me here. But there is nothing there but a small rising gust of wind.

Gradually the light evaporates from the moist air and the temperature drops. The last light of day ebbs out of the frigid air and the forest is absolutely black and still, waiting, pregnant.

Slowly I spread out my sleeping roll, which I have hidden inside my tarp in a plastic bag under a fallen tree, where the roots make a safe dry cave.

I lie here, looking out into the blackness, feeling the living earth under and around me. The forest is asleep now for the winter. The first flakes begin to fall, and to land like pin pricks on my upturned face, where they melt into small pools of cool water. The air is giving birth to her offspring — infinities of tiny, flat hexagonal crystals of ice that float serenely down, settling onto the crisp lips of last years leaves, where the frozen flakes cling and do not melt.

Slowly, slowly, like some unfolding drama, in a ritual procession of otherworldly significance, the barrage of flakes condenses out of the towering column of freezing air, which has arrived here, from the north. The first snow of winter.

I reach down and pick up a small brown stick with a cocoon stuck to one side and twirl it back and forth in my fingers. Some small insect inside has covered herself with a protective coat of spun fiber for the winter.

I need a new life. This one is no longer right.

I snuggle deep inside my sleeping roll, like a caterpillar inside her cocoon, and let myself be covered with snow all night long.

Chapter 40: Home on Leave

My brother, Paul, is home on Christmas leave from the Coast Guard. My dear parents are somehow dearer and more vulnerable than I remember them. Mother cooks a big turkey dinner. How she loves holidays, the pageantry and ritual of it, the gathering of family. I've missed Paul too, my baby brother all grown up, now in his Coast Guard uniform.

This evening Paul and I sprawl on the living room floor, like kids. Mother and Dad sit in their cushioned armchairs. We are silent, listening to Verdi's Requiem, one of our family favorites. The music pours around us, stirring us with its passion.

The dusty smell of the woven wool of the old maroon rag rug floods me with memories, as I lie, resting my head on my pale arm. Seen close like this with one eye, the rug, with its tiny filaments of red, blue, yellow and brown, fills my entire visual field. I see my brother's bulk over the horizon of my arm and remember the happy hours we played together on this rug when we were little.

The sacred music, with its deep primal chords, brings us close as a family, binding us into the pageant of birth and life and death, together. The grandeur and mystery of it, like volumes of ocean water heaving and falling, evolves and spawns, like some primal life form in a huge vast warm sea. The immense love that binds our tiny family together is a flickering candle flame of life that is passed precariously from one generation to the next.

On Christmas Eve my dad reads the Bible, the story of Baby Jesus, Mary, Joseph, and Herod. How many Christmases have we done this? How many times have I listened to this story? I remember how our family sailed together in the summers, shoveled snow together in the winters, ice skated on woodland ponds and skied through the Fells. I remember how every night my mom and dad would read us a bedtime story, tuck Paul and me into to our beds, kiss us goodnight, only to hear the nightly refrain, "I wanna glass of waader." Dutifully and patiently, they would bring us each our plastic glass, his pale blue, mine pale yellow, filled with tap water from the bathroom and we'd have an excuse for one last hug and one last, "Nighty, Night. Sleep tight. Sleep loose."

How many meals did my mother cook for us! Thousands of breakfasts, lunches and dinners. How many times did my dad come home from work and trudge up the cellar stairs to be greeted with shouts and hugs of joy! We could tell what kind of day he'd had by the sound his footsteps made on the cellar stairs, heavy and slow when he was tired and discouraged, lighter and quicker when happy, perhaps looking forward to the weekend. And I remember his horrible migraine headaches, which would send him moaning to bed for days, while my devoted mother would rub the back of his neck and bring him hot water bottles.

When Paul and I were sick with measles, mumps and chickenpox we stayed home and played together, with our stuffed animals, with which we made up great adventures. We would cover ourselves with a blanket tent. The blanket would encompass our entire world with its cozy protective covering. I can still see its plaid design, like fields of planted vegetables and grains in a farmers field, plowed in contours, making complex curves and bends, which to my resting eyes were beautiful.

On Christmas day Nana and Grampy and Mom and Pop would arrive. How happy we were! Nana would hold me in her arms and rock me and tell me stories about when she was a little girl. How safe and loved I felt. Then I was at home.

And now I'm living in Roxbury away from my family, in the city. I know with all my soul I do not belong there. That is not where I'm meant to be. But where? Where is my right life? What is my right life?

I know I have a life's work I'm supposed to be doing, but what is it? I can't find it? The closest I came to finding my own right life was on my westward journey. But I can't make a living sleeping under the stars thinking about the Divine. Who even cares about whether all that really exists is the Divine Creator or not? Who would even care about my other discovery that was even more astounding? It is as it is. We silly humans make up stories about the infinite and then fight over the stories we make up. What it really is is clothed in mystery, beyond anything we have ever thought... a miracle of such astounding magnitude that no one sees it at all.

Please, please give me some sign as to what I'm supposed to be doing... as to how I'm supposed to live in this life. I can't live as a woman in this society the way it is. I have to change it, but how? How? I can't give up myself. I can't fit into this trap. What am I going to do?

We decorate the tree, carefully unwrapping all the old decorations... hand blown glass that my mother had bought in Germany before the war, a star made of silver-plated pearls that my mother and father had used on their first Christmas tree in 1939, in the old apartment on Massachusetts Ave in Cambridge, before Paul and I even existed. How strange to think of the world going on before we existed. And the world going on after we cease to exist. How could Nana be gone and everything else still here? It's so weird, this idea of existing and not existing of being born, living and dying. My mind feels as if I've always lived and always will live. I have to keep reminding myself that this is not so. What do I want to leave for the world after I am gone? I want to give something to the world, to people, to all people everywhere, something that will make the world better and people happier. But what?

Handel's Messiah is playing and we sing along. Dad sings the bass, Paul the tenor, and I sing the alto and soprano. My mother doesn't like to sing. She says she can't sing. But when we all sit down at the piano, crowded onto the long bench, the cover of which lifts up so you can store sheets of music inside, Dad gets her to sing the Contented Camel song... She sings in her dear, wavery, off-key voice. She can also sing Adeste Fidelis in Latin. We all join in.

This Christmas glows with the love our little family has for each other. How different it is here in this house than any other place I've ever known, with our discussions of physics, chemistry, philosophy, religion and social issues, and the flood of music: Handel, Bach, Beethoven, Mozart, Brahms, and Chopin.

The telephone rings.

I jump up run into my mother's small den, a space eked out, in the hall that leads to the back porch, between downstairs bathroom and living room, and pick up the smooth, black plastic receiver.

"Hello?" I say, wildly hoping it is John, or someone with news about Moot.

"Hello?... Yes... Who?"

"This is Will, remember me?" The man's voice articulates with a slight drawl.

"Will!... Where are you?" I scream.

"Home for Christmas at my parents place." Will's voice sounds so familiar and so strange.

"I can't believe it! I'm so glad to hear from you!" It's been since summer of 1963, when we parted in Boston after our Nova Scotia adventure, since I've heard him.

"Any chance of seeing you?" he says.

I'm surprised and thrilled. My heart leaps up.

"Sure! I'd love to, when?" I reply

"How about tonight?"

"Sure! Where?"

"How do I get to your house?" he asks.

Somehow I always knew he'd come back.

So much for carol singing and the Messiah... I'm in the shower, singing and washing myself, steam everywhere, my hair sudsed, the smell of shampoo, the feel of rough terry cloth towel, the hum of hair drier and the directed blast of hot air, which is produced by the tiny electric motor inside the plastic handle, with its switches set at very hot.

Several hours later, the doorbell rings. In two jumps I'm down the stairs swinging on the railings, boom, boom. Thud! I land at the bottom with a house-shaking crash and pull open the door. There is rush of cold air, on my damp neck. Will, dressed in a dark-blue, wool navy suit, stands on the stoop! My old friend, Will, whom I had missed so much.

Spontaneously I leap to give him a hug as I would have John, but he stiffens and I stop in mid air, backing up instead, and pull the door wide open.

My parents have tactfully disappeared, Dad to his study upstairs, Mom to the kitchen to finish the supper dishes, Paul to his room where he is playing the New World Symphony by Dvorak, the strains of which can be heard faintly.

Chapter 41: The Proposal

Will and I walk shyly into the living room. In all the time we knew each other this is the first time he's visited me in my home. He seems nervous and awkward and I feel the same.

"Well how's the Navy?"

"Good, good," he nods.

"Remember the attic in the physics building?" I ask.

"Yeah, that was nice..." he responds.

"Remember Digby when they thought we were dead?"

"Yeah, yeah that was funny," he chuckles.

We sit and talk for several hours. He tells me he was engaged but she broke it off. I tell him about John's disappearance and Moot, and after swearing him to secrecy, about my plans to run the Boston Marathon in April.

"Why don't you come back with me to California?" he suggests at last.

"My mother and father would never let me go unless I was married," I said.

"Well?" he said.

I don't particularly want to be married, but where else do I have to go? I can't stay at my parents' house any longer. They have made that clear. I'm not happy in Roxbury. I have no way of earning a living and no real prospect of ever being able to earn a living. I hate secretarial work. I can't see myself as a primary grade school teacher, and I lack the training and inclination to be a nurse and I certainly don't want to work on an assembly line or as a laundress or some such thing, which are the only career options available to a woman.

Women graduating from college are expected to marry, as my mother had and as she never tires of telling me. You get engaged your senior year and married the next year. There really is no other option. Men expect this too and compete to get the best women, just as women compete to get the best men. Somehow all this had escaped me. I had actually gone to college to learn something. I had some intrinsic sense that I had a life's work, something I was meant to do, or to be, that was not any of these unsavory alternatives. I still have a gnawing empty sense inside that I have a life's work, but that not only will I never be allowed to do it, I will never even get to find out what it is. And I haven't even finished college.

I feel trapped. I am trapped, just as my mother had been trapped. I want to do my creative work... but I don't know how to make a living. Wal is offering me a way out, an escape, a way to be married but not married, to be with someone I love, and not to have to play the roles. With us there is camaraderie, a sense of equality... of brotherhood.

He had not, as John had tried to do, make me conform to the usual subjugated woman role and serve him as a house servant and child bearer, a second-class citizen over whom he exerted his male status and prerogative. It was Wal after all who had given me my first hunk of clay, and looked on in bemusement as I turned out sculptured head after head and filled our attic hide-a-way.

It was Will who taught me to play the bells in the Tufts chapel. It was Will who had led me on adventures, who had run with me out over frozen lakes in winter, who had slept in the lush, mossy Nova Scotia wilderness with me and listened to the wild, wind-singing trees.

It was Will who had listened to my elation about gravity and parabolic trajectories. Will is as wild as I am. He will never try to subjugate me...

True we had never made love, never even kissed. True we were more like brother and sister than husband and wife, but... maybe this is good!

He would leave me free to pursue my own life. We would just go on like that being pals. I had missed him. I had thought of him. It was months before I could open up to John because of my loyalty to Will. Perhaps I hadn't been fair to John. I was always comparing him to Will, to wild, untamable Will, and my romanticized recollections of our time together. And here Will is again, now offering me something different, offering me an escape, a way out, a way we can continue as we had been, a way I can find my own life and he can find his, as friends and equals... as we had been in college.

"Let me think about it," I say.

He shrugs, "I've got to be back on ship by January fifteenth."

We walk to the door and smile, but still do not kiss, "Think about it," he grabs my hand and grins, looking, for a moment, like a lost little boy in a play Navy suit.

Uppermost in my mind is my intention to run the Boston Marathon on April 19, 1966. I've already missed one year because of sprained ankles and since then I've trained a phenomenal amount, running every day, peaking with sixty-five miles of the Woodstock Hundred Mile in September, and now my thought is to maintain my peak through the winter from September to April without injuring myself again, and here is a way to do it, with a man I have long loved, with the man who indeed had opened me up to cross country running in the first place... a way to finish off my training in temperate Southern California with no snow or ice to hamper me.

I had known, that last day of my cross-country odyssey, standing on Stinson Beach, feeling the wild crashing of the huge Pacific surf, that I would be back. Perhaps this is God opening the door through which I am meant to pass.

Perhaps it is meant, perhaps the Divine is showing me the way I am meant to go, leading me from this life I am in, which I know is the wrong life, to the life I am meant to live. Perhaps Will is opening another door through which I am meant to go, even if I can't see the future. Maybe he is giving me another gift, as he gave me the clay and the cross country running, offering me a marriage, which is not, for either of us, a traditional marriage, but rather, a hope for something more, something better. I have, I realize, been in love with him all this time even while being in love with John, and Branden too.

Chapter 42: Whose Daughter?

After the compulsory meetings with the in-laws, the traditional hemming and puffing, the fatherly advice, the shopping trips with my mother, while I decided on "My bedroom image," ... the Bachrach engagement photographs, which are published in the local paper, *The Winchester Star*, with my engagement announcement, the day of my departure arrives.

I'd been to Will's parents house to visit the in-laws. I'd been there once before on one of our long runs to Blue Hill. The house is a modest cape cod in a working class neighborhood. I like the warmth and unpretentiousness of his parents, their efforts to be good people, their humility and rootedness. After the whirlwind skydiving with Branden, this seems grounded and stable, unassuming.

And now I'm leaving.

My parents seem small and wobbly. I slump in the back seat of our car, watching the gray buildings flip by the steamed up windows, as we make our way to the airport along my father's famous airport shortcut.

A thick coating of ice blankets the airport except for the runways, which have been scraped clear. Snow swirls down, gusts of wind lift the moored plane wings.

Dressed in an itchy wool skirt, several sweaters, a wool coat, boots, mittens, scarves, a wool hat and ear muffs, I hug my mother and then my father for the last time, board the plane, and we lift off into the storm.

My parents look at each other with trepidation,

"What have we done?"

"At least she is married,"

"Yes, at least she is married."

I imagine they are glad I am gone and on my way, safely married, provided for, and living according to the prescribed script, at last. Maybe Dr. Southgate had been worth it after all, getting me back on track, the track they thought I should be following for my own good. The track they and Doctor Southgate and all of society conspired to impose upon me. The only track that is open to a young middle class woman, to marry and to let her husband define her life for her, to have her very own kitchen and her children, and her little house in the suburbs and fill her head with shopping lists, home decoration, recipes to please her husband's boss, and whatever she has to do in the bedroom to keep her husband, if not happy, at least to do her duty whether she likes it or not.

Below me lies a bed of white cotton batting clouds and above me the bare blue sky with the single egg yolk eye of the sun radiating light and heat on the receiving earth.

When the plane touches down in San Diego my face is still pressed to the window, my eyes having registered every mountain ridge, every valley, and every dendritic pattern of water erosion for the last three thousand miles.

Palm trees!

How ridiculous I am, dressed in three layers of clothes with ear muffs, a wool hat and mittens, in the balmy embracing air of the great Pacific, under the intensely beating sun of Southern California.

The taxi deposits me at the El Cortez Hotel, which towers above the surrounding buildings, resplendent with a glass elevator, which levitates slowly along its outside wall.

Flowers cascade from every orifice: brilliant red bougainvillea, begonias, impatiens, ferns, poinsettias adorned with star-shaped red flower-like leaves, and birds of paradise. Orchids festoon the hotel rooms. My window looks out over the city and dinner is at seven.

I peek out the side door and find an alleyway where I run up and down, up and down. Stretching my cramped legs feels so good.

After showering and changing, I elevate to the elegant sky room for dinner in the glass elevator, which climbs majestically up the outside of the building revealing the panorama of the desert city, washed by the Western Ocean, spreading out beneath me. I'm in a time capsule, a transparent spaceship, which has alighted on some heavenly planet of the future with an advanced and peaceful civilization. The city lights sparkle below me, and to the west the huge orange sun sets into the vast sea, spreading a benign radiance of pink, gold and orange over the world.

"This sure beats life in Roxbury!" I think. "I've died and gone to heaven!" The afterglow of the sunset melts into indigo twilight and plunges us into the darkness of night, the same soft velvety darkness that I had loved that night on Stinson Beach, and to which I had known I would return. Sparkles of festive candles and flowers effulge on every white linen clothed table. My heart brims with happiness.

What a difference one decision can make! One minute I'm miserably trudging around Roxbury, lost, in the snow wondering where my life is going and the next minute I'm sitting in an elegant dining room looking out over shimmering city of palm trees and Pacific ocean, eagerly waiting to marry the man I love, or at least *a* man I love.

I sit down at my table in my simple skirt and blouse and take up the menu. I read the entrees and the prices, gauging one against the other, savoring each selection in my imagination, hungry after a long day; it is after all ten o'clock my time... my old time... Eastern time.

"Excuse me mademoiselle, your mother is here!" the maitre d' gives a short bow.

My mother? How did she get here?

The next moment the maitre d' returns with a tall statuesque woman, with an elegantly chiseled face, gray-blue eyes, her graying blonde hair pulled up into an upsweep, dressed in simple elegant black... an absolute stranger who looks more like me than I do.

"Thank you," she says to the maitre d' and she holds out her hand to me.

"Excuse me," she says softy, "The maitre d' said my daughter was here and led me to you. I'm Paula Hansom. May I?" she motions.

"Please sit down," I say, feeling an immediate rapport with this elegant woman who reminds me of myself, how I will be in say… fifteen years.

"I'm Bobbi Gibb," I muster.

She sits and begins to talk. Her diction is perfect, perhaps slightly European. She has just returned from Nevada, she says, where she was on business. What business is she in? Horse business, She raises thoroughbred racehorses, but that is not why she was there.

"I've just arrived myself," I venture.

"From?"

"From Boston."

"Oh yes, Boston, lovely city. I've spent some time there."

"What brings you to San Diego?"

"I'm getting married."

"Oh congratulations!"

Her voice falters and I sense a deep well of sadness brimming in her.

"May I... we've just only met... but I feel I know you, that we know each other ... that somehow we've known each other before... do you know what I mean?"

"Yes, I know, I feel that too," I say, feeling warm and a little frightened.

"When the maitre d' said my daughter was here, I... I've just returned from where my daughter was..." tears brim in her eyes and I feel reciprocal tears suddenly brim in my own eyes.

We sit there in silence for a moment.

"My daughter died..."

"Oh I'm so sorry,"

"She was killed... her husband shot her and then shot himself...I've just been out to take guardianship of the four children..." her voice breaks off again. I reach out and take her hand and we both sit there tears streaming down our faces. The maitre d' returns to take our order but tactfully fades away.

"He was a marine, back from Vietnam, under terrific stress. There had been other incidents... but she loved him, she couldn't live without him, she said.... I tried to warn her.... but maybe I didn't try hard enough. She was sure, she said, that he loved her... that nothing would happen... She had a temper too that's part of what drew them together....

"It just happened... a week ago today... so when the maitre d' said my daughter was here," she stops crying and looks at me, "Maybe you were sent to me for a reason."

"Yes, when the maitre d' said my mother was here, I didn't know what to think... I'm glad you came over."

As we eat dinner we talk about our lives, what we believe and how we feel. We are drawn closer together. "Is there another life after death?" she wonders. We speak of our relationships with men and our families. She is heir to one of the Midwest beer fortunes. My mother's family had, several generations earlier, made a fortune in the Midwest grain milling business. We both love the earth and we both love horses. We share a girlish delight in life, which flickers through despite the tragedy that has just occurred. I must come out to her ranch, she says.

"Where?"

"In Rancho Santa Fe."

"Oh that's where I'm going... to stay with Ewing Mitchell until my fiancée gets in from sea. Ewing is a friend of my uncle Fred."

"I'll drive you out... tomorrow... meet me at my room," She hands me a slip of paper with her room number scribbled on it, "Ten o'clock."

We embrace gently and go our separate ways.

As I walk back to my room I notice how everything is glowing with a warm light of benign meaningfulness and how aware I am of being in, of having the creature of God, DiMa, surrounding me, mysteriously creating itself into Itself at every place and time. I am filled with love for the Divine and feel Its love radiate from all of its self-creation.

It is as if having forgotten what I found on the mountain, now having talked with Paula about it, being back here where I first discovered it, my awareness of it is returning. It was this awareness I had been missing. It was this state of mind, this state of feeling, that I had been missing and had been seeking, dumbly moving towards It again. The full power of it rushes in around me as I feel myself, in this hotel spinning through the timeless, infinite universe brimming with celestial love.

To be in love all the time, not just to be in love with this or that person, but to be in love with everything, that's the way we're supposed to be naturally. Just to be in love… period. That is how I described it to Paula. That is how I feel it, now rushing in upon me, a joyous sense of life being right, of this incomprehensible love, out of which existence is continuously being born, permeating every molecule of every being.

After a delicious restorative sleep I awake just in time to grab a bit of breakfast, scrambled eggs and coffee, with universes of swirling cream, and read the Wall Street Journal, before finding my way to Paula's door. I knock shyly, so quietly she at first does not hear.

215

I listen to voices coming from behind the closed door, a discussion going on in animated, urgent terms between Paula and one or more male voices. I am embarrassed to knock again and stand there wondering what to do, when the door opens. Paula greets me in the most natural way and invites me in, as the man buttons his shirt and kisses Paula goodbye.

Chapter 43: *Vista Hermosa*

Paula and I motor in her jeep north on Route 101, our hair blowing in the warm wind, through the La Jolla hills, which are soft Mediterranean green with the January springtime, across the causeway at Del Mar, where the mighty Pacific crests in long lines of glistening white waves that break in thunder on the long sandy beach. We drive on past the Del Mar Race Track to Via De La Valle, up the hill on Camino Real. We wind through dripping, golden green eucalyptus groves, onto Linea Del Cielo, and down Rambla De Las Flores into a thickly wooded valley, across a bucolic bridge, over a stream to Vista Hermosa Farm, home of Crazy Kid, the fastest horse alive at three quarters of a mile.

Paula explains to me that Crazy Kid set a world record of one minute, seven and four-fifths seconds at six furlongs, and then went on to win the mile and one-eighth handicap in one minute forty-seven and three quarters seconds at the Del Mar Handicap four years ago.

Over us arches the brilliant blue of the freshly washed sky of a Southern California winter, which anywhere else would be called spring. Frogs chirrup in the wet places and crickets sing. I am filled with a sense of well being that I've not recently felt, a sense that my right life is opening before me as effortlessly as a curtain is drawn back by the unseen hand of God.

This is exactly the ranch that for so many childhood years my little playmates and I had pretended to own. Paula raises thoroughbreds.

"Wait 'til you see the Kid," Paula is like a little girl in her enthusiasm. She wheels the jeep left and we pass under a white wooden sign with "Vista Hermosa Farm" carved on it, past a sign propped up on a metal post with a cement base that says, "Drive Slowly, Cuidado." Chickens scurry out of the way. We drive past neat paddocks enclosed by white board fences that hold dozens of mares and foals. A rooster crows. We park by the white gambrel-roofed barn trimmed with green. Paula speaks a few words with the foreman in Spanish.

"We have a new arrival," she turns to me, smiling, and motions to me to follow her. My eyes adjust to the dimness; my nostrils tickle with the smell of sweet hay, grain, pine sawdust and horses. She pulls open the top half of the stall door. The mare whickers and nuzzles her newly born, warm, damp foal, which is lying crumpled in a tangle of its own long legs on a pile of fresh straw. A shaft of sunlight from on high lights the humble stable. This could be the manger in Bethlehem; it has a sense of blessed peace and holiness, which the barn and its creatures embody.

Paula opens the stall door and walks in motioning for me to follow. The mare nuzzles Paula affectionately and sniffs me warily. We bend over the foal who looks at us with glistening dark-brown eyes and listens to us with furry ears. With a sudden effort, the baby scrambles shakily to her feet. Paula runs her hands over the baby's soft body and turns to me with a grin. "A new baby girl! Isn't she a wonder?"

Tears brim in Paula's eyes again and I know she is thinking of her own daughter.

I nod, "Yes," and reach my hand out and touch the soft, warm, live fur of this little creature, who turns her whiskered muzzle towards me. Paula looks at me. The foal nuzzles under her mother's belly and suckles. Paula gently shuts the door as we leave.

From the open central part of the barn we hear the sounds of a horse whinnying and hooves hitting on the thick wooden floor planks, the entire barn shakes with the force of it.

"The Kid!" Paula exclaims, "What's going on?"

"Hey, What's going on?" "Que Pasa?" she shouts in Spanish rounding the corner in time to see the huge black stallion rearing up, pulling against the lead line, pawing the air with his hooves.

Three Mexican men are struggling to subdue the gigantic plunging son of Troy.

"Get away!" Paula commands. The men back off.

I watch in amazement as Paula stands absolutely still next to the plunging stallion and whispers something almost inaudible. The huge rearing horse comes back to earth, lowers his head and nuzzles Paula's side. She strokes his ears and he follows her out of the barn like a pet dog. I follow at a safe distance wary of his hooves, which can kill a person with one well-aimed blow.

"Watch this," Paula half turns to me as she opens the gate to the paddock, removes Crazy Kid's halter and makes a clucking sound. Over a ton of moving horse, Crazy Kid propels himself at amazing speed around and around and around the paddock. He loves to run. Just like me. His strength and power take my breath away.

"What a magnificent creature!" I breathe.

"Yes; Now you understand," Paula smiles.

We stand and watch his black glossy hide rippling, his hooves hitting the ground faster than you can see, his banner tail held high revealing some Arab blood in his ancestry. His huge size denotes the European cold-blooded lineage as well. Powerful haunches and high curving rump give him an advantage at the sprint.

The mares, seeing their stud, become animated and those in heat, those without foal, prance up and down along the sides of their paddocks tails held high, some of them rubbing against the fence trying to back up into him.

Paula and I lean our arms on the top rail of the fence and watch the Kid run. Inside I am feeling the urge to run, to run like this in pure exuberance at finding myself alive, the power and glory of it, to participate, to become part of life, to express this joy by running at full speed as fast and as far as I can go. I too am restless, eager to explore my new surrounding,

218

eager to embrace life in its fullness. I feel the way he feels, full of the vigor of life pouring through me.

"It takes my breath away when I see him run," Paula says.

"Yes, me too," I reply.

We stay here like this watching Crazy Kid run and feeling the joy of the deep love we have of life, even with all its sadnesses, tragedies and disappointments... the love of this life no matter what, and the joy of finding someone else who understands that joy, someone else who shares the sense of everyday wonder at the incredible, intoxicating experience of finding one's self alive, here on this earth. That is what we are seeing in Crazy Kid, and feeling in each other, the expression of the power and joy of this brief yet eternal life in which we participate to the fullest... the defiant brevity of it.

As we drive back out of the driveway after a delightful afternoon I read the handwritten words on the back of the sign, which we had passed on our way in that had cautioned, "Slow, Cuidado." The back side of the sign says, "Vaya con Dios." Go with God.

Chapter 44: On the Bridge

"Do you want to see the bridge?" Will asks.

"Sure!" I take his arm in mine and fall in love with him all over again. Will is always expanding my mind and showing me new worlds.

Squinting at the brilliant sun, I look up at the radar antenna going around and around, catching in its curved, metallic frame tiny electromagnetic packets of energy, tuning into some unseen information accessible only to machines and their human masters. There is an intelligence to it but it is not its own intelligence.

Here I stand in the midst of the most powerful, well-equipped, technologically advanced Naval fleet the world has ever known. I say a prayer, "Please let this marvelous force be used only for good, let it be a force for freedom from oppression, openness of government, for the value of each and every individual, for democratic government, of the people for the people and by the people... all the people, working together so that each and every person on this earth can live in peace, harmony and justice and fulfill the God-given potential that we are each given. Let it not ever become an instrument of oppression, greed or power, but preserve us, as a force for good, imbue us with caring, fairness, love, truth, self determination and dignity for all."

To see this fleet as a true force for good in the world moves me. To see America and Americans as committed to fairness, righting wrongs, freeing the oppressed, fighting tyranny, establishing freedom and democracy, healing societies, as we had done in WWII makes me feel proud. After WWII for the first time in the history of the world, the United States of America, the conquering nation, instead of taking booty, enslaving the populace, murdering the people as had been the modus operandus in every other war prior to this, helped friend and foe alike to rebuild, to heal, to become functional democracies with flourishing economies. When I remember this it makes me feel proud to be an American.

To suspect that our national purposes are being diverted by those with private agendas at odds with America's idealism, contrary to the American Dream of prosperity and freedom for everyone, purposes that are corrupt, fills me with a sinking sense of dread and sadness.

That scene from Camelot comes back to me where King Arthur, poor sweet, good, trusting, deceived and betrayed man, said, "...Not might makes right... but... Might *for* Right..." Yes to use might for right, to protect what is good and to destroy what is evil. That is the dream of the right use of power.

How will all this play out? In the long run I know that the only reality is God's unconditional, infinite love, but I also know that God does not coddle us, but leaves us the freedom to make mistakes and to stray off the path into the brambles of our own making. If this were not true we would not have freedom. This capacity to make horrific mistakes is the price we pay for having the ability to choose. This capacity to be tragically misled, by our own misconceptions and the misconceptions of others is the price we pay for being able to learn how to discern what is true and right.

I stand here my head flung back looking up at this radar antenna turning 'round and 'round, lost in these thoughts, when Will's voice interrupts me.

"Hey, my buddies in the radio room want to meet you."

Meanwhile in New Haven, outside of the Yale dormitories, snow swirls sensuously across the street, snaking and sinister, as John revs up his motorcycle. Many years later John relates to me this saga. The Reverend Richardson, John's interfering father, had sent him the engagement photo from The Winchester Star. John had enlarged the sad picture of me, multiple times, my face in red dots, plastered on the entire wall of his room, next to the bed where we had first made love the winter of 1964, over a year ago.

John had never answered my calls or letters and had not come to see me again or contacted me after that horrible day he fought with his father and disappeared back to Yale. I had drifted into a relationship with Branden, feeling lost, missing John even as I had missed Wal before him.

Somehow in the deep recesses of my unconsciousness I know it is John I am supposed to be marrying, but that natural and right impulse had foundered, first on the customs and stereotypes of the age, which would force our marriage into a mold neither of us could abide, and erase our natural egalitarian friendship, setting him as a master over me, giving him the power, and further reducing the small autonomy I would have as a single woman, to the even lower status of his wife.

It was a prerogative he enjoyed and I mistrusted this. I did not want to be a functionary, I wanted to be a full, complete, unique person and I wanted the same for him. I did not want to have to enact a preset, prescribed pseudo-relationship. I wanted to have a real face-to-face, unique relationship as best friends and equals, a love that suited us, which we could make however we wanted. I didn't want to have to play a role set out by some other authority. I wanted a real partnership the way we wanted it in a way that suited us as unique individuals. But that was not to happen.

I had seen the tragic consequences to my mother of the traditional role-playing marriage... she had little sense of self left. She felt empty and that is not how I wanted to live. But finding a man who could even conceive of this new way of relating as equals, with the woman not in a powerless, subservient role, was a formidable task.

John was, I was afraid, wedded to the old male expectations of his little wife to serve him, and do his bidding, and devote herself to maintaining him. His wife would be expected to give up herself and her life, as his mother had, as my mother had, as women always had... becoming in the process repressed, suppressed, unexpressed automatons.... reduced to mere household functionalities, not even respected by the husband to whom they had sacrificed themselves.

John and I had in fact a wonderful equal friendship as long as we were not married. Our impulse was good, but this natural impulse had been diverted, by our fathers... who were not in heaven... but were here on earth bent on keeping us apart, jealous, perhaps of our happiness.

I did not know for many years, for twenty years, that John had set out to prevent my marrying Will, set out into that blizzard that January 1966. He had wrapped himself in sweatshirts, jackets, gloves, and leapt onto his BMW cycle. He gunned the machine and roared out onto the highway, as we had done so many times together. Now alone, he was fighting the stinging bits of hard ice that cut his face.

"This is Sam," Will introduces me to a young man with an open face and a broad grin. "He's my best man."

I'm struck again with the friendliness and openness of these young navy men. Good humouredly they joke around with each other. These people are not interested in oppressing anyone or conquering anyone, but stand ready to help, to protect, whoever needs help and protection. I see that; I feel it. These kids are good kids caught up in someone else's war.

Will pulls on his running shoes and sweats. I change in the ladies room and we take off running along the San Diego waterfront. How wonderful it is to be running together again. How much I've missed him. With Will life is a perpetual adventure. We pass the Star of India, a three masted windjammer, and run along the quays.

"How do you keep in shape?" I ask.

"I don't really. I can't run as far as I used to."

To be following him along again, trying to keep up, brings back a flood of memories: our time together at Tufts, our hideaway in the attic of the physics building, our explorations of the back alleys of Boston, our runs out over the frozen lakes and along the railroad tracks, our adventure in Nova Scotia. I'm in love again with this strange, shy, poetic, lost, boy-man.

Chapter 45: Marriage

My parents, Mom-Christina and Grampy have flown into San Diego for the wedding and are staying in a suite at the El Cortez. They drive up to the Episcopalian Church in Del Mar where the Mitchells and I meet them. Will drives up from the naval base with several of his friends. Sam is his best man. Will looks handsome, but nervous, in his dark blue wool navy suit.

I feel awkward and tense in my white satin bridal dress... even the word scares me, denoting the bridle with which the wild horse is controlled, brought into submission. The seamstress, who had made many of my clothes, a French lady, in Rockport, had stitched the gown together. I had picked the fabric and the pattern and she had sewn an exquisite dress for less than I could buy it. I always enjoyed those trips with Mom-Christina to the seamstress's small stuffy apartment, which had a Continental flavor of depleted elegance.

Last night I had spent tossing restlessly in the Mitchell's luxurious guest room queen sized bed. Unknown to me, John was racing towards me through the blizzard. Plows could no longer get through. State Troopers were closing down the Interstate highways that were choked with snow. Traffic was stalled. John roared around the barriers racing along the deserted roads. He hunched into the icy blast, his hands almost frozen on the handlebars, his eyes stinging behind the goggles that iced up so often that he had slid them up on his forehead. On he rode all night until dawn, when, crazy with fatigue, he pulled off at a truck stop outside of Chicago and collapsed.

Here in the bright sun of California all the past seems washed away, washed clean and there is a sense of a new beginning. The service is moving and the music brings tears to my eyes as I reach for Wal's hand and squeeze it, meeting his eyes with mine as we kiss for the first time. I want to believe this can be a good marriage, that we can create something together that will be good. I want it to be so, to marry my best friend, to make something unique that will suit us. I want us to run together again. I want us to make a place as we did in the attic of the physics building where we can work on clay, study and talk. I want children too, eventually, and the thought that this man, who has been such a good older brother to me, will be a good father to our children fills me with tenderness.

When I look over at him, now and see him looking so nervous, and boyish in his navy uniform, I feel my heart rise up as it always did when he had come the through the door of our attic hideaway and had thrown his soft suede jacket over his chair. I do love him. I had loved him all this time, and missed him. He had become a glorious abstraction in my mind, and now I am faced with the reality I scarcely know. He looks small and pale and scared and I wonder suddenly if I know him at all. Suddenly he seems like a complete stranger.

After the reception and dinner at El Cortez Hotel, Will drives me to our new home on Hawthorn Street, in a friend's borrowed car.

"This is great!" I clap my hands and hug him.

An earth-shattering roar breaks the silence. I jump and cover my ears with my hands.

"What the....?" Wal exclaims... "Jets, right over the house!"

"Why?" I ask.

"So that is why the rent was so cheap," he laughs.

Our new home is right under the flight pattern for jets landing at the Lindberg International Airport!

I laugh too, "How will we ever be able to sleep?"

"Come on I have to meet Sam at the Watering Hole," he grins.

......

From the outside, the Watering Hole looks like a disreputable bar and girly joint in the bad section of town, a place where nice girls wouldn't go. But inside I am surprised to find how warm and homey it is. Girls in tiny pink bikinis slither around the tables gyrating in what presumably is an alluring way ... or would be to a man. To me it looks silly and put on.

After biology and life drawing class, I see the human body as an incredibly complex, beautiful natural biological expression of the divine creativity. I see where the clavicle joins the sternum, and note the epicondryl and ...

My thoughts are broken off by the arrival of an enfeathered bit of female protoplasm at our table. She inserts herself aggressively and talks with Will and Sam and the others in a familiar joking way that lifts their spirits and makes them laugh.

She leans towards me and confides that she is happy to see Will happy. "He needed to be married," she says. "Thank you."

"Thank you!" I think "Thank you?"

"These sweet dear boys," She continues in a motherly fashion, "Are giving their all to their country and they are so far from home, so homesick. If I can bring a little joy into their lives, then I've done something for my country, something for these lovely boys, many of who will have to die before this is over... You are doing something for your country too," she says looking at me directly.

I like her. I like her in spite of myself, in spite of all the previous judgments I had made about such women. I look around the smoky room at the beautiful young faces of these American boys, only eighteen, twenty, twenty-two years old, clear unlined faces. These boys, who were the hope and pride of their parents, whose voices had changed not too long ago, who had their whole lives, who should have had their whole lives stretching on ahead of them, but who sit here facing death, dismemberment, injury, terror, with dazed innocence and goodness.

Someone turns on Peter, Paul and Mary singing Pete Seeger's song, "Where Have all the Flowers Gone? Gone to Soldiers every one..."

"I hate this damn war!" one of the men whispers, "But I'm doing my duty."

"I hate those damn draft dodgers!" another says. Murmurs of agreement.

"This is where I wrote that poem I sent you," Will says.

"Yes. It was beautiful," I reply.

Several hours later we emerge into the tender embrace of the unexpectedly warm January air. I'm used to bracing myself against the bitter cold of a New England January.

"So strange to see Orion in my shirt sleeves," I observe looking up and out into the Universe, which I do on emerging into the night from indoors, as if to check my orientation.

"Will you be all right getting home alone?" Will asks. I've got to be back on board by midnight. We sail tomorrow early."

"Sure, I'll be fine..." I grin. "Be careful... See you when you get back."

"Yeah," he says with a shrug and a downward glance at his shoes.

Chapter 46: The Silver Strand

The next morning, eager to explore my new surroundings, I arise early and set off in the direction of downtown San Diego. Discovering a coffee shop, I engulf my usual coffee and muffin while reading the Wall Street Journal. Emerging from the human habitat into the sun, I head south to the Coronado Ferry. I watch the waters of the Pacific churn, deep and blue green, as the wide, slow ship makes the passage to Coronado Island. Disembarking, I pick up a slow run, noting on my right an elegant, sprawling red-roofed hotel. Winding my way south along the neighborhood streets, I am charmed by this place with its neat cottages and abundance of flowers. How exotic to see palm trees casually fanning the Pacific breeze.

Suddenly the buildings give way on my right to a brilliant silver beach, cresting with pristine surf. My heart leaps up in response to the primal beauty of the magnificent beach and I run on its crystal white sand, which gives way under my feet making me feel as if I am running in snow.

How different this is from New England. An image of barren, black trees forking to the cold sky contrasts in my minds eye to the huge soft warm Pacific shimmering peacefully under the sun that stretches out to the west.

Finally I have time to think again and to sort out all the thoughts about subjective experience and matter that have been welling up in my mind since my run on the banks of the Charles River and my scribbled notes at the end of the Woodstock Hundred Mile.

I drift into a reverie.

What if I ask: Where in the frog is the property of jumping? I look inside the frog and nowhere do I see jumping. Yet the frog is capable of jumping. Is it the same way with consciousness or the ability to experience subjectively? Is consciousness a property of the whole system; is the ability to experience subjectively a property at all?

The question at hand is: In order for consciousness to emerge, does some kind of innerness or subjective innerness of perspective have to be present in the constituting subsystems, or can subjective experience, and ultimately human consciousness, emerge from the compilation of subsystems that are completely external, purely extended, with absolutely no subjective innerness as is currently believed?

In the first case, that is, if in order for complex human consciousness to arise there must be some sort of innerness of experience of all the comprising subsystems, the unanswered question becomes: Why and how can the comprising subsystems have some sort of innerness; what would this inside perspective be; and, how can these innerness compile into more complex innernesses?

In the second case, that is, if human consciousness arises from the compilation of purely extended subsystems that have no innerness of point of view, the question becomes: How can a system capable of experiencing subjectively arise from the juxtapositioning of purely extended subsystems;

what would account for the innerness of perspective arising in the more complex systems; and, would these more complex systems necessarily entail living organisms with nervous systems?

In the brain many dozens and hundreds of neurons receive input from many hundreds of other neurons and in turn send output to many dozens of other cells, which in some cases eventually feed back onto the originating cell. So in some sense all these neurons are 'looking at one another'. But how do they look? They don't see something outside of themselves. They 'look' by being changed through interacting with something else. What they see is not something other than themselves. What they 'see' is their own changes of state.

There is a kind of logic to it. If neuron C has a certain threshold of input it needs in order to fire, and if both neuron A and neuron B, feed onto C excitatorily, if neuron A alone firing doesn't reach C's firing potential and if B firing alone doesn't reach C's firing potential, then, for the moment, assuming here that A and B are C's only input, both A and B would have to fire within some additive time frame in order for C to fire. So this is an 'and' gated circuit, that is, if C fires it means that both A and B fired.

In contrast, if neuron C has certain threshold it needs in order to fire, if both neuron A and neuron B, feed onto C excitatorily, if neuron A alone firing reaches C's firing threshold potential and if neuron B alone firing alone reaches C's firing threshold, then, assuming here that A and B are C's only input, if either A or B fire, C will fire. So this is an 'either or' gated circuit, that is, if C fires it signifies that either A or B fired.

In addition, neurons are brilliantly constructed to take the ratios of the firing rates of inputs. If neuron C receives an excitatory input from neuron A and an inhibitory input from neuron B, then the firing rate of C will reflect some function of the ratio or difference between the firing rate of A and the firing rate of B.

In many cases neurons in the brain are spontaneously active and their firing characteristics are sculpted by inhibitory input. In addition, the membrane characteristics of neurons can change, increasing or decreasing the amount of input necessary to reach their firing potentials. Furthermore, other types of neurons do not fire at all, but take on a range of membrane potentials. Add to this, the fact that the location of the input synapses on each neuron affects the firing characteristics of the neuron, and given the billions of neurons and astroglial cells, and their multifaceted properties and interconnections, I can see that the brain can generate mind-boggling numbers of complex logical functions.

Looking from the outside I, the observer, can tell what neurons have fired and in what patterns. I can deduce what C 'knows' in terms of its input and its output. A specific pattern of excitation in the auditory receptors is relayed precisely to the auditory cortex where it is 'heard' as the opening chord in Bach's Mass in B. But there is a fundamental difference between looking at a pattern of neurons firing from the outside and experiencing music from the inside.

I had seen that there is no 'conversion' from the patterns of neuronal firing into some insubstantial other substance that would comprise the subjective experience of that chord, but rather that the patterns of neuronal potentials are themselves subjective experience to the brain. But what in the brain has the subjective experience? Do the neurons that exhibit these patterns 'have' the subjective experience… or is it the auditory cortex as a whole organ that 'has' the subjective experience… or is it some higher center that experiences its own states subjectively, that is, to which its own states are, to it, subjective experience…or is it the 'brain as a whole' that has the subjective experience? Or all of the above? Or some or none of the above?

I see that, systemically, the neurons at each level feed onto the neurons in the next level of processing in ways that enable the next level higher to abstract more features from the comparisons of the firings of the neurons in the previous level than were available to the individual neurons at the lower level, and so the subjective experience of the part of the brain at the higher level is not just an additive function of the neurons in the level below, but is a new dimension in subjective space, so to speak, in which each level of subjective experience is appropriate to the structure and function of the type of complex structure at that level. In each case the actual neurons are similar, but the functions they perform are different in that at each level of processing a new dimension of subjective experience arises, not necessarily in the individual neurons but in the higher order brain structure as a whole.

For example, the photoreceptors that receive photons in the range of wavelengths from 650 to 700 angstroms do not 'see' red. They do not have the same subjective experience as the groups of cortical cells that subjectively experience the redness that we, who are, in part, our cortices, subjectively experience, but… and here is the question again: Do the individual receptors have some sort of inside subjective view or experience of the reception of a photon of light in their own way at their own level… Or are the receptors in effect 'blind' and empty, having no inside subjective experience of their own changes of state? Are the cells mere mechanical automatons, as is currently thought?

And, to extend the question one step lower, do the molecules of rhodopsin whose configurations change on the event of reception of a photon have some sort of innerness of view, some inside subjective, not sensation, as we would have, but some innerness of perspective and experience of their own changes of state?

The scientific community would of course unanimously answer 'no' to these questions. But this leaves the problem of where in the hierarchy of input-complexity does this innerness of subjective view arise and occur, since it does arise and occur? Is it only at the final levels of neuronal input and processing that some sort of subjective insideness of self-viewing takes place? Are there cells that are the final recipients of all the preceding processing and are these the only cells that can experience subjectively? Then how do their activities combine to produce the subjective experiences we have of seeing hearing, thinking, intending, remembering and so forth?

Each cell is made of compilations of complex processes of organizations, of organizations, of organizations of molecules. How can the compilations of molecules, however complex, have, or more radically, how can their processes and activities 'be' subjective experience? Or are all cells in effect empty and blind, that is, purely extended, and only the combination of the neuronal activities all together become subjective experience to the brain, whose activities and processes they are? Where in all this is the observer who perceives thinks, feels and makes measurements of the so-called physical world in which he or she finds him or herself?

I look out at the pure white crests of thunderous breakers crashing on the white sand and feel that I am at the very edge and beginning of the world.

Here again is that ubiquitous observer who has come back into physics in such a way so that every observation now has to be measured in terms of a specific observer who measures and thus who interacts with that which she or he is measuring.

But I'd seen from my contemplations on the Uncertainty Principle that each interaction entails two interactants and each interactant is privy to one half of the parameters of that interaction and so in some sense is an observer from its own point of view. More complex interactions can be analyzed in terms of pairs of interactants taken two at a time so that the basic interaction involves two participants each of which 'views' the interaction or 'experiences' the interaction from its own point of view in terms of its own internal changes of state.

Whether or not each has some sort of subjective experience of that point of view I don't know yet. How could I ever answer such a question since in order to know what the other entity experiences I have to be that other entity?

In my human interactions I can empathize and in effect feel and know what the other is feeling. Is there some cosmic interconnection that would allow me to know whether or not a photon, for example, that impinges on the Rhodopsin in my eye, from its point of view has some sort of inner or subjective experience of that interaction? Is the universe, in effect, full of tiny observers? If each interaction entails two observers, do these observers experience their own changes of state subjectively in some way?

The Silver Strand gleams like burnished silver. The light is profoundly intense, emanating from the solar disc and reflecting in brilliant array from the seething, roiling surface of this immense planetary ocean. I pause, bend down, touch the sacred water with my hands, hurl it upwards to the sky and watch the tiny globules break into dancing rainbows of color. Joyfully, joyfully the sunlight plays on the water, penetrating the liquid surface and turning the sand to gold.

Are these photon blind or do they, in their own way, feel, in their own way, the joy they evoke in me as they swarm and glitter in abundant array — the joy of pure existence?

I am thinking down both branches of this dilemma starting, on the one hand, with my subjective experience of mind, and starting, on the other hand, with my conceptual understanding of matter, and I'm approaching a junction where I can understand both in the same terms. But what are these terms?

I am seeing that mind is not an insubstantial 'mind substance' inhabiting the material brain, but rather that the brain itself a material object, in the sense that it is made of atoms and molecules, and yet it can think and experience subjectively. This is radical. The brain, a material object, so called, can think.

On the other hand, I'm seeing that matter is composed of atoms that are in turn composed of smaller entities that are in turn composed of smaller entities and that these smaller entities are not the extended hard bits of things that matter has been taken to be, but are rather systems of systems of systems of dynamical interacting parts that are in turn comprised of smaller systems of dynamical interacting parts, the smallest of which I've called 'interactons.' These interactons I take to be, not particles, or things at all, but rather, dynamical patterns of activity.

I look out over the Pacific Ocean and watch the light glimmer on the surface.

The quantum of light, that is, the photon of electromagnetic radiation, I think may be the smallest entity that can exist on its own. What is light then? The 'light' we subjectively see is a subjective experience generated by our nervous system when certain regions in the eye-brain system are stimulated. The 'light' that we take to mean the electromagnetic radiation that exists out there in the external world is, as we detect and model it, comprised of two fluxes that mutually create each other. The contracting magnetic flux creates an expanding electric flux; the contracting electric flux creates an expanding magnetic flux. These expanding and contracting fluxes are perpendicular to each other and perpendicular to the direction of motion of the photon.

Here is a system that is made of parts that do not exist until they mutually create themselves by mutually creating each other. The parts do not exist independently and then interact to form a system. Rather the system as a whole creates itself through the mutual self-creation of its parts. The system and its parts are dynamical organizations of interacting activities. To be exact, the photon is a dynamical self-creating, self-interacting self-activity.

Could this be the smallest system not made of smaller systems that is the basis of what in more complex organizations becomes what we have called matter? Could it be that this is what physicists have been looking for all along, the smallest system, made of no parts? Could it be that the quantum of light is the fundamental substance of the universe and, out of the interactions of photons, comes into being electrons, quarks and all the other subatomic particles and antiparticles? Could it be that this substance isn't a substance at all but is an activity?

Suddenly it strikes me that this may be so and that this would explain why light plays a crucial part in defining how we measure space, time and gravitation as well as electromagnetic fields, energy and matter. It would also explain the indivisibility of the quantum because when the light quantum is divided it disappears. It cannot exist in any smaller, more subdivided state than the mutually self-creating quantum of electromagnetic self-activity.

And here is the deeper meaning of the Heisenberg Uncertainty Principle, not only that we cannot simultaneously measure the position and the velocity or momentum of a photon or other very small particle because our interaction with it changes its position and velocity or momentum, but also because this uncertainty represents some fundamental indeterminance in the qualities of position and *motion as pertains to smallest constituents of matter, an indeterminance that is built into the very nature of space, time, velocity and the quantum of action.*

In a flash I see why this is. It is because space and time are not the correct fundamentals in which to explain the so-called physical world. Space and time are our ways of ordering, measuring, and even of perceiving events. But space and time do not really exist, especially in the tiny domains of subatomic entities that I call interactions, at the level of the quanta of action.

In a world where an emitted photon goes from zero velocity to the maximum allowable velocity for a massive entity in no time, where certain kinds of information can instantaneously span billions of miles of space, and where electrons are spread out around the nuclei of atoms, in short in a world of quantum dynamics, there has to be another fundamental basis than space and time, or spacetime.

If I, as I propose, I take action and interaction as my fundamentals, rather than mass, energy and spacetime, am I any closer to understanding what the so-called physical world is? If, as I think, more complex systems are built up out of quanta of action, and these mutually self-creating, self-active quanta are the smallest systems, then it is clear that these smallest systems, which have no rest mass, are pure self-activity. It is not the activity of something else. This type of activity is self-reflexive-self-activity and these self-reflexive-self-activities can and do interact with one another to build themselves into more complex systems.

These quanta are prior to time and to space and to spacetime, they create what we measure as space and time and spacetime, not vice versa. It is space and time and spacetime that must be explained in terms of these self-creating self-activities and not the other way around. Position and velocity cannot be used to describe these smallest entities because they do not have a position or a velocity. Position and velocity are terms in which we describe certain aspects of macro-systems with respect to our coordinate systems, but these concepts are inappropriate at the level of the quantum of mutually self-creating-self-activity.

So, if as I think, the fundamental constituent of the so-called material or extended world are these quanta of action, these quanta of mutually self-creating self-activity, then it is clear that the world is not made up of particles at all, but of interacting activities. And now the question becomes, and this is truly heretical, do these fundamental self-activities have, or are they to themselves, a subjective innerness of being? If not, then the questions will always be: How and at what level of complexity do systems with this subjective innerness of being arise, and how does such subjective innerness of being emerge in a world, which at the smaller levels of systemic organization is devoid of such innerness? If so, if these fundamental self-activities have, or are to themselves, as I think, a subjective innerness of being, then all of physics, philosophy, neuroscience and biology must change its basic precept.

In this new conception, matter is seen to be not fundamental at all, but arising out of our experience of highly complex systems of interactions of nested systems of patterns of fundamental activity. And mind is seen to be not an insubstantial mind substance inhabiting an otherwise extended object, but is seen to be the inner subjective experience of that complex system's experience of its own dynamical patterns of self activity. Mind and matter are getting closer and closer together. But there is still something missing. What?

I am running south along Imperial Beach with its closely spaced beachfront homes. On and on I run further and further south along the low tide mark. I cross a tidal outlet and past some kind of park, then an estuary of some sort that I wade across. Regaining my footing on the firmly packed sand on the other side, I extend my stride. I feel strong and fast today. To the left, far up near the high water mark, I notice a concrete bunker and a tangle of barbed wire and wonder if it is the remains of a wharf. I'm curious to see what is ahead.

As I run I am aware of a growing sense of unease. Something is different. Something is wrong. With growing apprehension, I turn back and head home, retracing my steps north along the beach. The tide has been rising and this time I am closer to the concrete bunker. When I reach the bunker some uniformed men, who seem to be American police or military personnel, intercept me and demand to see my identification.

"Identification? Why?"

"You are about to enter the United States," they explain gruffly.

"I thought I was in United States," I exclaim.

"No, you are in Mexico. There's the border," they point to the concrete bunker and the barbed wire.

I explain that I had just been running down the beach from San Diego and I didn't realize that I'd crossed the border. They don't believe me and suddenly I feel scared.

They escort me into the office and began to question me. I explain that I am married to a Navy man stationed here and I've just arrived in California. Could I call him? No, he's gone back to sea. Is there anyone I can call?

Now I'm really scared. What if they don't believe me?

"Ewing Mitchell," I say. "You can call Ewing, in Rancho Santa Fe." They glance at me dubiously, obviously not believing that a seeming ragamuffin, lost on the beach, could know anyone as famous as Ewing Mitchell.

One of the men grudging calls the number I give them, suspecting that I'm just toying with them. Ewing is a well-known actor who has played in many films and TV shows, including in Sky King, in a popular TV show.

Ring, Ring, Ring! What if he's not home? My stomach sinks. Click. "Hello."

"Is Mr. Mitchell at home?" the officer inquires.

I overhear a mumbled conversation and then the officer reappears relaxed and grinning and I know everything is going to be OK.

Friendly now, one of the officer drives me back across the border.

"How are you going to get home from here? Will you be all right?"

"Run," I say. "I'll be fine, thanks."

The heavy truck door slams with a metallic sound and I head off at a slow run weaving my way from street to street, finally picking up some railroad tracks that I follow north.

At last I arrive back in Balboa Park, which is near our cottage.

The immense size and grandeur of this park dwarfs both Boston Common and Central Park. The towering eucalyptus and fichus trees rise joyfully to the southern sun, spreading their smooth limbs in its warm embrace. I tilt my head back and watch the canopy of shiny dark green leaves wheel overhead.

Here the little potted fichus trees I'd seen back east grow more than one hundred feet tall, trunks eight feet in diameter, with smooth gray bark. Like the fichus, I was pot-bound there. Here, in the invigorating warmth of the open air, I can find my true potential and discover that I am not a tiny houseplant but have the ability to become a huge towering tree. This thought fills me with delight and anticipation.

Fichus leaves are pinnate, pointed ovals, like the beech but firmer and waxier. The fichus roots grow near the surface in a tangle of interconnecting limbs. I pause, look at the roots, and tilt my head back to view the massive gray trunk and the shimmering canopy, which is held aloft by wildly gyrating, gray arms and thin twig fingers that sprout leaves. I feel a spurt of love for this massive living creature. This is a sacred tree, a world tree, connecting and symbolizing all life on earth. It is a divine manifestation in all its glory, magnificent and holy. And, it grows here undisturbed through generations of us fragile, soft-bodied human beings.

The park is crisscrossed with running paths that extend for miles. Museums built in style of Spanish architecture with arched colonnades, a replica of the Old Globe Shakespearean theatre, and an immense pinkish tan organ grace the park. I'm charmed by this place.

Dappled, spotted shadows of light and color shimmer silently, shaded from the sun by fragrant eucalyptus trees. The scent of eucalyptus is familiar to me. Nana had used eucalyptus oil to sooth my rasping lungs during my childhood bout with Whooping Cough. She had put the oil in a small tray in a vaporizer and set it by my bed. She had hung a sheet over the headboard, to enclose me in a tent, which, filled with the steamy vapor, helped me breathe.

So here are the trees, which helped me to breathe, to survive, to live. Thank you trees! Thank you! Here in this valley they grow over seventy-five feet high, their huge peeling trunks shed strips of outer bark, and reveal an inner bark that is smooth and mottled with subtle shades of green, blue, orange, yellow, lavender, ochre, sienna and white. The tree produces hard, green nuts with gray-green powdery caps, which litter the moist ground beneath the tree. I stoop and pick up a hand full of nuts and hold them to my nose to inhale the pungent spice. I fill my pockets with them.

The trail curves around, descending steeply into a deep valley. Hidden birds sing in the leafy boughs. Twittering and chirping, the melodious mocking birds, finches and mourning doves flitter from branch to branch. Black crows caw raucously and terrorize the other birds. High above, circling red tailed hawks scream, making the doves cringe. A lizard scuttles across the trail. Here is a magical kingdom that has never known snow.

Tired, and lost in a reverie of motion, color, form, whirling earth, sky and shrubs, I am surprised by the sudden sound of feet running. I catch a glimpse of a man in shorts, his sinewy, tanned, long-legged, muscular, thin body moving fast. He slows down and I speed up and we fall into stride with each other.

"Hi, I'm Bill Gookin," the runner offers, looking at me with pale blue eyes, from behind thick glasses, eyes that remind me of my grandmother's pale blue Allen eyes.

"I'm Bobbi," I respond. He runs for San Diego Track and Field, he confides and asks if I'm new in town since he knows all the runners in San Diego.

We chat as we run. He is running faster than I am. I feel my legs tiring and my breathing speeding up as I labor to keep up with him. He inquires where I am running from. I describe my route, leaving out the part about the border guards and he figures I've run about twenty-five miles.

Chapter 47: San Ysidro

Ever since I looked out the window of the El Cortez Hotel and saw that enigmatic pale-blue, volcano-shaped mountain to the southeast, I've been wanting to run to the top of it. I don't know where it is or what it is called, but it has been calling me for weeks now.

I blink at the bright light of day and wrinkle my nose against the smell of diesel fuel. My face is pressed against the jiggling, warm windowpane as I watch my pale-blue mountain to the east following us along behind the lines buildings and houses.

San Ysidro! This looks like the nearest point.

The bus stops and I jump down the stairs.

The mountain beckons alluringly. I squat down, re-tie my brown leather nurses' shoes and head off through the suburbs of Mex-America towards that delicate, ephemeral mountain. Colorfully dressed children, with clear olive skin and jet black, straight hair, look at me with huge, limpid, brown eyes, as I trot through their neighbor out along the streets to the desert. "What beautiful children!" I think, wanting to gather them in my arms and hug them.

I slip quietly from town to desert. The fragrance of the February flowers intoxicates me. Ceanothus, wild lilacs, and sage breathe in the noonday sun. Underfoot, the gravelly desert floor makes little scraping noises on each shoe. My body warms up, my pace picks up. Soon I am singing along, lulled by the cadence of my own body in motion.

Perfumed air, tiny flowers, purple legumes, fancy hanging ovaries are delicately fringed with yellow and pink lace. Female fertility! And the male, on the wing, finds her, embeds himself in her, making himself one with her, sacrificing himself to become the next generation. He loses himself, a tiny grain of pollen, impelled by some life-death wish, impaled in a tiny womb, the two forever entwined, joined in new life, becoming together a seed, which grows into a new plant with roots that suck up dirt and water and leaves that eat sunshine.

My eyes are fixed on the pale blue mountain in the east. What is that? I look to my right and see an area that looks as if it has been raked smooth. Why would anyone rake the desert? Perhaps it is something else, a road or a landing strip. After almost an hour of steady running in the vast expanse of high desert, in the fecundity of the spring bloom, under the wide blue sky and midday sun, the mountain looms larger and darker, brown now with deep purple-blue shadows in the valleys.

The day rolls on as the earth turns lazily over onto her belly. Under the sun, golden-brown, flecked with dirt, bits of green appear; living green plants that find every crevice of moisture and grow here, having perfect faith, knowing that the sun will find them in their hidden places and grace them with a touch of solar elixir, out of which they will weave themselves so delicately, here on the desolate shelves and ridges of this empty mountain unknown by busy city-dwellers.

I climb, straining against the heaviness of the earth, pulling her with each breath up the mountain. Inside, the tingle in arms and knees tells me I'm running low on oxygen. I breathe harder. The tingling subsides. The sun beats down making me squint my eyes. I know the hot blazing force of that sun, the blue sky, which contains it, the line of earth in my vision moving up and down with my stride and the dry desert gravel. Blood rushes into my lungs and out to my arms and legs in rhythmic pulses. Over all arcs the all-seeing blueness of the atmosphere. Bits of high altitude dust absorb the longer wavelengths and let only the short, energetic rays pass.

My body belongs to the earth from which it arises. I have no more idea how my heart beats or how my liver works than I do how the earth turns and the seasons follow one another. It is given to me. Life itself is given. Nor am I ever separate from that which gives it. I am the Oneness, of which the earth partakes, taking yet another form. The Oneness that spawns the earth is but taking another form in me.

Thank you for this! Thank you for this joy, for this aliveness, for this strength. Thank you for bringing me to these mountains.

On all fours now, smelling the close dust and the dank of the actual rock, I climb. This is not the granite I know from New England, but sandstone—soft, crumbling, holding within it the skeletons of tiny animals from ancestral seas, thrust up now into the sky, the same sea that we carry in our blood, the surging tide now as my heart pulses deeply, belonging not to me, but to this from which it came.

All of us are under the sun's eye now, in this silent rain of photons from this medium sized star, in a cozy corner of the galaxy. Its very quietness feels heavy. I pause and look back down the mountains and across the desert, which looks like a long beach extending to the sea. The wide flat plain full of blue haze stretches back towards the Pacific. The whole earth is a shimmering planet, basking in the immensity of its own blueness.

A Presence surrounds me now, and joy rises within me. Its love is present in the blueness above and in the hot sun. The earth is breaking into fragments of mountains as if billions of years are compressed into the present moment. Being, brimming with a sense of purpose and self-existence, is vibrant, as if the veil of everydayness is drawn aside revealing a world resplendent with divine significance. Why bother with all this? Why manifest in this way and not some other? Why does it exist at all?

I know that I, the small one climbing this mountain, am part of the larger Being who the mountain is and who the desert is, who the immensity of blue is, and who the heaviness of gravity is. I feel this wholeness. I feel this divine ecstasy implicit in the very act of being.

Shades of brown, rich with reds, purples and ochres, glistening quartz and soft mollusk shells glitter in the floors and walls of this primal palace. The quiet is immense and hot as this stray planet rolls over and over, ponderous in such profundity, such unimaginable beauty, in this strange, stray, desolate rock. An incandescent star burns in the vacuum of intergalactic space, one star among countless billions. One planet. Turning... majestically.

Such an immensity of longing for the Being of all creation fills me, such longing for the infinite love of the Divine Creatrix. Here now, at every place. This celebration of being, Her divine being is here. Her very being is the body of the earth. Her very being is the sun. Her mysterious being is the gravity itself, and the endless blueness of the sky. Her being is Being itself. The Divine Creator is the ground of the being we think we perceive, everywhere creating Itself into existence. It is impossible! Yet it is.

The only thing that ultimately exists is this divinely, miraculously, paradoxically Self-Creating Being and this Being is the self-creating-self-acting-self-existing wholeness.

I experiment thinking of the feminine aspect of the Divine. At first it feels strange and unnatural, but then, even as my image of the Divine is changing, so is my image of women. I begin to see her, not as the downtrodden captive that she became, but as the powerful creative force for good that she once was and can be again if she rediscovers her true nature.

Her mystery is absolute. She is here now. This is Her. I am looking into the face of the Divine... running across the body of the Divine, this hot, dry Earth, this gleaming, dark-shale mountain here. This is the Ultimate Creator. Here. I touch Her. Her mystery is absolute. How? Why? What is all this wonder? What is all this joy?

Who am I? A tiny fragile speck of living dust, an unlikely concoction of biochemical processes, tenuously balanced, rising against all odds, out of the universe, looking out, looking in, seeing the Divine in every perfect crystal of being.

Why did the Divine choose to manifest in this particular way, in rock, dust, planetary dryness, a universe of stars? These are but what I see. What is really here is the Divine Self-Creator. The Divine Self-Creator exists at every moment prior to and outside of my conceptions of time and space in this paradoxical act of being. This is who I really am, one tiny manifest of all this wonder.

The Divine Self-Creator manifests existence not as something separate. She is all that truly exists. She sees herself through the myriad eyes of her own creation. Why?

Because Her mode of Creating is through this Divinely Self-Creative act of Being. She is both transcendent to the existence we think we see, and She is that existence as it really is. She is both and neither male and female. This that we see and touch and taste and feel is the reality of Her being. My abilities to perceive and to conceive are Her. My perceptions and conceptions of object, space, time, and all the myriad forms that She takes are Her. But what really exists, behind all this that I think I see, is Her, the paradoxical, Divine Self-Creating Self-Existing, infinitely dear, infinitely loving.

This was what I was losing. This is why I returned. Not to a place, but to a state of mind. I had stopped seeing existence as Divine.

Why?

Because I was on the wrong path. I needed to be healed, to be saved. I needed to know once more that the All-Loving Creator is at hand, on all sides, all around and within us.... I needed to return to feeling and knowing that the All-Giving Creator loves each one of us unconditionally and with infinite forgiveness.

The top beckons, and I turn from my reverie, on hands and feet now because the way is so steep. I am the Divine as me, climbing the Divine as rock up-thrust by cataclysmic forces deep within the Divine as earth. I climb like some ancient quadruped snuffling along this old, old trail, this cooled crystalline, molten rock, millions of years old, and I only twenty-three, but my own body containing DNA from ancient life forms, this life being passed on from generation to generation like the fire that passes from torch to torch in a relay, for four billion years. I am as old as the Universe. And as young as today.

Once I was a single-celled organism swimming in a warm amniotic sea that covered the now dry rock sea floor. It was I who laid down my life, a thousand million years ago as one tiny mollusk encaptured here on this mountain slope. I was there then in a different form, but that form is still deep inside me in my own genetic memory.

I carry myself within, as fragments of evolutionary Deoxyribonucleic acid, through the evolution of each species as it developed new characteristics and abilities. I was here before there were muscles, hearts and livers, before there were eyes. I was here in the softly undulating delicately coordinated cilia. I was here in the very metabolic machinery of the living cell; the same metabolic machinery that now fuels my own cells and sends me galloping joyfully across the plain. I was here and so were you! How incredibly intelligent divine evolution is to build itself so miraculously, so chaotically, and yet so inexorably into such complexities of living forms. What intelligence creates the world so that it can evolve ever-new forms?

Finally, the top! Exultation bubbles up inside me. I feel as light as air. I am happy in some fundamental, primal way. *I am the sunshine. I am the wind. The earth is my being. I am the whole cosmos stretching out into infinitely and eternity.* I hurl my arms to the sky and throw my head back; turning a full circle I see the entire expanse of the horizon—blue above, brown below. Crinkled mountain ridges to the east and south, flat desert to the west, and very far away, the vast Pacific shimmering like molten gold that stretches across a quarter of the globe. I am alive here on this planet now.

It is quiet, so quiet I can touch the silence. Silence becomes a thing itself, and this Presence, this benign loving presence, always here, is around me now and within me. I am it. It is the planet earth. It is the sun; it is the infinite care with which everything is made.

I've come back. I've returned again. I find the Divine Self-Creating Miracle again here in the wild way I did in Nevada that night on the mountain. But then Moot was with me... my sweet dog....

I remember standing on that mountain in Nevada and understanding for the first time that all that exists is the Divine Self-Creator and that It is continuously creating Itself into Being.

I lie down on a huge, warm, flat stone and feel the earth beneath me. The earth takes away all my fatigue and leaving me calm. Here I am now on this rock at the top of a desert mountain, looking out at all the vast earth, a tiny speck floating in the endless, soft universe. I haven't a clue why it is all here. I think of the other side of the earth wrapped in night, turned away from the sun, facing down into the dark infinities of stars and galaxies, falling away to infinity below me, falling away to infinity above me. I feel the whole earth floating in the unknown immensity of creation and me pressed lovingly on it, my body on its body.

Standing up with a rush of dizziness, I turn slowly around again letting my eyes play across the entire horizon. I breathe in the air, which comes from far away places. I think of the wind encircling the globe and the solar wind blowing through the planets.

I stand for a long time gazing west towards the afternoon sun, letting thoughts run through my mind.

Suddenly it occurs to me that what I've been looking for is what I've already found. The fundamental substance that explains both mind and matter, the fundamental substance of physics, the smallest and the largest is the paradoxically, divinely Self-Creating-Self-Activity Itself. The fundamental substance of thought, perception, and this subjective innerness of self must also be the Paradoxically Divine Self-Creating Being. This would have to be true, if the Divine Self-Creating Miracle is all that really exists. It would have to be the basis for both mind and matter simultaneously. It would have to be both external and internal, in fact, since there is no outside to all that is, its entire being would have to be internal to itself.

Here is the monistic substance for which I've been searching. It was right in front of me the whole time. The monistic substance must be the Divine Self-Creating Being Itself, which is all that really exists and it must be prior to and inclusive of both what we call mind and what we call matter. It must be prior to the subject/object split, prior to the observer/observed split, prior to the object/action split, and prior to the noun/verb split. It is, after all, the unitary substance from which everything else derives and in which everything else has its ultimate being.

Can this be so? Can it be that the Self-Creating Divine Miracle is the fundamental activity and being of all that exists and that it exists prior to the mind/body split; it exists in a way we have not yet conceived?

This dynamism must be fundamental to the nature of existence. What exists is not the things that we think we see out there. These are just the constructs of our nervous systems. What exists out there and what exists subjectively is this self-creative-self-activity. How would this view affect my understanding of physics, philosophy and biology?

What we know immediately are our own thoughts and subjective experiences. We take on faith that something exists out there. If all that exists is the Divine creating itself into existence, then the kind of existence it has must include thinking, that is, it must include not only this self creative, self formative power, but also this subjectiveness, this inner subjectiveness of experience.

When I interact with something, I experience, subjectively, the changes that occur in me as a result of that interaction, but I attribute an external existence to the other thing with which I am interacting. In effect I have an inner, subjective view of the changes that occur in me and from those subjective changes I construct a percept or concept of the outside of the thing with which I'm interacting. The subjective and the objective are different points of view on the same interaction. But what if that with which I'm interacting also has a subjective experience of the changes that it has as a result of it interaction with me? It would in effect "see" the inside subjective activity of its own changes, which it would take to be the "outside" of me. Matter, then would be the concept of the outside of something other than myself, and Mind, or the Subjective would be the inside experience of my own changes… and this would be true for every interactant.

But does this mean that the cosmos is conscious, or that things like photons and trees are conscious?

That depends on what I mean by consciousness? If I mean the human experience of consciousness, then I'm talking about the inner experience of the human brain. But this is a very circumscribed anthropic view of a particular kind of subjective experience characteristic of the human brain. If this is what I mean by consciousness, then by definition no other system except for the human brain has it. But if I take a wider view of consciousness, meaning any sort of subjectivity of experience, then I use the word "conscious" to mean any sort of subjectivity of experience and this would include at least animals with nervous system, and what I am being led to conclude is that perhaps even molecules and photons have an innerness. Whatever definition I take, I need to be clear and consistent.

What is at issue is not the word I chose to define, but the quality of that inner subjectivity of experience or perspective.

This is nothing anticipated by physics or biology or even philosophy.

I'm not saying that there is no such thing as matter. I'm just saying that matter is not fundamental; matter is not the fundamental substance. Matter is our name for a certain level of organizational complexity as viewed by us. Matter is not fundamental and neither is mind.

Mind, as we experience it, is the inner workings of our own brains, as perceived by us, who are the inner workings of our own brain. That is to say, the brain's subjective experiences are, in fact, its own processes and activities as experienced subjectively from the inside of the system whose processes and activities they are.

I'm saying that there is only one fundamental substance and this substance is not a thing but is an activity, and this is the Divine-Self-Creating-Self-Activity creating itself into existence. This unitary substance has to be the reality behind both what we call matter and what we call mind. But how is that reality manifested?

Consciousness is a type of subjective experience. I need to find another term since the word consciousness is so ambiguous. Meanwhile, I'll call this inner subjectiveness of view 'subjective experience', which is simply that inner, self-identical self-reflexivity that exists prior to the subject/object split and I'll acknowledge that there may be as many types of subjective experience as there are types of systems capable of subjective experience.

Since I am aware of the subjective experiences of my own brain, or to be more accurate, I am that thinking, which identifies itself as me, and this is the only activity of which I am directly aware, I can never know if the outside world exists or not. I only know that I think it exists. But that, which I assume to exist out there, is only the projection of my perceptions and conceptions of my interactions with it. So in some sense all that I know is subjective experience. My concept of matter is just that, a concept that I project back onto the world and endow with some kind of external reality. Thus, this primal self-activity of nature includes the capability for certain kinds of subjective experience to emerge, wherein certain types of natural system experience their activities subjectively from the inside.

Clearly since we are systems that arise naturally in the universe, the universe is of such a nature that systems capable of experiencing subjectively, and indeed capable of having human consciousness, can evolve, because we have. If the fundamental substance of existence is the Divine-Self-Creating-Self-Experiencing-Self- Interacting-Self-Activity, then human consciousness or human subjective experience does not arise in a world that is purely extended matter.

How then would the complex subjective mode of experiencing that we call human consciousness evolve, occur or emerge?

If as I suppose all that really exists is the Divine Self-Creator creating Itself into existence, and this is the fundamental self-creating-self-activity, then it must be true that the smallest constituent part of existence would include this capacity for self-experiencing in some primal modality. This would include for example the photons of light.

This would mean that a photon of light would have, or be, in some sense this Divine Substance, or as I conceive it, Divine Self-Activity, which includes some sort of subjective innerness of view. It would not be conscious in the way we are but it would have, or be, a subjective innerness, in its fundamental nature.

Could this be true? This would mean that all self-creating natural systems would have insides as well as outsides, that is, they would have an inside perspective on their interactions with the rest of existence, and that inside perspective would be subjective, not a complex perception as we with our complex brains have, but never the less as a subjective insideness comprised of their own internal self-activities.

But wait a minute, just because the smallest self-activities contain the potential to interact to create more complex systems that are capable of self-experience, may not mean that the smallest self-activities themselves have that property, any more than atoms have the property of jumping just because the frog comprised of atoms has the capability of jumping.

241

Atoms must at least be of such a nature as to allow jumping to emerge as a property of more complex systems. What then must this imply about the nature of atoms? That they be capable of motion, of activity. Were the capacity for activity not fundamental, the world would be absolutely static and no system however complex could jump or move at all.

So can it be the same for subjective experience? There must be at least a universal principle that says that, for systems of certain degree of complexity, the ability to experience subjectively emerges. And yet I've just discovered that the fundamental substance must be this Divine Self-Activity, which contains within it the potential to evolve into complex systems that experience subjectively, that is, which must have, from its own point of view, some sort of self-reflexive innerness of perspective, from the beginning.

This is, as far as I know, an entirely new view of nature and of the natural world, with astounding implications for physics, biology and philosophy.

From the outside, I the observer see activities, and interactions. But my ability to see activities and interactions arises from the fact that whatever I am observing interacts with me in a way that changes me, or more indirectly, changes my measuring tools in a way that I can detect when I interact with my tools in a way that produces a change in my nervous activity that I can interpret. So the final interaction that provides me with the information about the system that I am observing occurs subjectively in my nervous system and brain.

I have seen that nature is comprised of nested systems, that is, systems of systems of systems, of systems made up of subsystems. Interaction defines form through defining the boundaries of interaction. Each participant in the interaction is its own inside, figuratively speaking, has its own perspective, on the interaction. So whole systems have insides that are defined by the very interactions through which the systems form themselves.

At each level of complexity of the compilations of nested systems, new properties arise. And yet these properties that emerge must be consistent with the nature of the whole of the Divine Self-Creating and with each of its parts. Since the Divine-Self-Creating-Self-Activity is fundamental, in order for subjective experience to arise in more complex systems, there must be a proto-subjective experience or a primal subjective innerness in the most fundamental of the constituent parts and this must be in some sense fundamental to being. This means that as systems evolve in complexity as viewed from the outside, the subjective experiences of which they are capable from the inside must also evolve. How is this possible?

There must be a universal law or principle that says, first, that simple systems are such that they can come together to form more complex systems and, second, that these systems have both outsides as viewed by something other than themselves and insides as viewed self-reflexively by themselves. This is to say that in every interaction there are two halves giving rise to two perspectives on the same interaction. Furthermore as the systems, seen from the outside, compile in complexity, their subjective inner experiences compile in modality and dimension. This entails that each level of systemic complexity acquire an "as-a-wholeness" in which the system functions dynamically as a *whole that is capable of interacting with other systems and with its environment as a whole. This whole system develops properties according to its own functioning as seen from the outside by something other than itself, and it also develops new dimensions of subjective experience as it experiences its own processes and activities from the inside subjectively as a whole.*

So these whole systems of nature in fact do have insides that are capable of self-experiencing, but this is not yet a sufficient condition to show that the compilation of these systems, as subsystems of more complex systems, explains how more complex systems become self-experiencing in new ways. In order for the next level of organizational complexity to develop a self-experience appropriate to it, there must be a general principle in nature that says that as systems compile in complexity and gain in functional capacities as viewed from the outside, these same systems must also be able to gain more complex self-experiencing capacities as they experience themselves from the inside. Moreover, this inner self-experiencing must be fundamental to the system.

In terms of the human nervous system this would mean that the neuron experiences subjectively in its way, the auditory cortex experiences subjectively in its way and the higher centers, or combined activities of many brain areas, experience in their own ways. At each level of organizational and functional complexity the system is experiencing itself from within itself in the manner appropriate to its level of organizational complexity and specific to its dynamical structure and activity and is experientially accessible from the inside only to that system as a whole.

What would this imply about the whole of existence? Would it too have, or be, some kind of subjective innerness, some kind of subjective viewpoint, something closer to what we would call thought than matter?

My head is spinning with this rush of thoughts, but I must stop here. The afternoon shadows are lengthening and I have a long way to run back.

Reluctantly I turn to leave. I leap down from boulder to boulder, cautious, knowing that if I slip and fall, no one is within miles. Who would ever think to come out here and look for me? Who knows when, or if, the next person will be this way? Months, perhaps. No one knows I am here. Who would I tell? Funny, I never feel alone.

Suddenly something inside of me says. "Stop! Don't move!" I stand, teetering on the edge, just about to jump down to a ledge some four or five feet below me. My rational mind is just about to override my irrational mind when, an alarm clock goes off with sudden violence, and the rattling, as of dead bones, screams out, shattering the hot silence.

I've never seen a rattlesnake before. Looking down at a coiled, gray-brown snake I see it poised to strike. Very coldly, and matter-of-factly I back up and make a wide circle around the place. Excuse me, snake. There is no shot of adrenalin, only perfect calm. I tiptoe away very softly, leaving the alarm clock ticking on the mountain shelf.

Thank you! Thank you, whatever it is, whatever it is that warned me. Thank you, you blind instinct. Thank you God, Divine Father, Divine Mother, who or whatever you are, the Universe, retinal motion detectors. Thank you, myself for listening to that part of me, that more primitive brain that somehow knew the snake was there. Only later does the shot of adrenalin course through me, constricting my blood vessels and making the tiny blonde hairs on my arms stand up and my hands tingle as I realize what could have happened.

Shadows deepen and lengthen in the afternoon sun. Fifteen miles back. I am hungry and thirsty. This must be a thirty-mile round trip jaunt. After about half an hour of trotting west, I see a tiny cloud of dust on the horizon. What is that? Some kind of small tornado? It gets bigger and bigger.

A jeep! There are no roads. What's a jeep doing out here? And after what seems a very long while, the noisy vehicle pulls up in front of me. Two men with rifles jump out and walk towards me. I smile wearily.

"Border Patrol," they announce gruffly. "We've been tracking you for fifteen miles... We never expected to find a girl out here. We thought we were tracking a wetback."

"What's a wetback?" I ask not knowing.

"An illegal alien from Mexico." They point to the raked area I had wondered about. "That's the Mexican border."

"Oh no," I say, "I ran out here to see the mountains."

"You ran fifteen miles?" they exclaim, shaken.

"Oh yes. I'm training for the Boston Marathon and I saw these beautiful mountains and I just wanted to climb up on top of them. I just wanted to see them, to touch them."

They look at each other and then look at me, confused and amused. They offer to drive me back. Eagerly, I clamber aboard into the back of the jeep, and we head west into the golden slanted rays of the late afternoon sun.

Chapter 48: The Jewel

Several days later, tired of running into borders, I board a bus and go north through Pacific Beach to La Jolla. In this magical place, flowers bloom all year 'round. "Cottage City!" I think to myself, an entire city of cottages. Every cottage is covered with cascades of flowers, bougainvillea, trumpet vines, honeysuckle, petunias, geraniums, birds of paradise, ferns and flowers I've never seen before. I am entirely enchanted with this wondrous place and decide to live here forever.

In downtown La Jolla I find Harry's Restaurant on Girard Street, a friendly place, which serves breakfast all day long.

"A blueberry two by four, and coffee with lots of cream," I tell the waitress. I feel as if I'm back on my westward trip in the VW with Moot. Moot. I miss Moot. I love that dog. I watch the cream swirl and think of the Usher's kitchen, filled with light and love, where I first drank coffee, where I first learned about the Boston Marathon, where John and I sat.

Wal is excited about my plans to run Boston and seems supportive. "I have to do some serious training here. Boston is only three months away!" I had told him urgently.

I stroll through La Jolla, digesting breakfast looking at the Spanish architecture. "Lovely," I think as I stroll past the Christian Science Reading Room, and glance at the Bible passage for the day, and on by the Valencia Hotel, perched, elegantly pink, above the palm-tree-lined park and the Pacific beyond. This reminds me of Hamilton in Bermuda that spring after I had dropped out of Antioch. Lenny, dead, it doesn't seem possible, killed in a car crash, Pop gone, Nana gone, Moot gone.... But somehow a new life is opening up before me, as if I too have died and been reborn in this distant exotic place three thousand miles from my parents.

The vast blue Pacific stretches off to China in the west and heaves itself rhythmically in and out of the Cove. I remember the frozen snow on the headlands in Rockport. How brutal is the winter Atlantic, steaming arctic fog and knife-edged frigid wind, which blasts unmercifully unchecked from the North Pole, tearing relentlessly at the solid granite with its salt foam teeth. I remember Mom-Christina and our fireplace fires together.

Pelicans! Archaeopteryx! The ancient birds fly like Pterodactyls, old, much older than us upstart humanoids. I watch their curved necks and large-pouched beaks extended horizontally. Their huge, beating, mottled brown wings pull in delicately at each stroke, fanning at the tip. They follow each other in ragged "V" shapes as they have been doing for a million years, dark, against the light sky.

The La Jolla Cave has been carved by the ocean, which washes the yielding sandstone cliffs. I look at the gift shop and pass by.

My legs itch to get running.... Mt. Soledad! That will be a good hill workout to start the day! I follow the winding road up past houses nestled in lush gardens, slowly, slowly; it pays to start slowly. I push against gravity; my legs feel tired and sluggish.

I will run to the top of this mountain!

I listen to my body. I don't push. I let it pull me, as I pick up the steady rhythm: breathe in two, three, four, breathe out two, three, four; I count each stride and feel my heart beat. I bring all four into synchrony: my heart, legs, arms and breath. I watch the gardens roll very slowing by, and the lovely homes, as I fall into a reverie.

If, as I had seen, the fundamental substance, the monistic substance, for which I've been seeking, to explain the emergence of both mind and matter at higher levels of organizational complexity is the Divine Self-Creating Being, and it is characterized by this self-active ability to self-create, to self-experience, and to self-act; and if, as I had seen, the self-active parts interact to form more and more complex systems, which then act as whole systems, and these self-active, self-creating whole systems have not only outsides, but also insides as defined by each and every interaction; if, furthermore, at each level of complexity these self-forming whole systems subjectively self-experience in ways appropriate to their own level of dynamic organizational self-activity, and self-interaction, then the questions remain: How does this unitary Divine Being divide itself into self active parts in the first place? What makes the interactions of those parts possible? And, how do the parts remain part of the unitary whole even while being parts?

What is this 'as a wholeness' that characterizes these sorts of systems that are capable of this sort of inner self-experiencing?

Natural systems create themselves through the interactions of their parts, but those parts do not exist as parts until they are created within the context of the whole system that is creating itself though the interactions of its parts. I'd seen this kind of circularity in the moss, and in all living systems. I'd seen this kind of self-creative interaction in the photon and in chemical reactions. And I'd seen this paradoxical self-creation in the Divine Self-Creator.

To build a frog, you don't take a frog's leg and a frog's arm and a frog's eye from the workbench and put them together the way a mechanic might assemble a bicycle. The frog's legs, arms, and eyes don't exist until the frog as a whole exists. The frog starts as a single cell and differentiates into more and more cells, which interact with each other to form tissues. Through these complex interactions the frog builds itself, by building all is parts and orchestrating their interactions. But paradoxically it doesn't exist to build itself until it builds itself. What is this self building-as-a-wholeness that characterizes so many natural systems?

The photon creates itself through the mutual self-creation of its parts. But its parts do not exist until the whole system comprised of the parts exists. Here is this same paradoxical quality in which the system does not exist to create itself until its parts come together to form it, but its parts do not exist to come together until the system as a whole exists. Moreover, its parts are not things at all, but are mutually self-creating self-activities.

Activities of what? Here again is that paradoxical self-reflexivity. The activity is a self-activity, that is, it is the activity of activity. Our language requires that a verb have a subject. What jumps? The frog jumps. There must be something, a noun, that jumps, that is active. But here in the case of the fundamental activity, the activity itself is the subject of its own action. Being is. The act of being is both the verb and the subject of its own action.

It strikes me for the millionth time how mysterious and wonderful is this existence. It exists in a way that we have not yet conceived. How marvelous are these atoms, which are designed, or rather, design themselves, to fit together so nicely to make molecules. But, if they design themselves, how is it that they have the capacity to design themselves? What designed them to be able to design themselves? What could have ever thought up such an amazing system?

It is the Divine Self-Creator, creating Itself in this incomprehensible way into this miraculous universe. There is nothing ordinary about it. Everything, from the tiny photon to the specks of dust on the road, to the far-flung galaxies is this wondrous Self-Creating Miracle, All-Present, All-powerful, All-loving, joined together as One, yet each one individual and interactive.

This binding together, this intrinsic oneness, is the most intimate of relationships, which is a love so vast and incomprehensible that we don't even see it.... until we pause and look.... and then we see it, we feel it inside ourselves, we sense it all around us, and it fills us with sublime joy, right in the midst of our everyday ordinary lives, which are extraordinary.

I am surrounded by and filled with a profound sense of joy, even as I run up this morning mountain, Mount Soledad.

I pause and look out over the vast blue Pacific Ocean and feel the fresh sea wind on my face and arms.

What about whole systems then?

The brain exhibits this natural 'as a wholeness' in which the system forms itself through the interactions of its parts that do not exist, as such, until the system as a whole acts to form them. The system is the activities and processes and interactions of the parts, but the parts do not know how to form the system. It is only through the interactions of parts that the system forms itself, and yet the parts cannot interact in the ways to form the system until the system exists.

This paradoxical ontology characterizes natural systems that act as a whole.

When I look at the brain, I see complex dynamic systems of interactions of living cells. I see dozens of types of neurons repeated over the over and over. I see the surrounding astroglia that nurture and support the neurons. I see a multiplicity of tissues. I see neurons making new synapses as the brain encounters new experiences. From the outside I would have no idea that this brain has an insideness of view, that is, that it is subjectively experiencing its own activities and processes, or more precisely, that at least some of its own activities and processes are to it, subjective experience.

From the outside the brain looks like any other type of self-formative living system. Neurons grow physical processes that join other neurons and form synapses. That growth is in response to chemical cellular signals and reflects some input that signifies, for example, something learned, and remembered by the system. From the outside it looks like a purely physical process. From the inside I experience a mathematical equation or a remembered tune.

The brain is a system that creates itself through the interactions of the multiplicity of its parts, and has miraculously evolved over the billions of years of life on earth. It exhibits the self-formative intelligence of nature. It is self-active, self-building, self-operating and it is an example of the Divine Self-Creator evolving itself, and becoming itself as this particular natural system. It is also a system that experiences subjectively, which we all know first hand, because each of us is that system experiencing its own processes and activities, and that system is, in its ultimate nature, the Divine Self-Creator becoming Itself in this particular form.

What is then this as-a-wholeness I see in all of nature that characterizes self-experiencing self-active systems of interacting parts, which themselves are whole and yet part?

How can I explain how parts come together on their own, without benefit of external mechanic, to form more complex systems? If I assume that the parts are fundamentally separate, like the parts of a machine, I am at a loss to explain how they come together to form systems.

The only way I can explain the emergence of complex systems is to understand that what is primary is this as-a-wholeness, this unitary divine being. The parts are never separate from the whole. The whole gives rise to the parts and the parts remain part of the whole, just as the billions of cells in the human body and brain remain part of the whole body and brain. In living organisms the parts derive from the unitary fertilized egg cell, so in the cosmos the parts must derive from the unitary Divine Self-Creative Substance, which is self-experiencing, self-creating, self-interacting and self-acting. Otherwise I am at a loss as to explain how the parts come together to form wholes or how these whole can self-experience.

That parts can come together and form larger more complex systems must be a general principle of the cosmos. And that these more complex systems can function as unitary wholes and acquire properties not possessed by the parts that comprise them must reflect this general principle. Each part, however small, contains, in its very act of being, the totality of the whole. In its essential being, every part is the Divine Self-Creator creating Itself as a whole, as all that exists. It is not that independent parts come together to form wholes. It is that the whole, the unitary, self-creative whole, is primary and the parts differentiate from it, and yet, retain their relationship with the unitary wholeness of the entire Divine Self-Creating Whole. And this wholeness includes not only the external aspects that an external observer infers, but also includes the subjective innerness that I've seen is fundamental to the Divine Self-Creating-Self-Activity.

So if, as I think, this as-a-wholeness is fundamental to the universe and to existence, then the idea that one can explain the origins of the universe by finding a smallest particle are entirely misled. All that is is a unitary wholeness, like a fertilized egg cell. This is primary. Just as the egg cell divides itself into parts and those parts into parts again, the fundamental Divine Self-Activity divides itself and divides itself again and again into parts, which then interact to build more complex systems, even while remaining part of the original whole. So in some very real sense I see physics as a biological *study. Rather than, as Dr. Payne suggested, we explain biology in terms of physics, I think it is the other way around, we need to explain physics in terms of biology or more precisely, in terms of paradoxically self-creating systems, in which the parts that comprise the system do not exist until the whole system exists, just as the photon does not exist until the electric and magnetic fluxes interact to create it, but the electric and magnetic fluxes do not exist until the photon exists. And, in the same way, the living system does not exist until the parts interact to form it, but the parts cannot interact to form it until the self-forming living system exists. There is this paradoxical circularity to nature. The Divine Self-Creator is creating Itself into existence as all that exist, but until it exists, how can it act to create Itself? This is the nature of nature, I believe.*

My legs are feeling the strain of the long climb. At last I'm at the top, where a large cross has been placed in memory of those who died in war. I turn and look back out over the vast Pacific and feel elated. This is how Balboa must have felt when he rounded the horn, and emerged into the Pacific Ocean.

I descend by a different route and find myself on La Jolla Shores Drive, which I follow along the coast by the Scripps Institute of Oceanography and up a steep hill.

Can a machine ever be designed to think and to experience subjectively?

If complex systems can develop the ability to have subjective experiences from the juxtapositioning parts, then one might think that eventually machines could be made complex enough to think, especially these new mainframe computers that take up an entire room filled with circuitry.

But wait a minute, there is something fundamentally different about a machinist building a machine and a natural system forming itself through its interactions. In contrast, to biological systems, which build themselves, a machine is designed and built by something other than itself. Whether it is a cash register or a computer, human beings manufacture the parts and then assemble those parts into the machine. There is no self-interacting, self-formative intelligence required by the machine at all. All the intelligence and activity is in the human beings. This is the mechanistic model that has carried over and been superimposed on the concept of the natural world that we have inherited in both science and religion.

So can a machine ever experience subjectively? Or is the most it can do mimic outwardly the responses that the subjectively experiencing human creator programs into it?

A machine lacks this paradoxical self-creating as-a-wholeness that characterizes the kinds of natural systems that I believe can subjectively experience their own activities and processes. The machine is not self-active, self-designing or self-creating, and so it is highly unlikely that it can ever be self-perceiving. But I don't rule out the possibility especially in terms of biological machines.

What I have discovered is that as the complexities of natural self-creating systems compile as viewed from the outside, the sophistication, modality and dimensionality of their systemic subjective experiences compile and evolve as viewed from the inside by the system whose activities and processes they are, and that the capacity of natural systems to self form systems that act as unities derives from their intrinsic participation in the unity of the cosmos as a whole.

Clearly this is a view not endorsed by, and in fact would be scoffed at, by the scientific community. At present I see no way to prove such an hypothesis, since there is no way of getting inside another system and experiencing it subjectively without being that system. Furthermore, the idea of a Self-Creating-Divine-Nature that acts as a unity is completely foreign to current scientific, religious or philosophical thought.

But if what I think is so it would open the question whether the whole cosmos is capable of experiencing itself subjectively in some way.

I need to learn more. I need to go back to school and to learn everything I can about biology, physics, matter and mind and philosophy... I have been a solitary thinker and now I want to know what other people have thought about these matters.

I've wound my way to the top of the second hill. My thoughts are interrupted by the loud growl of an earth moving machine backing up towards me. I look up at its yellow hub, huge caterpillar wheels, and gigantic shovel and jump back out of the way.

What's this? I look around and ask one of the workers. It's the campus of the new University of California, which is just being built on the top of this hill, up above Scripps Institute of Oceanography. New buildings are going up among mounds of dirt, and huge earthmovers.

As I look around in amazement at all this activity, I'm filled with the powerful sense that this is where I belong. I know this as certainly as I know I am supposed to run the Boston Marathon. This is where I'm supposed to go to college.

Disheveled as I am by the long run, I poke around until I find an intact building, which says, "Admissions," on the door. In I go. The receptionist asks if she can help me. ... I wonder what kind of help she has in mind.

"How do I apply?" I burst out, knowing nothing but that I am meant to be here.

She explains that I need to take two courses and to get a "B" or better. That plus my transcript from the Tufts School of Special Studies and Museum School will get me in provided my grade point average is a 3.6 or better. I can sign up for Extension courses, which have already started. She hands me the necessary application forms. A biology course in California Native Flora and a creative Writing course with Ronald Kaiser will do the trick.

Revelle College, she informs me is the first of twelve planned colleges to be built on this campus. Revelle specializes in science, but, she adds, the philosophy curriculum has been integrated into the science program so that they can cross-pollinate each other.

"Wonderful!" I exclaim. "Brilliant!"

My heart is singing! This is exactly what I want!

Chapter 49: Paula

By the time I arrive, Paula is already at the barn saddling up her black gelding. I jump out of the jeep, which Paula has kindly loaned to Wal and me, until we buy a car of our own. I'm dressed in my running gear: a black tank top bathing suit, shorts and my nurses' shoes. "I'll ride with you after I run the marathon," I explain. "If I were to ride now, my leg muscles would be all out of kilter for the race." Paula smiles at me. She mounts and we take off together. I run next to her horse and feel the power and warmth of this huge gentle beast running next to me. The clip clop clip clop of the sound of the iron-clad hooves of her horse blend with the light tap, tap, tap sounds of my own feet on trail.

The day is warming. Mist rises from the low-lying coastal lagoons and swampy, green fields that are luxuriant with sweet, new spring grass. The scent of horses, mud, moisture, and newly-made oxygen molecules tickle the inside of my nose. The cool ocean breeze flaps our shirts and blows the horse's mane and tail sideways, lifting the long fine hairs like a lady's long tresses.

Through the languid eucalyptus groves we walk, listening to the melodious sound of birds that flit from branch to branch in the long trailing veils of the harlequin-brown, gray and white eucalyptus trees.

"What's that beautiful song?" I ask.

"The mocking bird?" Paula answers.

"Yes... But there's another that sort of rises up high folds up and in on itself like tumbling water, hear it?"

"Yes, the house finch, often erroneously called the red start out here for some reason.

"I love the sounds of birds, don't you?"

'Yes, I do," Paula agrees. "Being in nature heals, doesn't it?"

"Yes," I agree.

"I love this place. It is like the Garden of Eden. Look, an orange grove, and over there, an avocado orchard! When Hank and I first discovered the Ranch it was just a dusty, horsy place filled up with little ranches. Most everyone had a horse or two in their backyard. Many of the streets weren't even paved. You could ride for miles. It was wide-open space.

"Then I saw the Kid and fell in love with him. He'd just broken the record at three quarters of a mile and I bought him. This was the perfect place to raise thoroughbreds.

"After Hank left, I hired Gabor to manage the place. He'd managed racing stables in Hungary before the War. I had four kids, one still in high school and two off at college but home for vacations and one married, so the Ranch was perfect," Paula shares with me.

"I've always dreamed of a horse ranch. When I was a kid, I'd play horse ranch with my girl friends," I confide.... "But you've made it a reality!"

"Being heir to one of the largest beer fortunes helped," she laughs. "I've always felt guilty because I never drank."

"Me neither... true confessions. Beer tastes like fermented hay and liquor makes me sick. I tried it once and it was awful... like poison. Never tried it again," I agree.

The sweet scent of orange blossoms wafts on the gentle air that caresses us as we perambulate under the warming sun, with spring gloriously unfolding all around us. "Same with smoking," I continue. "I tried it once. It was a poison and made me sick. Never did it again. And drugs, I would never even think about. Who would do that to their body let alone their brain? What a waste!"

"Yes, so true," Paula nods in agreement. "Why would anyone deliberately hurt themselves like that? I do everything I can to stay healthy and well."

"Me too," I agree.

After a pause I continue, "Several generations ago, back in the mid-1800's my mother's family made a fortune in the mid-western grain milling business. My mother grew up in a big mansion in Cleveland Ohio. The male side of the family has done very well, but the female side hasn't renewed the fortune very well, I'm afraid. For some reason, I've never been able to get very interested in money... and neither has my mother. I think she always felt guilty about having so much, when so many people had so little."

We amble, finding our way along the narrow dirt trail, which descends to the golf course, where it flattens out and widens. Eager to run, I look up at Paula. She signals her horse and we take off at a crisp trot. She posts up down up down English style. Blood races through my veins making my arms and legs tingle with energy as I keep pace with the horse. We feel the wind on our faces and a rising sense of the joy that freedom brings.

On the other side of the rolling golf course the trail rises abruptly and leads out to a stunning view to the east across miles of rolling green hills to the mountains of Del Dios. Something in these mountains speaks to me with a thrill of recognition. With Paula on her horse and me on foot, we race out across the field. I'm struggling to keep up and am breathing hard. Blue sky over us, and miles of untouched land enfold us in delight.

"How wonderful to have someone to share this with... someone who appreciates it as much as I do!" Paula exclaims.

"I was just thinking the same thing," I reply breathlessly as we come to a grateful stop at the top of the far hill and look around us at the oceans of space stretching away into purple mountain ranges, one behind the other, fading into pale blue on the horizon. I remember the mountains of Nevada and how Moot and I ran to the top of them that one spectacular day and night.

"You must stay for dinner," Paula insists as I follow her into the barn after the ride. "We'll let Carlos and Pablo finish up here," she says, as we pat her horse and feed him sweet bits of carrot and apple.

With a final farewell pat, we turn and walk together up the well-worn path to the white house on the hill, noting how the golden light of afternoon lights up the yellow acacia bushes along the far pasture fence and makes the brilliant red bougainvillea, which cascades over the front porch of the house, glow. The sharp scream of a male peacock greets us as we turn the corner and see the cock strutting. His feathers fan out in an iridescent crest while the indifferent brown hens ignore him, pecking for hidden particles of grains among the flowerbeds and between the uneven stepping-stones.

Opening the back door, we're greeted with the strong odor of pinesol. Maria has scrubbed down the back hall floor and it is still wet. We tip toe across it to one side and open the inner door to a flurry of dogs barking, Australian Shepherds—gray, brown and white.

After showering in the guest room bath, I find my way down stairs to the living room where a glossy black grand piano sits closed, looking lonesome and unused. Gingerly, I sit on the bench, lift the cover and timidly play a few scales listening to its woody reverberation. It's in tune. Softly I begin to play the Moonlight Sonata. Suddenly, unexpectedly, the clear memory of my dad intrudes, out of place in this new environment. A recollection of our family at twenty-seven Sargent Road washes over me with a knot of homesickness, even in the midst of this elegant setting. I've finally left home and found a life of my own... not the one I expected but much, much better than anything I could have planned, as if the Universe simply opened it up to me, once I made the decision to live my own life.

I play on, lost in the primal sounds of the moonlit swamp, where the first life is gestating in the womb of warm, wet darkness. When I finish and come back to present reality, Paula is standing in the doorway quietly listening. I turn and there are tears in her eyes. I know she is thinking about her dead daughter again and that somehow I'm filling an empty place in her life.

As it turns out Paula is twenty-two years older than me and she had her first child, a son, at age twenty, not with Hank, but with her first husband. She's had three husbands in all. The break with Hank had devastated her and she'd spent several months recovering in La Paz, where she has a place... her retreat. I must come with her some day and see it, she says.

Dinner in the formal dining room with just the two of us at first seems too stiff, too elegant, but with a fire crackling in the rounded, adobe oven, four dogs lying on the carpet and candles on the table, with the patio door ajar so we hear the night sounds of crickets and frogs and the occasional squeal of horses in the paddocks below, the large, carpeted room becomes warm and homey.

"Someday, I'd like to build an adobe house," I say, "I want to sculpture the whole thing myself by hand." I lift up my hands. "I'll make an interior courtyard, and patios, and porches, bougainvillea, and plants everywhere... and a fountain...."

She smiles, "That's something they don't have in New England, adobe houses."

"Yes, they'd melt away with all the rain and snow," I laugh, thinking of New England under a blanket of crystal white snow, pristine, cracking cold, with long dark nights, juxtaposed against this balmy, sweet evening.

I take a forkful of mashed potato and savor the salty herbs, sweet texture and comforting sensation in my mouth as I let it slide down my throat.

We talk on into the night about our lives, our loves, our thoughts and our spirituality.

"You must tell me more about your journey," Paula exclaims.

Our thoughts are interrupted by Maria, who brings the dessert and the after-dinner coffee.

"Come, let's move closer to the fire," Paula exclaims motioning with her arm.

Maria wheels the dessert tray over to the couch by the fire and pours out two cups of coffee into delicate demitasse china. The aroma of the coffee, the chocolate pie, the cracking fire blend into a bouquet of contentment as we each flip off our shoes and nestle into opposite ends of the couch.

"What did you find on the mountain?" Paula asks, curling her feet up under her.

"It was the most extraordinary, almost nonsensical thing that came to me."

"What?"

"Well the first thing that came to me was in the mountains in Wyoming. I was seeking a whole, unitary concept that was neither matter nor spirit, but embraced them both.... A monism, to replace the dualism. I felt that this idea of a material world and a separate immaterial deity that creates and may or may not inhabit the world, depending on whether you are a deist or an atheist, was somehow damaging."

"So what did you discover?"

"I realized that what really exists, beyond our conceptions and perceptions of it, is in fact the Divine Creator. That is all that exists and it is physically present all the time. It is all that exists and it exists in a way that we haven't yet conceived that is beyond matter, beyond spirit and beyond mind, but embraces all three... but there's more."

"What more?" Paula encourages me.

"I'm almost embarrassed to say it."

Paula smiles so warmly, I lower my defenses and begin hesitantly. "I'd been wondering: If there is a God who creates the Universe, what creates God. I'd already realized that what I was feeling and following wasn't a separate supernatural deity, but was somehow the whole of everything. But this made no sense. I wondered: If the Creator creates, or created, everything, how did the Creator get here?"

"Yes," Paula urges.

"Suddenly, on a mountaintop in Nevada, it hit me in a flash that if there is a Creator of All that exists it must create Itself, because there is nothing else to create It. And, this Self-Creating Being must be in fact all that truly exists. It's not a separate supernatural deity and it's not the universe we think we see. It's a sacred mystery beyond anything I had yet imagined... and yet at the same time... I knew that this too was only a model of it... a new model... perhaps... but still a model. What exists directly and immediately is something that on the one hand we can never know and on the other hand is all that we know."

Paula sits in silence for a long time. She is the second person with whom I've ever shared this. John, the first person, had not been very receptive. I feel a bit nervous and hope I haven't offended her with my wild thoughts.

"We all seem to be connected to this larger sense, but some are more aware of it than others. You seem to be very aware of it," Paula observes.

We sit silently taking small pieces of chocolate pie on our forks. The sweet, rounded, mellow sensation of chocolate melting in my mouth sends messages of pleasure through my body, relaxing me and filling me with a sense of well-being. Paula and I glance up and our eyes meet. I feel that I want to share with her the secret source of joy and wonder that I've found.

"When you come into the present moment, you realize that everything exists," I continue shyly, "Then you ask: 'How does all this come to be?' And then you realize that all that exists is creating itself into existence in this completely paradoxical way right before your eyes. It is even creating itself as your eyes that see. Then you think, 'This is impossible.'"

I pause and gaze deeply into the orange crackling fire, listening to the sound that the small wind in the fire makes, the sound of the air moving rapidly as the heat of the fire pulls cool air into it and rushes sparkling up the chimney. I hope I'm not making a mistake sharing this that I've never shared before, with my new-found friend, a woman who is rapidly becoming something between a soul-sister and a spirit-mother to me.

I push on slowly, "And you realize that your brain that thinks, is also it. Then you say, 'Well how can it create itself until it exists?' And then you say, 'How can it exist until it creates itself?' You realize that this is impossible because it can't create itself until it exists, but it can't exist until it creates itself.

"Suddenly you are beyond what it is possible to think and you feel a shift inside... a spurt of happiness.

I pause again, looking sidelong at Paula to see what her reaction is. I'm so used to people thinking I'm nuts with all my far out ideas and discoveries. She is smiling softly and gazing into the fire. For a moment I'm reminded of Nana. I continue carefully, "It's a direct spiritual experience in which you feel the Divine Self-Creating Mystery immediately present as everything around you and as you too and as everyone else too. You feel it actively creating itself into existence everywhere at all times, even creating what we conceive as space and time as it creates itself. You don't explain away the mystery. You experience it directly and it fills you with a sense of awe and love… and peace… at least it does me."

Another long peaceful pause fills the room that is growing warm with the steady, bright heat of the fire.

"I sense that, too," Paula says. "I've never thought of it in those terms, but I feel it very much… especially when I'm with horses… a kind of all-embracing love that is everywhere."

"Yes, that is it. It's wonderful isn't it, just to feel it. To know it without having to give it a name or have some kind of doctrine around it. Just to let it be."

"Yes," Paula agrees. "That's what makes life worth living."

"Yes," I agree. "That's why we are alive, to feel the mystery and to let it guide us and join us with all that is… It is all that is."

We fall silent and gaze at the fire. The feeling of Divine Presence fills the room to bursting with its love.

"What do you think happens when we die?" Paula's question interrupts my thoughts.

I know she's thinking about her daughter again. I pause for a moment, then begin slowly. "I think that the death we think we see is just our materialistic sense of things. But that sense is incomplete. We are seeing only our interpretations of our interactions with what is there, which we can never know.

"We don't begin to understand this existence, what it is, how it got here, or the nature of the Divine Self-Creating Existence. All we have is our human models of it… even this one. We know that the nature of this existence cannot be purely material, because of the subjectivity of experience, something that could not arise in a purely extended materialistic world."

"Yes…?"

"If what I am thinking is right, then who we really are is not just this small form we think we are, but we are the Divine Self-Creating Existence becoming Itself as us. So when we die, we are still what we were all along, the Divine Self-Creating Existence, creating Itself into existence."

"So," Paula adds, "Perhaps something persists that is uniquely us, just as we go through all the transformations in life from infancy to old age and yet we have the same identity, the same self… so it is very likely that this same self persists in another form after the material body drops away."

"Yes," I agree. Suddenly, I remember Athena. I had not understood what she meant when she had said that she was not afraid of death because it was only a change of form, not a non-existence. But now I am seeing that perhaps she was right. "Existence is itself the Divine, and so is infinitely miraculous, mysterious, and holy. We are all forms of this fundamental divinity, all forms of this basic divine existence, which is continuously creating itself into existence, and this mysterious divine self-creative activity is prior to mind and matter. This never ends, so we, who are It, never end either. We may change form but we do not end."

Paula reaches over and takes my hand in hers, "I'm so glad I found you."

"Me too," I say.

Chapter 50: The Application

The next day after my run, after my piano lessons, after my creative writing course with Ronald Kaiser, I sit in my living room and write a letter to the Boston Athletic Association asking for an application form to run the Boston Marathon. The letter goes something like this:

"Dear Sirs,
Would you be so kind as to send an application form and information to me?
Thank you very much.
Sincerely,

I sign my name, my new married name, which still seems unreal to me.

I address the envelop, seal it up and place in on the shelf by the front door, so I can mail it on my way out tomorrow.

Tonight I am happy. Will is coming home!

I have bought him a present... a pink camper truck. The vehicle is composed of a plywood hut built in the back of a pick up truck, painted bright pink. Its name, "Baja Bomb," is etched across the front part that sits up over the hood of the cab with ventilator windows opened. It's a sturdy truck with big tires and an eight-cylinder engine. It cost fifty dollars, more than a month's rent. I hope Will will like it. We can go camping in the mountains, in the Cuyamacas up behind San Diego, to the east. We can go see the desert bloom in March... the Anza Borrego. Maybe sometime we can even drive up to the Sierra's and walk where John Muir walked.

I'm so excited to see Will again. It's been a month since he's been home. I want to show him all the sculpture I've been doing and the paintings of Paula's ranch... the newborn foals, Crazy Kid running and the wild flowers I'm sketching for my native botany course, which are laid out over the dinning table for him to admire.

When he arrives I am out. I'm at my music lesson. The instructor reminds me of Miss Parkhurst, my music teacher in sixth grade, a fragile thin elderly lady, with tiny nimble hands, who played Chopin with unexpected passion and strength. What is it about the piano, the flat white keys interspersed with black narrow key, the touch of ivory and ebony, the sound of the soft padded hammers inside hitting the strings that makes my insides reverberate with its magical sounds? I touch the keyboard and music fills the room.

Somehow the billions of neurons in my brain have learned which fingers to move to get which sounds.

By the time I get home, Will has gone out with Sam somewhere, probably the Watering Hole. I see his navy coat thrown across the armchair and his navy bags half opened with clothes hanging out as if he'd rummaged for something to wear.

My heart leaps up eagerly. Oh good he's home at last! I see where he's pushed aside my drawings to make room for some piece of equipment he's put on the dining table.

Quickly I shower and change and get out all the good things I've bought to make for supper, hamburger to make a meat loaf. But... no Will. No phone call. No nothing. Seven o'clock. I am eating cold meatloaf at the dining table alone, reading *Anna Karenina* for my writing class. Mr. Kaiser had said, "If you want to learn how to write, read Tolstoy."

After a half hour I pick up *Memories, Dreams and Reflections,* and continue to read Jung.

Setting the plates aside, I read in my biology book for a while. I identify native wild flowers and sketch some that I've picked and put in a vase on the table. I label them with their Latin names. Eagerly I sketch the Brown-Eyed Evening Primrose, with its four light-yellow petals surrounding its extended pistols and stamens and the Camissonia claviformis ssp.peirsonii, Bigelow's Monkeyflower. Oh dear, it's all wilted. I'll have to get another one, maybe this week I'll run out to Black Mountain and pick up some creosote bush and sage and wild lilac... and get in a twenty-mile workout.

It's late; I'm getting so sleepy my eyes feel filled with grainy sand and my brain is slowing down. Discouraged, waiting for Will, I fall into bed into a deep sleep.

The next morning I wake up and no Will beside me in bed. Where could he be?

I open the door into the living room and there he is asleep on the couch. My heart leaps up. Will! I'm in love with him all over again.

"Hey want to go for a run?"

He looks at my paintings especially the one of the mare with a foal inside her with no comment.

We drive the swaying, pink Baja Bomb out to the mountains. Slowly it moves up hill. It feels strange being with him like this, linked together in a prearranged relationship defined as he the husband with his roles and obligations and me the wife with mine. It doesn't feel as free as when we were in the attic of the Physics building.

He's still a strong runner. "It's amazing how you stay in shape," I say in admiration as we take a hard run in the mountains. "I train and train, and even without training you can still keep up with me."

"I get a lot of exercise on ship."

I think again of the ship, his ship, the tight quarters, the guys in the radio room, nice guys, fun-loving, good-natured, kidding each other, all-American boys, peaceful and easy going doing their job.

"You sure have a nice bunch of guys on board," I comment.

"Yeah," he says, "If we don't all get blown to kingdom come."

"Are you going where it is dangerous?" I say alarmed.

"I can't say where we are going or where we've been."

"OK," I say. "Just be careful," I look at him feeling so much love brimming up inside me. I reach for his hand, but he moves it away and I feel hurt and withdraw inside me.

That night he sleeps in the bedroom for the first time. For a while he lies next to me, but nothing happens and I feel confused. He rolls back to the other side and we lie there in the dark until I hear him breathing heavily and know he's fallen asleep.

The next morning our talk is casual and sporadic.

"How long are you here for?" I ask.

"A few days."

"A few days? Oh no... That's all?"

"Yeah, sorry."

A few days later I wake up and his clothes and bag is gone and so it he. I don't know where he's gone or for how long. Suddenly I feel a rush of loneliness. I remember how it was when John went back to Yale.

Chapter 51: The Reply

Each morning in the days that follow, I dash expectantly to my mailbox and rifle through the mail looking for the Boston Athletic Association envelope. Ronald Kaiser has assigned us more Tolstoy to read and given us some writing to do. With Wal gone, I've pulled my sculptures and paintings out of the closet and am working happily on a painting of the flowers that grow in profusion around our little cottage. The sun fills the yard with dappled colors. I am happy in my new life.

Ah what's this! I reach into the mailbox and here is a letter from the Boston Athletic Association! Eagerly I rip it open and pull out the epochal epistle.

"Dear Mrs. Burgay," I read... Mrs. Burgay. How strange that sounds, this eponym, as if I'm now someone else. Who is this stranger I've become with the same name as Will's mother, Mrs. Burgay, the middle class housewife, desperately trying to maintain an identity of my own through my art work, which now has to be surreptitious... me the apostate romantic... he the neglectful, nugatory nuptial. The letter reads something like this:

Dear Mrs. Burgay,

We have received your request for an application for the Boston Marathon and regret that we will not be able to send you an application.

Women are not physiologically able to run twenty-six miles and we would not want to take on the medical liability. Furthermore the Boston Marathon is a men's division event. The rules of International Sports and the Amateur Athletic Union, do not allow women to run races more than the sanctioned one and a half miles.

Sorry we could not be of more help.

Sincerely,

Will Cloney

A dark prickly sensation rises inside me.

What?!

I read the letter again. Women are not allowed to run! This is an outrage! It's supposed to be open to any person in the world. That's what they said. Any Person. Women, evidently, are not persons!

A thick dark weight presses down on me.

Women are not able to run twenty-six miles! I feel a blinding fury rising inside me. I crumple the letter in my fist. What are they talking about? I feel my sense of reality stretch and warp. I can run forty miles at a stretch! Do they really believe this? Is this what everyone believes?

Yes, this is reality to them, not only to them but also to everyone else in the world evidently. Women are thought incapable of running more than a mile and a half. Not allowed by whom? The international rules of sport, the Amateur Athletic Union... whatever that is.

I am not allowed to run a marathon because I'm a woman!

I feel a blinding fury rising within me, an outrage at injustice in the core of my being.

"AAAAAARRRRGGGGGS!" I let out a scream of frustration and outrage, I hurl the crumpled letter across the room. I tug on my nurses' shoes and slip into my black bathing suit, shorts and shirt. I slam out of the house, reminding myself of how many times I'd slammed out of twenty-seven Sargent Road, outraged at some injustice.

I run blindly at first. After a half dozen miles I realize I am headed for Del Mar. On and on I run zigging and zagging through streets past Mission Bay up through Pacific Beach and La Jolla. I push up the big hill by Scripps Institute of Oceanography, and run out along the cliffs, by the dusty riding ring next to the new Salk Institute, across the soft, moist, grassy turf of the Torrey Pines Golf Club, to Torrey Pines Park, where I flop down under a gnarled Torrey Pine tree to rest on the carpet of fragrant tan pine needles.

It's now afternoon. I don't know how many hours I've been running.

I am stunned, flabbergasted, shocked, dismayed, disappointed, outraged, upset beyond all bounds. My hopes are dashed, my dream destroyed. This is wrong! Every fiber in my being cries out. This is wrong!

A door is slammed in my face, shut tight, and locked just like every other door. I can't be a doctor or a lawyer or a statesman or a president or.... or even have an equal partnership in marriage. Everywhere all the rules and customs conspire to the same end... the subjugation of women.

Why? Why are women condemned to a life of servitude, stunted, like bonsaied houseplants, kept forever from developing our bodies or minds as people, as unique individuals? Only to be used in the service of men, like the slaves of old, captured in battle by men and dragged off to serve them as slave wives, never having full rights, never having a chance to be anything else?

This entire edifice of prejudice and custom is based on a lie... the lie that women are not able to do these things. Well how are you supposed to prove you can do something if you are never allowed to do it? How can you even know you can do it if you are never allowed to try? The entire thing is insane! Anger boils in my blood. This has to stop. I can't live in a world like this. It has to change. I can't live in the world the way it is.

Looking up into the whorling branches of the immense coniferous plant towering over me, I feel the benign radiance of the sun shimmering down, dappling the land with golden pools of numinous love. I want to go away somewhere and live in the deep forest away from the world of man, close to the divine, somewhere where I can bask in the glorious creative power of this beautiful world whose nature is pure love.

I run down the steep, brush-covered slope to the beach, where foaming white breakers curl and crash, smashing themselves on the flat sand as they have for the last four billion years. How brief is one human life span. How tiny in all the eternity of space and time. What does it matter really?

I plunge into the crashing surf and feel its strong heavy pull on my body as it tears my arms and legs in every direction. I dive low under each huge breaker into the sand-filled, churning water.

Ah, I am healed, cleansed by this baptism in the holy waters of the earth! I fling myself into the hot, loose sand feeling its warmth penetrate my body.

I lie still now with my head on the sand. The beach is now my entire world. I feel the breakers pound the beach, which is my body. I smell the damp sand and watch a stream cut a channel out across the beach, which is the body of the earth.

I watch the stream become flat and quiet.

This must be what death is like.

It's just this simple, this individual stream, alive, cascading down the mountain, now having run its cycle, from raindrops pelting on the earth, channeling into its own form, raindrops condensing from vapor breathed up by the sea, now finds its way home to its source.

Gratefully with a small rippling quiver, seeking its own source again, willing its own death, which it does not see as death but as reunion with itself. Its individuality disappears even as its true nature becomes manifest. It thought it was a stream, but it was the sea all the time. It is the entire cycle of birth, life and death. Even as it churns and toils, gurgles, delights, sparkles, ripples and tosses, exalting in its own being, as a stream, it is the sea.

Still this death is no death but is new life, the small self reuniting with the larger self, which it was all along, perhaps to emerge as a stream again, somewhere else at some other time, perhaps to reach into the sea canyon depths, its molecules scattered.

There is no death in You. Different molecules tumble down the same slope and follow the same channel that it has cut through rock and earth to make itself. Living on in what it left of itself for other molecules to follow, as it had followed in courses left by earlier molecules. It is in the flow that form evolves, in the flow against the bank the sculpture has carved itself, just as the wind and water have carved these towering golden cliffs that border the western edge of America, the western edge of the North American continent, washed by the majestic Pacific Ocean, each small stream tumbling from its finite form into its infinite Self, each small life yearning for the larger Life of which it is forever part.

I lie still like this until I fall asleep in the warm sand.

I'm awakened by the sounds of children laughing. Opening my eyes I'm surprised to find myself in absolute darkness. Where am I?

It is night. Human bodies move in the dancing firelight, which casts long shadows on the sand. I watch the sparkling, bright orange firelight gyrate its wild dance, rising defiantly against the vast, warm, velvety darkness of a Pacific night. "Stay out of the water," a mother yells. Children run shouting joyfully in the sand.

I sit up. Where are my shoes? I rummage in the dark patting the now cool sand with the palms of my hands until I feel one familiar, stiff, worn leather shoe and then the other, the laces broken and retied, my faithful Red-Cross nurses' shoes.

Brushing off the sand and shaking my head to get the sand out of my hair, smoothing my rumpled clothes and hair with my hands, shoes dangling from one hand, I stroll off barefoot down the dark beach wondering hungrily what to eat and where to sleep. I'm running away from home... or maybe I'm once again trying to find a home. And it is nighttime.

I wander on the Del Mar beach, feeling the way I did as a child when I ran away from home—disoriented, unreal.

Clusters of people are making campfires and cooking supper on grills. It is picnic night, family night. Why can't I have a normal family? I feel like an outcast, an outsider wandering with nowhere to go. I look up into the dark of night, soft and comforting, out over the vast earth-sea, which has gestated life in the warm amniotic fluid of its being.

Suddenly a curious thought strikes: the timeless, eternal, infinite Divine Mystery of existence must be terribly lonely, pouring out infinite love, creating, by Her divine act of Being, all this splendor, with no one to love Her back. No one even notices her or cares about the stupendous job She's doing.

People talk with me and I am surprised at how cheerful and light I sound, just as if I am one of the happy picnickers. We chat about trivia; the sound of the human voice is comforting. Someone offers me a hot-dog on a bun. Californians are so friendly and open. I love them. Funny how a little warm food and conversation can mellow me out. I guess I'm a Californian now too. If I'd come from another country, I'd say Americans are the most friendly and generous people in the world.

As I eat and talk and listen, I look at the kind faces of these lovely people. I don't feel lost anymore. I feel at home everywhere, part of the human family, part of these people here. The beach is filled with a benign sense of divine love.

"Look at the phosphorescence!" one lithe, young girl cries excitedly. The waves are lighting up like neon tubes as they curl and crash, bright with the bioluminescence of microscopic creatures, which glow in the dark the way my Mickey Mouse and Donald Duck pictures did when my father held them up to the light in my room at night, before he tucked me in. I must have been six then, centuries ago. I remember our sailboat, the East Wind, and the way Paul and I used to pull the pail up and down at night under water and watch the trail of phosphorescence.

After several hours of talking with my new friends, I stroll off into the night looking for a place to sleep. I smooth the sand, clear away the crisp dried seaweed, and dig a little hollow for my hips and shoulders. I lie down on the beach, pressing my body into, the cool, comforting sand. I listen to the lullaby of the eternally crashing breakers. Suddenly I don't want to go back to Boston. I don't want to run the marathon at all. I just want to be here, feeling this infinite peace, and the power of this love, the love out of which all this wonder comes. I just want to lie here and rest in Nana's lap, on her beach, the beach where we played when I was young.

It's cold at night with only a shirt and shorts in the rising mist from the sea. I scoop the sand around me to make a buffer from the wind. I know it never freezes here, so I'll be OK.

I drift off to sleep.

The first light of dawn wakes me. I'm here on the fog-enshrouded, gray beach with its endless wash of waves. The sun rises quickly sending its halo of rays across the face of the earth. Flowers, sensing its new presence, unfurl and open themselves to its living light. The fog rises in thin white wisps. The beach smells sweet and moist, dripping with the half finished dreams of night.

The waves wash in. I follow the line of breaking surf with my eyes. A few surfers try their skill, walking on water, longhaired like Jesus. I watch the waves curl, crest and break in sensuous lines of white foam. I pick a wave way out there, out where it is still a soft, subtle hump, and watch it as it approaches, as it begins to crest.

I watch the breaker, following with my eyes the entire life cycle of the wave.

I am lost in thought. A raucous gull demands to be fed.

The mist melts away.

What to do today? Run? There's no more point to training. No more single-minded goal to run Boston that had served as a beacon for two years, guiding me to find my own hidden potential and strength, bringing me joy, leading me across the continent to a revelation on the mountain and then to a new life here.

I sit in silence as the earth turns and the sunlight glides down the beach shortening the shadow of the cliff behind me. Time has ceased now and this moment hangs in perpetual silence forever.

Suddenly out of the depths of despair a fragile bubble of excitement is born and gurgles happily up through my body to my solar plexus where it bursts with joy into thought.

I must go back and run the Boston Marathon!

I see that now. I cannot... not run.

Now it is more important than ever to run, to run, not just for my own challenge and happiness, but to run to set women free, to overturn the old myths and prejudices, which have kept women enslaved all these centuries… to prove that a woman can do this.

If women can do this that is thought to be impossible, what else can women do?

The humor of it strikes me and I laugh out loud. How amazed everyone will be when I, a woman, trot right along with the men for twenty-six point two miles! It will change the way people think! It will demonstrate once and for all the truth. It will topple the entire lie which keeps women ... and men too... in bondage.

My stomach growls and I realize I am starved. I wonder if my favorite cafe is open yet. I make my way to the small shack under the gigantic eucalyptus tree that drops its fragrant nuts on the ground, where, crushed by parking cars and trucks, they emanate that enlivening aroma. A friendly middle-aged Mexican couple who have taken on the position of my surrogate parents, give me extra food and charge me half the price. I feel exactly like a huge stack of pancakes, with syrup and melted butter!

Chapter 52: April 1966

Who should arrive home just as I am about to leave for Boston but Will. He is acting strange. I don't know what is going on. He leaves long letters lying around the house addressed to me, which are garbled and make no sense. With a sinking feeling, I fight down the realization that this is not working.

Now it is April. I have to go or I will miss the Marathon. Will and I fight about it. He refuses to drive me to the bus station. I yell at him and grab the motor scooter, which I had bought, leap on and race downtown to the bus station. I buy my ticket and, as I wait around, I wander out to the street where I see a shoe store. Bill Gookin, my friend from the San Diego Track and Field, suggested I get boys' running shoes since women's shoes are not made. The nurses' shoes are too heavy to run a race in.

A huge, smiling man, full of energy, tries shoes on me. We talk about the marathon. He tells me he is a Baha'i and they take the "good parts of many religions," he says. He shines with a kind of inner light that makes him radiate love and beauty. His smooth, black skin glows. He sells me the shoes and gives me a big hug and wishes me well.

I can afford the bus, just barely.

I board the bus and sit in front near a window. A large friendly woman smiles and asks if she may sit next to me. She must weigh over two hundred pounds.

"Of course," I smile and move over to give her room. She takes up one and a half seats. Lucky I'm thin.

The bus takes off with a roar and cloud of toxic diesel fumes. We settle in for the long ride. She's going to St. Louis to see family. We chat on and off during the rest of the day as the desert rolls by outside.

"Watts is gunna to burn!" She exclaims, "You just watch. Watts is gunna to burn."

Watts did burn last August 1965 in the Los Angeles riots.

We talk about civil rights and women's rights. I tell her I'm going to run the marathon.

"Good for you missy. You show them folks girls can do it too."

Night falls and I lean my head against the window and fall asleep. Later that night I wake up; something soft and warm is over me. I sit up. The woman is snoring softly next to me.

What is this thing over me?

It is her coat! She has taken off her coat and draped it over me. I look over at her dark, shiny face as she sleeps and feel a tender love for her. I want to give her something back, something to keep her warm and safe and happy, too.

In St. Louis she gets off. I miss her. It is empty without her next to me. The bus hurtles on night and day. I sustain myself by eating bus station chile and apples out of a plastic bag I've brought with me.

Finally the scenery that has flipped by my window for the last three thousand miles stops. I look at the familiar scene: Boston. Outside the trees are bare, the ground is bare and the air is cold and damp. Stiffly I pry myself out of my seat and disembark. It is April 18th one day before the marathon, and I can barely walk. Outside it is cold, gray and desolate.

From the old bus depot in St James Square, I put my dime in the clanking wall telephone box and tell the operator my number, "Parkhurst 9 -3808"

"Hello?" my dad answers.

"Hi Dad! It's Bobby Lou."

"Well! Hi Deah! Is everything all right?"

"Yeah great! I'm in Boston!"

"Boston?!"

"What are you doing in Boston?"

"I came back to run the Marathon."

I hear muffled voices as he tells my mother with his hand over the mouthpiece.

"Bobby Lou?" It's my mother's shaking voice, which makes my insides knot up with anxiety... her anxiety.

"Hi Mom. I came home to run the Boston Marathon."

"Where are you?" She asks, her voice quavering.

"At the bus stop in St James Square. I don't mind taking a bus to Medford and walking."

"We'll come pick you up, you just stay there." I imagine that they put in a call to Dr. Southgate.

"OK. Thanks." I sit a read for a half hour until they arrive looking pale and worried.

Mom makes a huge meal of roast beef, apple pie and potatoes that evening. No one mentions the marathon.

Chapter 53: The Big Day

Spring comes slowly to Boston.

Patriot's Day, April 19th, 1966 dawns clear and cool.

This is the day for which I've trained for two years. This is the day I'm going to change the way people think about women. I'm nervous, tense, on edge.

Breakfast... I should eat something... but what? The roast beef, cheese and apple pie I ate last night is still sitting in my stomach in a hard lump.

What should I wear? I tear around the laundry room and pounce on my brother's Bermuda shorts. Too big. I grab some brown string, loop it through the belt holders and pull it tight, rippling the tan fabric around my waist. Of course my tank-top bathing suit, I always wear that under whatever else I'm wearing. And, a hooded, dark-blue sweatshirt to conceal my femininity as long possible.

What I fear most is that they will stop me, that the police will arrest me, that the officials will pull me out and I will not have a chance to prove that a woman can run twenty-six miles, which is what I have come to prove.

Once they know that women can run, I am sure that they will open up the race to women.

I know that once this prejudice, which everyone—men and women alike—take as true, is overturned that it will call into question every other prejudice about women.

They think the world is flat. Well I'm going to show them the world is round!

OK.

Now how do I get to the starting line?

I don't have enough money for a taxi. I have no idea about bus service but I doubt that a bus even goes to Hopkinton. My Dad thinks I'm delusional and somehow I think I'm going to run the marathon. He has forbidden me to leave the house. My Mom has called doctor Southgate. My Dad is afraid that if I actually do try to run that it will kill me. I don't want to bother Gail who is busy with her three kids and husband.

Breakfast is tense that morning. I cram down some orange juice and a piece of toast.

"Well who's going to drive me to the start of the Boston Marathon?" I hazard.

"You are not going to run any marathon, and that is all there is to it!" Dad spits out between his clenched teeth. Turning to my Mom he says impatiently, "Get me those sandwiches. I'm late for the regatta already."

She hands him the sandwiches.

"I am going to run. If I have to take a taxi I will," I state emphatically, my voice rising.

"This is insane! I will not have you running any twenty-six mile race with a bunch of men and that's final!" my Dad slams out the front door.

I turn to my Mom in desperation, "Mom, I have to do this. I have to run the race. Don't you see? It's to set women free! No one believes women can run twenty-six miles. If I can run it, it will change what people believe. They'll say 'We were wrong about this, what else can women do... what else can people do?' The sky's the limit. They'll be women who go hundreds of miles in all kinds of races. They'll be women geniuses who can get an education and put their minds to work. They'll be women rocket scientists and women engineers. Women senators and presidents. They'll be women doctors and lawyers and business executives. Children will see their mothers being what ever they want—being who they fully are making the world a better richer more wonderful place."

"Who'll take care of the children?" my Mom queries.

"Having children and raising children is the most important work in society. I know that. Women and men who chose to do that will be respected, supported and valued. Both parents will share the children. Think how much men are missing. They don't even get to know their own children.

"Don't you see? The way it is now men and women are each half of who they are meant to be. Women don't get to use their minds or their bodies. Men don't get to have feelings. Men and women can both be full people: both men and women can have feelings, and both women and men can have minds, and both men and women can raise their kids, and both women and men can work at what they love ... And both can run marathons... together... sharing life... being all they can be.

"We don't have to be crammed, or cram ourselves, or cram each other into stereotypes... we can be who we really are at last! And do what we really love!"

My mother frowns.

"Mom, don't you see. This is so important. I have to run. I've trained for two years for this. I know a different reality... a truer reality. I need to share it with the world. If they already allowed women... if everyone knew women could run... it wouldn't be so important. It could just be my own personal satisfaction and challenge, but no one believes a woman is capable of running twenty-six miles. Don't you see... not even women believe it. Women themselves don't know they can do this because they've never been allowed to try. This will be the trigger point in the creation of a whole new world. I have to run... I can't not do this." I feel the passion rising within me.

My mom is listening intently. I see her lip begin to quiver.

"OK. I'll do it," she relents.

I leap into the air and give her a big hug, which I haven't done for years. At last, after having to fight against her all these years she is on my side!

"So how do we get to Hopkinton?" I grab a map. "Let's go into Boston and follow the route out. I've never seen the course. This will give me an idea of what I'm up against."

We get an early start in order to get to Hopkinton before the roads are closed for the race.

My mother is driving and talking, and as she talks, I realize that I've never really known her at all. She has always played a role with me and never really opened up before.

"When you were born. It was a beautiful November day. The sycamore trees along Memorial drive along the River were yellow gold. I'll never forget the sound of your first cry. It was the most thrilling moment of my life. I'd never held a baby before.

"I had a fever so they put us in a private room, with a nurse. She was a big comfortable woman. She saw you, a day old, lifting your head and looking all around and she exclaimed 'I've never seen a baby so alert, so bright. If you raise her right she'll do remarkable things.'

"For all these years I've felt like a failure because I could never seem to raise you right. I could never force you to conform to the standards I thought you should conform to. You were what Gail said.... an untamable spirit, galloping like a wild horse beyond the limits of most of us. I was obsessed with breaking that spirit. It was the behaviorist psychology we were taught, before Dr. Spock.

"But secretly I admired your unbreakable spirit and wished I could be like that. I felt I'd failed myself and I'd given up, in myself, what you refused to give up. After you left, I had a break down. Now I'm drying out and beginning to see clearly for the first time in years."

I am moved and feel closer to her than I ever have before. "That's the best thing I've ever heard... I always felt you weren't there. That's why I was angry at you because you weren't you. I've always loved the real you, I'd get glimpses of you every now and then, and I wanted to rip off the gray glob that sat on top of you and covered you over, that awful glob that was so thick you didn't even know who you were."

She smiled, "Well I'm coming back. But it takes time... years sometime to rebuild what was lost."

"I'm rooting for you. I've always been rooting for the real you," I confide.

I look out the window and note the lay of the course, the hills and turns and flat places. It seems as if we drive for hours, hundreds of mile.

"I never knew twenty-six miles could be so long." My stomach is tying itself in knots.

The urban landscape gives way to affluent suburbs and then to another semi-urban area, "Framingham," the sign says, and then to countryside.

Chapter 54: Hopkinton

Hopkinton is a small New England village. We park on the edge of town. I get out of the car.

"I wish I didn't have to go to this damn regatta!" It's the first time I've ever heard my Mom swear. "I'll be thinking of you and praying for you," she says shyly.

"Thanks!"

"Bye. Bye. Good luck."

"Bye. Thanks."

She drives away, leaving me standing there alone.

I look around me. Hopkinton, where the race begins is built around a common, with a white church that has a green roof, a cemetery, with thin slate stones and huge, dark conifer trees pushing up between the stones that breathe of bygone eras. Large comfortable homes ring the common.

Barren trees, still wrapped in winter gray, brush the April sky with pastel shades of mauve and lavender. People in brightly colored clothes mill among the trees, talking and clustering in groups. Children dart in and out playing tag, laughing and squealing.

I suddenly feel naked standing all alone in this strange place, a place I've never been before.

What am I doing?

The reality of it hits me. This is a real race and real people; they really do not allow women. I am about to do something I'm not supposed to do, about to transgress customs and laws that are centuries old. There are policemen here who can arrest me. I have no idea what I am getting into.

I'm faced with the reality of this insane double bind. How can I prove I can do something I'm not allowed to do?

I have to hide myself until I get into the race. If I go into the pen with the men, I'll be seen and dragged out. My greatest fear is that I will be stopped, prevented from demonstrating that a woman can run twenty-six miles. I trot slowly around the town getting the lay of the land. I see the starting pen. I run around the common looking for a way to get into the race without being stopped.

Next to the common I find a little hollow, which smells dank and dusty with last year's leaves. Earthen vaults, with rusting doors remind me of the ammunition storage vaults my ancestors used in the Revolutionary War, almost two hundred years ago, on Patriots' Day. A stonewall encloses a little hollow and early flowering forsythia bushes adorn the two granite posts that mark the old gate with shocks of brilliant yellow.

"This will be a good place to hide," I decide. If I'm detected and prevented, no one will ever know that a woman can run a twenty-six point two mile marathon. A sense of urgency grips me.

I circle the hollow. The race won't start for another hour or so.

After three nights and three days cramped on the bus, I need to move around.

I find an alley and run up and down for three quarters of an hour or so to warm up for the race. As the starting time approaches I return to the bushes and pull the hood on my sweatshirt up over my hair. How many other women writers, artists, scientists, and soldiers have had to disguise their femininity so well that history still has not discovered?

A policeman backs the gathering crowds away from the rope barricades.

On the far side of the Common I see a flurry of white shorts and undershirts. The men are gathering in the starting pen. A preoccupied race official runs, notebook in hand, toward the starting gate. I sense the growing tension.

If I can prove this prejudice wrong I can call into question all the other false beliefs that have been used to keep women subjugated for centuries. This will be a pivotal point, a shot heard 'round the world. This will catalyze a social change. This will change social perceptions and will begin to free women. I have been given an opportunity to change the world for the better and it is a huge responsibility.

I want to do it in an upbeat, non-threatening, inspirational way that will encourage people, both men and women to take up running and to relate with one another as friends and equals. I want to show that men and women can share life's challenges and opportunities.

 I crouch down hidden in the bushes. The curled, dried leaves, rotten from last fall, smell like nutmeg. The dead litter rustles under my new running shoes. My heart is beating fast inside my warm, sweatshirt. I feel the restless energy in my legs and thighs. I wait, poised, ready to leap.

"Bang!"

The sound drifts across the light spring air like the first "shot heard 'round the world," one hundred and ninety-one years ago. A cheer goes up from the spectators. The white mass of runners springs forward with a roar, like foaming water released from a breaking dam. I wait until about half the pack has gone and then leap out of the bushes into the middle of the pack. My legs unfold and my feet hit the pavement running hard. The physical exertion of the other runners surrounds me — the flailing arms and legs, the intense concentration, the heat, the sound of soft, strong foot falls on the road, like rain, the smell of human bodies. This too will be a shot heard 'round the world.

Overhead, the noonday sun beats down through a clear and indifferent sky, which smiles benignly on whatever is happening on earth, whether it is love or hate, war or peace, effort or repose. The sun magnanimously dispenses its affluence on sinner and saint, on success or failure, on all of human endeavor, on all of human error. The vacant blue sky arches over our small twenty-six miles.

What am I doing?

I've fallen in love with this ultimate challenge.

I've trained for two years never questioning that this is what I am meant to be doing.

When they said I was not allowed because of my sex, and that women were not physiologically able to run, I said... "All the more reason to run... to prove that women can run."

And here I am running the Boston Marathon out of that love, love, which I believe is the basis of all meaningful human endeavor, love that is incomplete until it is shared with others.

Crowds line the streets cheering and shouting. The other runners press around me, arms and legs churning strongly. I'm swept along in a tide of runners; my own arms and legs pick up the rhythm.

In a few moments I feel a studious silence as the men concentrate on my anatomy from the rear. I hear the men behind me talking to each other in hushed tones.

"Is that a girl?"

"It sure looks like one."

"A woman running?"

There's a long pause.

"Excuse me..." one calls out to me.

I turn and smile.

"It is a girl!"

"Hey, it's a girl."

"Hey, a woman's running!"

The news spreads like pheromones wafted on the summer's day.

"A girl's in the race!"

"Are you going the whole way?" the lanky man running next to me asks.

"I hope so," I respond, laughing.

"Great! I wish my wife would run," one of them says. I see how much they want to share their passion for running with the women they love.

We run on like this stride for stride into Ashland.

"I'm gettin' hot in this sweat shirt, but I'm afraid if I take it off and they see I'm a woman they'll throw me out," I say.

I know that if these men are unfriendly, they can easily shoulder me out of the race. I want to do this in an upbeat way to win over the officials and to inspire people to find in running the sense of health, wholeness and peace that I find. I want men to support women's efforts to expand.

I'm a shy, private person used to running by myself in the woods and here I am now running in front of all these people. Not just running, but making a statement, trying to prove something, trying to change people's prejudices.

The weight of responsibility presses on me. I know if I fail to finish I will end up setting women back, I know that if I fail, people will say, "You see, this is why we don't let women run. Women really are not capable of these things," and the door will be slammed even more tightly against women.

I have to do it in a graceful, feminine, upbeat way. I don't want to have to become a man. I want to be able to do everything, and still be a woman, and still love men and still be loved by men. I want this war between the sexes, which exhausts both and leads to nothing, to end. I want men and women to love, respect and honor each other, as equals, not identities, but as valued unique individuals, not as functions, or stereotypes, but as whole people.

The men are friendly and supportive. What a relief!

"Go on take it off," Alton urges. His name is Alton Chamberlain, from Connecticut. I like him.

"It's a free road," the man behind me asserts.

"We won't let them throw you out," they agree.

The brilliant, noisy world of color and cheers disappears into a dark blue, muffled world of warm, familiar fabric, as I reach my arms up and pull the sweatshirt over my head. For a moment I want to stay there, safe and protected. I don't have to do this. I could have stayed in bed this morning; it would have been easier. It would have been easier not to have come by bus three thousand miles. It would have been easier not to have trained for the last two years. It would have been easier not to have taken a six thousand mile odyssey in search of what?

For a moment, the images of that journey run through my mind, the entire continent, New England, the Midwest, the slow meandering Mississippi, the great open plains, the rough-peaked Rocky Mountains, the nights in Nevada, the Sierras, the shimmering Pacific Ocean, Moot, Debbie and her baby, the car crash. And the return, art school, Branden, Kirk, Gardner, then California, Will, Paula, Crazy Kid, And before that, John, the Willards, my mom and dad, my brother, Nana and her gardens, Mom Christina and her fireplace, Pop, Grampy, my cousins, Uncle Al telling me I float when I run, Audrey and summer camp, a kaleidoscope of color and form, brief and almost tactile.

I feel the thin air and bright light again as if being born, as I throw the sweatshirt to the side of the road like a discarded husk, a cocoon, out of which I emerge blinking into the sun, ready to fly with my newly unfolding wings.

The stunned crowd is silent for a second.

It is scary to do something so far outside the social norm. You never know how people are going to react. Will they be hostile?

"It's a girl!" one woman screams.

"Hey at a go girly!" a big brawny man in a tan jacket claps.

"Hey girly! Go get em!"

"There's a girl running!" shrieks another woman.

It is here, in Ashland, a few minutes from the start, that Jerry Nason, a reporter from Winchester first sights me. He calls on ahead, sensing that there is a story in the making here.

"What's your name?" one of the men asks me. "The reporter wants to know."

"Bobbi Gibb," I reply.

"Where are you from?"

"Winchester."

"Parents?"

"Professor and Mrs. Gibb."

The information is relayed out, runner to runner, to the reporter.

News travels fast. Soon it is being broadcast on the radio: A girl is running the Boston Marathon!

The news has also been relayed to Will Cloney, the executive race director, the same man who had written me the definitive letter, which had reached me in California, informing me that women are not physiologically able to run a twenty-six mile marathon and that, furthermore, they are not allowed to do so. It is against the rules that govern the world of athletics.

"Will she finish? How long will it take her?"

Jerry Nason is monitoring my progress and reporting to a stunned public. The reporters from the *Record American* are also alert and following my run.

"Framingham," the runner beside me announces.

"So soon?" I am surprised. I've been so busy talking with the men around me I hardly noticed the time. We are on a sub-three hour pace. We whisk by the car sales lots, across intersections and vacantly blinking lights.

A friendly police officer calls out to me, "Hey slow down so he can catch you." Another one calls out, "He went that a way," and laughs. The policemen, whom I had feared, smile and wave, and I smile and wave back.

How rude to run right by, when all these nice people are calling out and wishing me well. I want to appear graceful. I am still a little uneasy about sweating in public, and in fact I am running well under my speed, knowing that if I go too fast and fail to finish I'll end up supporting rather than demolishing the prejudices and false beliefs I am trying to destroy.

Kind people keep offering me water and orange slices. Tables with cups of water loom up periodically and the other runners grab the small cups, drink quickly and drop the empty cups on the ground making a sea of wet pavement and cups. But, thinking that drinking while racing will give me cramps I politely refuse the water and the fruit.

We speed on through Natick, the ten-mile mark. I am feeling great. Then on into Wellesley.

It seems effortless. I am having fun. I feel like cavorting across the road. This is a celebration of life!

Chapter 55: Half Way

Up the long hill to Wellesley College. Almost half way through already! I'm not tired at all, not out of breath. We're churning off a mile in a little under seven minutes. I want to go faster, but I keep reining myself in, aware that, with all this resting on me, I can't risk going too fast and not being able to finish.

In the distance, I hear what sounds like a day on the beach, people laughing and screaming with delight.

I look questioningly at Alton.

"The tunnel of love," one of his friends replies.

"The best part of the race," another responds.

We run on together sweeping up the broad hill.

I can see in the distance a colorful blur of people huddled together in the middle of the road.

As we come closer, the sound of happy screaming becomes louder.

We are now running by Wellesley College and the road is filled with beautiful coeds, jumping up and down, hair streaming in the spring air. The men are disappearing into the knot of laughing women.

The Wellesley women have been listening to my progress, which is being broadcast on the radio, I later learn. Eagerly they've been scanning face after face looking for me. They sense that this is a definitive moment in history and a turning point for women.

When the women see me, the intensity of their screaming increases several decibels.

"There she is!"

"A woman is running!"

I look at these women and see how much my running means to them. Some of them are crying.

About two dozen women are standing, in two parallel lines, facing each other, with their arms up over their heads, hands meeting, to form a long tunnel, through which the runners pass. The men lean over and run through. I follow, passing through the living, laughing tunnel. I glance from side to side, meeting their eyes, looking at their faces. Women are screaming, "Great! Great! Keep on running! God, a woman! A woman is running! Do it girl! Go! Go! Go! Go!"

Emerging from the tunnel, I catch my breath.

Over to one side I see a woman with several children clinging to her ample overcoat.

"Ave Maria!" She shouts. "Ave Maria!" Tears are streaming down her face. I can feel the passion in her voice. In her heart, she knows that her daughters will be free in a way she never dreamed possible. She senses that this is the beginning of a new world of accomplishment and opportunity, that the old prejudices are dead; that never again can anyone say a woman cannot do this.

Our eyes meet and I feel a surge of tears at the contact. Does she know that in my heart I want children; that I respect her for her devotion, patience, and her strength? She has undertaken, without thought of fame or reward, the most difficult, most important human endeavor of all.

On we run into Wellesley Hills, past the fifteen-mile mark. We are coming down hill; I can feel it on the front of my legs. I have no watch but someone shouts that I am on a sub-three hour pace. We descend down into Newton Lower Falls.

At the bottom, we cross the Charles River; I smell its coolness and feel its ancient, liquid body snaking under the bridge.

Now we are climbing up out of the valley. I hear tires on pavement, the silent scream of traffic moving at speed on an asphalt highway—the sound of the modern age. We are running so primitively up and over the bridge across Route 128 like a displaced herd of wild animals. So strange to see modern civilization from this perspective.

Through the staid suburbs we wildly careen, half dressed, as if some ancient tribe set loose in this well-mannered place. People cheer and clap. This is my vision, the return of some wild ancestor, the re-integration of the body with the mind, the acknowledgement of our own animal being, not in some derogatory sense but in the reality of it, the integrity and nobility of it, this sense of aliveness and vigor it brings.

"Heartbreak Hill...." I hear the fragment of conversation around me. I pass and am passed by small clumps of runners.

"Heartbreak Hill coming up."

"I hate Heartbreak."

"It's a killer."

"What is Heartbreak Hill?" I wonder. I feel the tension in the runners around me.

We run on into the Newton Hills. I look up and read the sign; we're on Route 30, Commonwealth Avenue, through Newton Hills. Seventeen miles. I feel great. We're running on an open broad road, with a grassy center strip. I cavort onto the strip to ease the heat I am beginning to feel on the soles of my feet. I am not used to running on pavement and my new shoes are rubbing.

At last we begin to climb. What a relief to be going up after miles of descent hammering our legs. I feel myself begin to push against the road and against the pull of gravity.

I watch the pavement, and draw within me, focusing, balancing, keeping my center. The incredible strength and endurance it takes to run a marathon, to live a life with integrity. You are surrounded by other people running, but no one else can do it for you.

You have to do it yourself. I watch the patterns and sparkles in the pavement, and I am filled with a sense of their beauty.

The road is going up. I wonder if this is Heartbreak Hill. Up and up we go to the top. Well that wasn't so bad, nowhere near as long or steep as Black Mountain.

But what's this? We're going up again! Maybe this, now, is Heartbreak Hill. The pace has slowed as runners strain. I feel the edge of fatigue for the first time, no longer reining in, but pushing to keep going.

Ah at last, the top! That's a relief. My pace picks up again as the road flattens. But what is this? Another hill! We're going up again. Maybe this finally is the legendary Heartbreak Hill. I dig in and push up the hill. Yes this is Heartbreak!

Finally it crests and we start down. A view of Boston opens up. The Prudential tower shows clearly, closer that I thought. Boston College and a church with lovely spires slides by. Only five miles more to go I hear someone say.

Chapter 56: The Finish

"Five miles! I can run five miles in my sleep," I think. I feel like Caesar crossing the Rubicon. I feel like Caesar standing on the brink of conquering Gaul. Such a feeling of elation and success! I feel as if the race is over; I'm almost in Boston. I'm as good as finished.

But as usual, life is never what I think it will be. The marathon is no place for smugness.

The steep downhill slope rips apart my legs. The blisters on my feet have burst, and now raw flesh is rubbing on my nice, new, stiff boys', size six running shoes, which I did not know I was supposed to break in. The roast beef, cheese and apple pie from last night's feast has become a cannon ball in my stomach. And having taken no water or electrolyte replacement for twenty miles, running in the heat has left me seriously dehydrated.

Down, down, down we descend into hell, it seems. A graveyard then trolley wires, tracks and rough footing. Store fronts then rows of brick buildings with protruding windows, peaked roofs, lots of big trees, and turrets give me the sense of castles, then suddenly we're in a medieval village, Coolidge Corner, Tudor-style buildings with a series of peaked roofs surmounted by a tower. I expect to hear a town crier announcing the news. Instead I hear the clapping of the spectators. The people who line the streets are as much a part of the race as the runners.

We're almost in Boston now. My pace drops off. If I could have quit, it would have been here. But quitting does not enter my head even as a theoretical possibility. I am locked on to this race. I will finish or die trying. I will make it across that finish line if I have to crawl, no matter how long it takes.

We pass over into Boston, a ragged bunch of survivors. Bus loads of men who have dropped out wave and cheer at us. The huge red Citgo sign in Kenmore Square looms above everything else.

"One more mile! One more mile," the crowds chant. "Come on you can do it. Keep it up. Keep it up." I feel like a gladiator, who has been mauled by the lion, struggling to get up and keep fighting. My pace has dropped off. I am barely moving, tiptoeing along, each step sending a searing jolt to my brain. My blistered feet feel as if they are cut through to bone. The bottoms of my feet are on fire. I am running across beds of hot coals, slowly, slowly, slowly, slowly.

And this is where I discover the real meaning of fortitude, to go on, to keep going in the face of disappointment; to see your hopes dashed but to keep on anyway; to finish what you set out to do even if it isn't what you had hoped.

Interminable. This last mile takes me longer than the preceding five miles. I watch my pace drop off and my time spin out. My three-hour marathon is left dead on the course; my hopes of winning had long ago died a hero's death.

The Citgo sign in Kenmore Square is still hanging in the sky above me. I am caught in a space time warp, out of which I cannot get free. Eons of time pass and still I am running by the same Citgo sign. Four billion years pass, as life evolves from a tiny, self-sustaining chemical reaction, to the first one-celled creatures, to multi-celled diversity, cascading into the infinite miracle of life on earth, today, and still the Citgo sign is hanging there.

At last, after four billion years, just as human life first appears on earth, the Citgo sign passes into oblivion. I wonder if anyone will still be at the finish when I get there. I follow the scattered herd of runners along Commonwealth Ave. As I turn right, into the brick canyon of Hereford Street, music plays. People are hanging out of windows holding beer cans and screaming. So many people crowd into the street that only a small passage is left through which to run. I look at their faces and see such incredible beauty. In the end, nothing is as beautiful as the human face.

I turn left, on to Boylston Street. Suddenly the road opens up. Thousands of people line the streets. Bleachers are packed. A roar goes up. The press truck rolls along beside me, flash bulbs, the announcer and police. I pick up my pace and trot across the finish line in a time of three hours and twenty minutes I'm told, ahead of two thirds of the pack. Not bad. Alton comes to welcome me. Some kind soul throws a wool blanket around my shoulders.

I reach up and shake the hand of a nice looking square-built man in a dark blue wool coat. He is the Governor of Massachusetts, John Volpe, who has come down to congratulate me!

I feel supremely happy. It is the end of a long journey for me, which I hope will change the world for the better, and begin a new journey for our times toward a better world for all.

After the Race, I am whisked off to a hotel room where the press surrounds me. I've never met a newspaper writer before and I am enthralled. I like all these nice people and want to ask them what their job is like.

They interview me and I hope they will understand the loving spirit behind my running. I try to keep it up-beat and non-confrontive, knowing that this is the only way I can hope to win support and to inspire other people to run. I want people to say, well if she can do it so can I. I want everyone to find the healing, stress-relieving, physical, mental, spiritual benefits of running that I have found. And most of all, I want everything to open up to women, including, but not limited to, the Boston Marathon. I don't want to antagonize or threaten people. I want to inspire them and free them. I take off my shoes to relieve my burning, bleeding blisters, and sit talking with reporters.

Alton and his friends want me to come with them to the post-marathon stew. We walk to the door, but I am not allowed in. No women are allowed. Alton apologizes and I can see he feels badly about it. I'm hoping that people like Alton and his friends will begin to take steps to end this type of discrimination. It is clear that his view of women has forever changed and I hope that everyone else's has too.

I walk across the cold damp parking garage alone, realizing that there is still more to do to break down the subtle and not so subtle prejudices, which are truncating the lives of women... and of men too.

I reach into my bathing suit and un-pin the money my mother gave me. A taxi pulls up.

Chapter 57: After the Race

As we turn onto Sargent Road I'm surprised to find that the entire street is jammed with parked cars. I wonder what all the cars are for. Perhaps someone is giving a party? My street looks like a parking lot. As we approach my familiar gray house, I realize that there are dozens of people crowded into my house and yard. What is going on?

I walk up the front steps and I realize that the house is full of newspaper reporters. I catch a glimpse of my parents who are standing in the living room, utterly bewildered. The phone is ringing. It's my dad's colleagues from Tufts, Professor and Mrs. Mead, the Fontneaus, the Burleys and the Harrisons. "Congratulations on your daughter! You must be very proud!" My dad is completely confused. My mother is trying politely to serve tea.

I sit with my mom and my dad, my shoes comfortably off, reading the paper, while the photographers take pictures. Then the photographers want me to dress in something feminine, as if to reassure the readership that the "shapely blonde housewife," as they describe me, really is feminine. So I dress in my dark blue and white polka dotted dress and make fudge with one of my parents' guests from the regatta, while the flash bulbs pop purple spots in my eyes. More reporters arrive.

"Hub Bride First Gal to Run Marathon!" The headlines will blare the next morning. Word goes out, by wire, around the world a woman has done the impossible and run the Boston Marathon.

My dad puts his arm around my shoulders and says something like, "We knew she could do it!"

I laugh and say, "It's those Gibb legs, Dad."

By now it is suppertime. I'm hungry and feeling overwhelmed by the events of the day. I excuse myself from the reporters, slip out the back door and jog up to the Willard's, barefoot, leaving my mother and dad to cover for me with the lingering reporters.

Gail and I sit by the fire. Dick isn't home so we make a pizza. I crawl around on my hands and knees giving piggy back rides to Lisa. Jimmy wants to play the "tiger who eats kitty cats," so I growl and pretend to catch him, which makes him giggle with delight.

After the kids are in bed, Gail and I sit quietly by the fire.

"So now you're famous!" Gail observes.

"I didn't mean to be. I just saw something that was wrong and I tried to change it."

"Well, you changed the world."

"Good! It needed changing."

"And what about you?"

"I'm going to go back and finish college."

"Good. But does it have to be in California?"

"I never felt smart enough for college and I was afraid I couldn't do it, but now after running the marathon I feel that maybe I can do it.... even if it takes me a long time. Education is important and there are some things I've been thinking about and wondering about..."

"Like what?"

"Like— How can we do this?" I open and close my hand. "How can my thoughts activate the nerves that activate my muscles?"

Gail looks surprised.

"Isn't it extraordinary that there can be a mass of billions of neurons all made of atoms and molecules, all with trillions of changing electrical and chemical potentials and out of this comes the subjective experience of which I am directly aware. What does this say about the nature of the universe that such a thing can and does evolve? To me it a wonder beyond anything imaginable."

"Yes. But why California?"

"The thing I like about the University of California in La Jolla is that the physics and biology departments are mixed in with the philosophy department so they can share ideas and cross-pollinate. I want to learn things and to help heal the world," I say. "So much of the world seems to be steering by an antiquated, false map that will fetch them, and everyone else...up on the rocks... so many false beliefs causing so much suffering and damage.... like so many wars.... all so unnecessary.... but that's a whole other harangue.... and it's late..."

"You must be exhausted! Twenty-six miles!"

"No curiously. I'm invigorated and excited; I don't want to sleep. Besides... it's only six o'clock California time."

"California time.... yes..." Gail looks sad again. "I'm a night owl," she sighs.

"I've missed you," I say.

She looks up and says wistfully, "It hasn't been the same around here... with you gone."

"This was the best home I ever had." I say "... I wish I could just spend the rest of my life here in the coal bin, sleeping out, being with you guys..."

When I say it like that.... we both see it out in the open, we know that it can never be... I have to move on... to find myself in the larger world.... to have kids of my own some day... to finish college, to do my life's work. Gail has her children... and her husband.... and her home... this is her life and her life is good...

We sit gazing into the fire for a long time.

Suddenly the memory of sitting by the fire with John, feeling the passion of love sweep over us, comes upon me with an intensity that takes me by surprise. I remember the time we fell asleep on the floor and Gail covered us with a blanket. I remember how we crawled around with kids climbing over us. I remember how he was, the feel and smell of him.

"You never heard from John?" Gail says softly, reading my thoughts.

"Nope."

"Any idea what happened?"

"Not a clue. I called him and wrote him and wrote him some more. I felt hurt and angry... I felt sad... but nothing."

"You two were such a great couple..."

I gaze in silence at the fire. A rush of sadness washes over me. I miss John. I listen to the sound of the wind in the fire, flam, flam, flam, like the sound of wind in your ears when you run.

"But you know what, Bobby Lou, you have your own destiny, your own path, your own authentic self, your own inner guide that you listen to and follow, no matter what. He has too. He admired you and wanted to be like you, but he just couldn't." Gail puts her hand on my arm.

"I kept hoping he'd have the courage to go for what he really loved," I sigh.

"Maybe in time he will, but meanwhile, you have to move on. You have to follow your own destiny, not his."

I nod and turn and look into Gail's blue eyes and smile, and I know for the first time that I'm following a new path that is opening up before me. I'm finding myself in a way that I never could as John's wife.

Gail continues, "Follow your own unique path and discover what you are meant to do and do it; find what you are meant to give and give it; find what you are meant to be and be it."

"Yes," I smile. "I will." I throw another log onto the fire and we watch the burning cinders fly up, out and away.

Afterword

Bobbi's courageous run in 1966 changed the way men thought about women and the way women thought about themselves. Her feat help to galvanize the women's movement. Two months after her 1966 run, the National Organization for Women was founded. Her run was a pivotal event that changed social consciousness and helped to inspire both the running movement and the women's movement. For a decade Bobbi was known as the "Matron Saint of the Boston Marathon."

She returned and ran again in 1967, finishing about an hour ahead of the other women competitor, Kathryn Switzer. Bobbi returned again in 1968 and finished first among a field of about five women. Until 1972, when, following a change in AAU Rules, the first sanctioned women's division race opened at Boston, all women were unofficial entrants running in an as yet to be sanctioned women's division race. From 1969 to 1971 Sara Mae Berman was the unsanctioned women's winner, and in 1972, Nina Kuscsik was the first official women's winner of the first official Women's Division Boston Marathon.

Bobbi graduated from the University of California at La Jolla (now UCSD) in 1969 with a major in philosophy and a minor in mathematics, having completed courses required for a pre-med degree.

During the 1970's Bobbi continued to run every day and to attend law school at night while working on epistemology and color vision with Jerry Lettvin at the Massachusetts Institute of Technology, in Cambridge, Massachusetts. She also remarried and started a family.

In 1976 she founded the Institute for the Study of Natural Systems and continues as president. In 1978 she became a member of the Massachusetts Bar and practiced law for the next eighteen years.

She published *"The Art of Inflation"* in 1980 and continues to write on the topic of natural systems, including systems that can think. In 1980 she co-produced a film on Amory Lovins entitled, "Lovins on the Soft Path," which is still relevant today. She also joined by invitation the United States affiliate of international think tank that addresses global problems.

Bobbi was inducted into the Road Runners of America Hall of Fame in 1982.

In 1986 after qualifying in the New York Marathon, Bobbi ran her beloved Boston Marathon again to celebrate the twentieth anniversary of her first run. She co-founded the Worldwide Running Club for Peace and ran the Boston Marathon to support world peace, understanding and friendship among all the peoples of the earth.

In 1996, on the thirtieth anniversary of her first run and the one-hundredth anniversary of the Boston Marathon, Bobbi was awarded a medal for her three wins and her name was inscribed with the other winners on the Boston Marathon Memorial in Copley Square. The official times for her three wins were: 1966, 3:21:40; 1967, 3:27:17 and 1968, 3:30. She was also included in the BAA film, "Blood Sweat and Cheers," a moving documentary on the history of the Boston Marathon.

Bobbi has made numerous TV appearances and has been featured in the HBO Documentary, "Dare to Compete."

In 2000 she produced her own documentary, "Where the Spirit Leads."

In 2001 Bobbi ran the Boston Marathon again to help raise money for research on neurodegenerative diseases. She then became associated with the Cecil B. Day Lab, where she studies neurodegenerative diseases and aging, primarily focusing on Amyotrophic Lateral Sclerosis.

She pursues a career in sculpturing. Her work has been included in the National Art Museum of Sport, NAMOS, and in private collections. Germain Glidden the founder of NAMOS says of her work, "It captures the human spirit in bronze."

She is a member of the National Sculpture Society.

In October 2009 she was honored by Tufts University and awarded a Special Achievement Award. She has been included in Who's Who in the World, Who's Who in America and Who's Who in Women.

In June of 2011 Bobbi was inducted into the TD Garden Sports Hall of Fame in Boston, Massachusetts.

Bobbi continues to run an hour or two a day, to write and to publish books, and to sculpt. She is working on a full-length, theatrical, cinematographic presentation of her story.

Her hope is for a better world in which all people will find health, peace and love, and lead happy, creative lives, doing what they love.

Special Thanks

Special thanks to those friends who helped me bring this book to you: Claudia who helped me edit the preface and the first two chapters; Leif who had faith in my vision and who set up my website; my cousin Rich for his guidance and writing instruction at the very beginning; Jim for his critique of the earlier versions of this book; Dave for his encouragement of my writing; Richard for his support and many years of friendship; and Linden at the Harvard Book Store for bringing this book into printed form. Thanks too to all the people who are in this book, whose real lives are forever woven into my heart. Thank you to all my wider family and friends for being an inspiration to me. And thanks to you dear readers for your time and interest. May this book bring you joy and new discoveries!

Bobbi Gibb Art

Bobbi Gibb is an exciting contemporary artist who creates bronze sculptures of the human form in action and portrait busts; vividly colored murals; and subtle, impressionistic landscapes, which reflect her deep love of both humanity and nature.

Bobbi's artwork reflects the human and divine spirit and her point of view on the transcendent source of all being. From life-like busts and full body sculptures detailing the human form in an exacting manner to expansive murals that display an explosion of nature as she sees it in her imagination, Bobbi's work explores all facets of nature.

For more information, or to commission artwork, visit:

http://www.bobbigibbart.net/

Bobbi Gibb
Marathon Sculpture Project

Join Joan Samuelson, Bill Rodgers, Meb Keflezighi, and a dozen other Boston Marathon winners by making a donation to the Bobbi Gibb Marathon Sculpture Project.

Boston currently has several sculptures of male marathon runners, but none of women runners. Your contribution will help support the creation of a sculpture by the Boston Marathon's first woman runner (Bobbi Gibb, 1966) that will honor women's running and the proud tradition of women in the Boston Marathon.

To donate, visit FirstGiving.com and search for "Gibb sculpture" or send a check to:

Bobbi Gibb Marathon Sculpture Project
c/o 26.2 Foundation
P.O. Box 820
Hopkinton, MA 01748

Thanks for your help!

Printed in Great Britain
by Amazon

27137584R00170